Who

Art

Thou?

Unveil the Divine Mystery of Your Existence for

Self-discovery, Deliverance and All-round Fulfilment

Who Are Thou?

@ May 2021 DR D.K OLUKOYA

ISBN: 978-978-820-232-4

A publication of **Mountain Of Fire And Miracles Ministries**

Press House

13 Olasimbo Street, Off Olumo Road, P.O. Box 2990, Sabo, Yaba, Lagos, Nigeria.

08095423392, 08095419853

Email: *mountainoffireandmiraclespress@yahoo.com*

Websites: *www.mfmbooks.co.za*

Cover illustration: Pastor (Mrs) Shade Olukoya

Typeset, designed and printed at: **MFM PRESS**

13 Olasimbo Street, Off Olumo Road, By Unilag 2nd Gate, Onike, Yaba, Lagos, Nigeria.

Contents

INTRODUCTION

Life is full of secrets and mysteries. Many people are a shadow of what heaven created them to be. This is because, even after three or more decades on earth, they are yet to discover their correct identities and begin their journey of destiny fulfilment. It is so disheartening! A bird will keep struggling in the water whereas it is ordained to thrive in the air, and the fish that compares itself with the bird will never make it in the air.

Many people are engaged in wrong occupations and careers; some are married to spouses that are completely incompatible with them spiritually; others are addicted to food, drugs and drinks that they should never taste because of the peculiarity of the assignment that heaven has for them.

Why are all these happening? It is because such people are ignorant of who they are. They do not know their correct identity. A lot of people will struggle from the cradle to the grave if they do not seek God's face, discover who they are and align their lives to match heaven's expectations. Some will die poor, unknown, unsung and unfulfilled until they make God's blueprint the compass and roadmap for their lives, instead of living as copycats or following the wisdom of men.

So many people have attempted to know who they are and what they should do in life. Some of such people sought the vital information from stargazers, palm readers, the occult, witchdoctors, magicians, philosophers, and so on. The information they got led them nowhere and they discovered that those who claimed to know tomorrow actually do not. Beloved, only God, your Manufacturer, has the correct information of who you are. Seek His face in the prayer of faith and He will reveal to you great and mighty things that you do not know (Jeremiah 33:3).

The truth is that your deliverance, victory, healing, breakthroughs, progress and fulfilment in all areas of life are tied to the discovery of who you are, what your purpose on earth is, and how you should go about fulfilling it. The Bible says that by knowledge shall the righteous be delivered. The truth you know and apply has the power to set you totally free. (John 8:32, 36).

Those who are fortunate to access and use divine information wisely often succeed phenomenally and rise like meteors. God is light and He is all-knowing. He is also the custodian of secrets, and He reveals them to those He loves. The Bible affirms that the secret things belongs to God and those that are revealed to us belongs to us and our children (Deuteronomy 29:29).

The patriarchs, Job and Abraham, had access to God's secrets. The Bible affirms that the secret of the Lord was upon Job's tabernacle (Job 29:4) and that God would not conceal His acts from Abraham (Genesis 18:17). Our Lord and Royal Master, Jesus Christ, also had unrestrained access to God's secrets. John 5:19-20 affirms, " *Then answered Jesus and said unto them, Verily, verily, I say unto you, The Son can do nothing of himself, but what he seeth the Father do: for what things soever he doeth, these also doeth the Son likewise. For the Father loveth the Son, and sheweth him all things that himself doeth: and he will shew him greater works than these, that ye may marvel.* " With the proper use of the divine secrets they had, these notable Bible characters lived exceptionally impactful lives and fulfilled their divine purposes.

As a believer, God wants you to have access to His secrets and use them to dispense His grace, enforce His dominion and reign in life. Jesus said to His disciples, and that includes you, *"It is given to you to know the mysteries of the kingdom of heaven, but to them, it is not given"* (Matthew 13:11). He also said in Luke 11:25, *"Father, I praise You because these things that you have hidden from the wise and prudent, you have revealed them to babies."*

It is your responsibility to seek and find beneficial secrets about your life and destiny. When you have access to items of divine information and use them positively, you will begin to live a mountain-top Christian life.

Peter became a new person as well as a world-changer when Jesus revealed His correct identity to him. He realised that there was more to him than being a professional fisherman. He was to be a fisher of men. When he used this information from heaven correctly and keyed into his assignment, he became a great force to reckon with. The same is true of Saul of Tarsus, who became Apostle Paul and wrote two-thirds of the New Testament. It is also true of Mary, who saw herself like every other ordinary lady until the angel of the Lord told her, *"You are highly favoured. Blessed art thou among women. You are going to conceive and have a child whose name shall be called Jesus because He shall save His people from sin."* In the Old Testament, Gideon's might and fame were unknown and lying fallow in him until the angel of the Lord said to him, *"Hail thou, you mighty man of valour."*

Today, angels may or may not appear to you, but when you pray destiny-changing prayers, God will reveal secrets and mysteries to you. As a result, the battles of your life will be demystified and surmounted, and your stubborn enemies will bow to you in defeat.

You need secrets to confront and conquer the enemy, spiritually and physically. That is why nations spend fortunes on espionage and secret services. Lack of the right information is what has deformed many lives and destinies. I want you to remember that if you can pray, you have a God that will answer you and do exceedingly abundantly above all you can ever ask or think (Ephesians 3:20). The Bible says, *"Hitherto you have not asked for anything in my name. Ask that you may receive and that your joy may be full"* (John 16:24). Finally, as a believer, you have an assurance that God will answer your prayer. The Bible, affirms this, *"Ask, and it shall be given to you; seek, and ye shall find; knock, and it shall be opened unto thee"* (Matthew 7:7).

One of the essential steps for ministering and obtaining deep deliverance is to first gather the right items of information and to attack the issue from the roots or from the womb. Seeking and knowing who you are as well as addressing womb-related secrets are necessary for total deliverance and all-round victory.

Some of the information you need may take you back to while you were in the womb, the circumstances surrounding your conception, where your parents visited for help before you were born, and where and how you were born. The more of these mysteries heaven helps you to unravel, the deeper your deliverance and the greater your breakthroughs in life.

Once again, beloved, I implore you to be violent and persistent. The devil is a strong man and he does not release his captives easily. Pray and keep praying until you get your desired results and testimonies. I pray that the mercy of God will prevail for you and that the God of all possibilities, who answers by fire, will give you the beneficial secrets that will set you free and make you sing a new song, in the name of Jesus.

Chapter One

SELF-DISCOVERY: THE KEY TO DESTINY FULFILMENT

Self-discovery is a fundamental component of personal growth and development in both the spiritual and physical areas of life. It is a lifelong journey of exploration through prayerful enquiries and attempts to discover who we are, our potential, our purpose in life, and what core principles are guiding us to take different paths in the journey of life. Someone said that a person who finds himself loses his misery.

The reason many people are overwhelmed by spiritual problems and strange battles is that they are yet to discover who they are. Their ignorance makes them easy prey for the devil, his demons and his human cohorts. Discovering who you are today is the first step to being who you will be tomorrow.

Have you ever inquired from God, Your Maker, about who you are? Joseph was fortunate that, as a young man, heaven revealed his correct identity to him through his dreams

(Genesis 37:5-11). Jeremiah also got to know his correct identity from God (Jeremiah 1:4-12). An angel told Jacob and Gideon their correct identities through special encounters that each of them had. Through the ministry of His angels, God also revealed the correct identity of Samson, John the Baptist and Jesus Christ to the mothers of these Bible characters. It is important to note that, apart from Samson who failed to use the information properly, all the others obeyed God's instructions and followed His divine blueprint to run and shape their lives. Each of them became heroes of faith and world changers for God.

Beloved, if you can pray fervently and demonstrate unwavering faith in God, He would reveal great and mighty things to you. The beneficial secrets about your life that will guide your journey to all-round fulfilment and make your destiny speak gloriously will be made known to you. The more you pray, the more you discover! The more you discover, the more you recover and the more you recover, the more you experience fulfilment.

In other words, you need self-discovery to take your place in destiny. You must discover who you are. This is what will enable you to obtain and enjoy your inestimable heritage in Christ and achieve your divine purpose.

The Bible affirms that through his dreams, Joseph discovered himself and his destiny path. Genesis 37:5-11 underscores this important point:

> *And Joseph dreamed a dream, and he told it his brethren: and they hated him yet the more. And he said unto them, Hear, I pray you, this dream which I have dreamed: For, behold, we were binding sheaves in the field, and, lo, my sheaf arose, and also stood upright; and, behold, your sheaves stood round about, and made obeisance to my sheaf. And his brethren said to him, Shalt thou indeed reign over us? or shalt thou indeed have dominion over us? And they hated him yet the more for his dreams, and for his words. And he dreamed yet another dream, and told it his brethren, and said, Behold, I have dreamed a dream more; and, behold, the sun and the moon and the eleven stars made obeisance to me. And he told it to his father, and to his brethren: and his father rebuked him, and said unto him, What is this dream that thou hast dreamed? Shall I and thy mother and thy brethren indeed come to bow down ourselves to thee to the earth? And his brethren envied him; but his father observed the saying.*

In the end, with God's help and by living in righteousness, Joseph fulfilled his destiny. In Genesis 45:5, he told his brothers, *"Now therefore be not grieved, nor angry with yourselves, that ye sold me hither: for God did send me before you to preserve life."*

Prophet Jeremiah also got beneficial visitation and clear revelation from God on his true identity, life assignment and destiny path.

> Jeremiah 1:4-12: *Then the word of the LORD came unto me, saying, Before I formed thee in the belly I knew thee; and before thou camest forth out of the womb I sanctified thee, and I ordained thee a prophet unto the nations. Then said I, Ah, Lord GOD! behold, I cannot speak: for I am a child. But the LORD said unto me, Say not, I am a child: for thou shalt go to all that I shall send thee, and whatsoever I command thee thou shalt speak. Be not afraid of their faces: for I am with thee to deliver thee, saith the LORD. Then the LORD put forth his hand, and touched my mouth. And the LORD said unto me, Behold, I have put my words in thy mouth. See, I have this day set thee over the nations and over the kingdoms, to root out, and to pull down, and to destroy, and to throw down, to build, and to plant. Moreover the word of the LORD came unto me, saying, Jeremiah, what seest thou? And I said, I see a rod of an almond tree. Then said the LORD unto me, Thou hast well seen: for I will hasten my word to perform it.*

The truth is that when you successfully obtain beneficial secrets about your life and destiny and utilise them properly, your life, achievements and testimonies will bring glory to God, the same way the lives of Joseph, Jeremiah, Peter, Paul, and other Bible heroes and heroines did.

THE GREATEST DISCOVERY

There are great discoveries in life, but the greatest discovery that anyone can ever make is self-discovery (knowing who you are, your purpose in life, what you have, what you can do, and so on). In the New Testament, the Bible underscores the importance of knowing one's identity. Two of these instances stand out:

> Matthew 16:13-18: *When Jesus came into the coasts of Caesarea Philippi, he asked his disciples, saying, Whom do men say that I the Son of man am? And they said, Some say that thou art John the Baptist: some, Elias; and others, Jeremias, or one of the prophets. He saith unto them, But whom say ye that I am? And Simon Peter answered and said, Thou art the Christ, the Son of the living God. And Jesus answered and said unto him, Blessed art thou, Simon Barjona: for flesh and blood hath not revealed it unto thee,*

> *but my Father which is in heaven. And I say also unto thee,*
> *That thou art Peter, and upon this rock I will build my*
> *church; and the gates of hell shall not prevail against it.*

Jesus knew who He was, where He came from, where He would go back to as well as His mission and purpose on earth. He also wanted His disciples and other people to know His correct identity: Christ, the Son of the living God. If this knowledge was not pertinent, Jesus would not have bothered about asking His disciples the salient question in Matthew 16:13-20.

> *Matthew 16:13-20:   When Jesus came into the coasts of*
> *Caesarea Philippi, he asked his disciples, saying, Whom do*
> *men say that I the Son of man am? And they said, Some*
> *say that thou art John the Baptist: some, Elias; and others,*
> *Jeremias, or one of the prophets. He saith unto them, But*
> *whom say ye that I am? And Simon Peter answered and*
> *said, Thou art the Christ, the Son of the living God. And*
> *Jesus answered and said unto him, Blessed art thou, Simon*
> *Barjona: for flesh and blood hath not revealed it unto thee,*
> *but my Father which is in heaven. And I say also unto thee,*
> *That thou art Peter, and upon this rock I will build my*
> *church; and the gates of hell shall not prevail against it.*
> *And I will give unto thee the keys of the kingdom of heaven:*

> *and whatsoever thou shalt bind on earth shall be bound in heaven: and whatsoever thou shalt loose on earth shall be loosed in heaven. Then charged he his disciples that they should tell no man that he was Jesus the Christ.*

John the Baptist also knew who he was. When he was asked about his true identity, his answer left no doubt.

> *John 1:19-23 And this is the record of John, when the Jews sent priests and Levites from Jerusalem to ask him, Who art thou? And he confessed, and denied not; but confessed, I am not the Christ. And they asked him, What then? Art thou Elias? And he saith, I am not. Art thou that prophet? And he answered, No. Then said they unto him, Who art thou? that we may give an answer to them that sent us. What sayest thou of thyself? He said, I am the voice of one crying in the wilderness, Make straight the way of the Lord, as said the prophet Esaias.*

The response of John the Baptist to those who enquired about his true identity was unambiguous. He knew who he was. He also knew that His purpose was to serve as the forerunner of Jesus Christ and to be subservient to Him.

From the foregoing biblical examples, it is crystal clear that a person can be clueless about his divine identity. One of the deepest causes of problems and failure in people's lives is ignorance of who they are. If you are still ignorant of who you are and, as a result of that, your status in life and rating in God's programme are a far cry from what they ought to be, I pray that God will damage your ignorance today, open your understanding to know who you are and empower you to recover all that ignorance has denied you over the years, in the name of Jesus.

THE DEVIL'S DEVICES

The Bible warns that we should not be ignorant of the devil's devices (2 Corinthians 2:11). Unfortunately, many believers are. The devil is an expert at making people ignorant of their true identity. He is also an expert at making people doubt who they truly are. Matthew 4:3 reveals that he tried it on Jesus, *"If thou be the Son of God, command that these stones be made bread?"* What was the devil trying to do? He wanted Jesus to doubt His identity. The devil tried again at the Cross... *"If thou be the Son of God, come down from the cross"* (Matthew 27:40).

Beloved, knowing who you are and being convinced about it helps to strengthen your faith as well as make you stand in faith and Christ, no matter the storm that the devil brings against you. When the devil makes you doubt who you are or makes you lose the truth of your correct identity, he will defeat you. You must not allow him to achieve that agenda in your life. For instance, as a born-again child of God, the Bible reveals your identity as a saint of God, pardoned, sanctified and redeemed. The Bible also says that you are more than a conqueror through Christ (Romans 8:37); you are God's righteousness through Christ (2 Corinthians 5:21) and you are seated with Christ in the heavenly places far above principalities and powers (Ephesians 2:6).

You must take time to discover who you are as a person. You can achieve that through self-reflection – a phenomenon that allows you to think about and examine your actions, preferences, feeling, values, beliefs, emotions, and tendencies with the word of God as well as effectual prayer. As a believer, you must embark on the journey of self-discovery, know who you are as well as your God-given assignment and focus all your spiritual and physical resources on successfully and excellently completing your divine assignment. You should be able to declare, as Apostle Paul did, that, *"I have fought a good fight, I have finished my course, I have kept the faith: Henceforth there is laid up for me a crown of righteousness, which the Lord, the righteous judge, shall give me at that day: and not to me only, but unto all them also that love his appearing"* (2 Timothy 4:7-8).

BENEFITS OF SELF-DISCOVERY

Self-discovery will help you to gain better insights into yourself. It is a way for you to explore your personality, natural preferences, values, beliefs preferred styles and tendencies. It is also an all-encompassing journey of getting to know yourself better, what makes you tick, and how you go about life.

The truth is that when heaven gives you the beneficial information about who you are, and you utilise the information obediently and faithfully, all areas of your life (academics, career, health, marriage, finances, ministry, etc.) will not only be fruitful but also manifest the glory of God and produce testimonies of His wondrous works. For instance, as a young person, the knowledge of your divine identity will guide you on the course to study in the tertiary institution and the career to take up afterwards.

QUESTIONS YOU MUST ANSWER

Beloved, you and I need to find the answer to the question: Who am I? That answer is so important that it will serve as the key to open your heaven, doors of breakthrough and give you divine acceleration. Self-discovery will lead you to self-mastery, self-actualisation and self-development.

As a believer, by asking some salient questions and prayerfully seeking answers to them from God, you can know who you are as well as who you can be. Some of the other soul-searching and self-discovery questions include:

Why am I here? The truth is that every person on earth is here for a purpose. It is your responsibility to find out what that purpose is and how you can fulfil it. It is also your responsibility to put everything you have into ensuring that you fulfil your purpose in life. You must get to the core of your life's mission by asking this all-important question. Many who failed to ask and get properly guided ended up wasting decades of their lifetime pursuing wrong agenda and running the race that heaven did not set for them. For example, Moses was 80 years old before he encountered God in the burning bush and got to know who he was and God's purpose for him. He had been a shepherd all his life, but little did he know that heaven's record of his correct identity was that of a General and deliverer of God's people. Saul of Tarsus, who later became Apostle Paul and an extraordinary builder of God's Kingdom, spent several years persecuting Christians and working against the Church of Christ until he encountered Jesus Christ on the road to Damascus. The Lord revealed who he was and his divine assignment to him. Thank God that Paul did not disobey the heavenly vision he received.

Dearly beloved, self-discovery is the key to your destiny fulfilment. Ask yourself these questions and seek the face of God, not man, an oracle, soothsayer, or any medium, for answers to them:

1.   What will be the most important mark I will make on the world?
2.   What would I like to learn?
3.   What brings me joy?
4.   What am I most afraid of?
5.   What is one step I can take today to move closer to my ideal life?

SHOW YOUR IDENTITY

Identity is who or what a particular person or thing is. Your identity is your personality. Your look, shape, complexion, behaviour, language and nationality can be described as your physical identity. You also have a spiritual identity. It refers to who you are spiritually. It is also who God, your Creator, has made you to be.

The tragedy of life is that many people are ignorant of who they are. Some people have false identities and are living fake lives. It is not surprising that, for most of such people, life is unpleasant and unfulfilling. Beloved, you need to know your identity and heritage in Christ.

Gen. 1:26-27 and Gen. 2:7 tell us that in the beginning, God created man in His own image. It means that God gave man a physical identity. He made man a reflection of His glory.

Life without Christ is meaningless, dark, without direction and without divine identity. The Spirit and presence of God in us makes complete our identity in our Maker.

Sin destroys the image and glory of God in man. God asked Adam, "Where art thou?" (Gen.3:7-9). Sin removed God's image from Adam and his wife. It destroyed their spiritual identity. Similarly, in Gen. 32:24-28, the angel of God asked Jacob, "What is thy name?" For the first time in his life, Jacob discovered that he had a wrong identity – his name. The sons of Sceva, though of a priestly family, lacked God's Spirit and power (Acts 19:13-16).

The presence of the Spirit of God in us is power, purity and love. The Spirit Himself bears witness with our spirit that we are the children of God (Rom. 8:16).

WHO TOLD YOU?

Beloved, who are you? Is the knowledge you have about your identity correct? If you claim to know who you are, the big question from the Almighty God is: "Who told you?" Who told you to engage in your current career or occupation? Where did you get your instruction from and whose orders are you obeying? Beloved, if the information that is presently guiding your life is not from the infallible God, it means you got it from a source that can be wrong or make mistakes. The implication is that you are travelling in the wrong direction. You need to turn to God, change to His lane and receive the information for your journey from Him.

PERTINENT QUESTIONS

The question, "Who told you?", now transforms into some other 12 pertinent questions:

1. Why are you doing what you are doing?

2. What is God's purpose for your life?
3. What is your appointed or ordained future?
4. Toward what end were you born?
5. What has God predestined you to be or become in His divine will?
6. Why were you born?'
7. What is the expectation of heaven for your life?
8. What is it that is written in heavenly records concerning you?
9. What does God have in mind when He created you and allowed you to come to the world?
10. Do you know the sum total of who the Lord created you to be?
11. Are you aware of your inevitable necessity?
12. Do you know the divine decree for your life?

RELEVANT SCRIPTURES

The following scriptural passages are important for you to know. They will help to show your correct identity. I advise you to read and meditate on them:

> John 18:37 *Pilate therefore said unto him, Art thou a king then? Jesus answered, Thou sayest that I am a king. To this end was I born, and for this cause came I into the world,*

that I should bear witness unto the truth. Every one that is of the truth heareth my voice.

Matthew 26:24 *The Son of man goeth as it is written of him: but woe unto that man by whom the Son of man is betrayed! It had been good for that man if he had not been born.*

Isaiah 45:3 *And I will give thee the treasures of darkness, and hidden riches of secret places, that thou mayest know that I, the LORD, which call thee by thy name, am the God of Israel.*

2Timothy 4:7 *I have fought a good fight, I have finished my course, I have kept the faith:*

Luke 23:28 *But Jesus turning unto them said, Daughters of Jerusalem, weep not for me, but weep for yourselves, and for your children.*

You can have the mind of Christ when you meditate on the word of God. Meditating on the word of God will also flood your soul with the light of God and fill your life with His wisdom.

FOOD FOR THOUGHT

Pay close attention to the following important and deep statements:

1. You did not come to the world to hang around.
2. The moment you are born, your time begins. Time does not wait for you.
3. Many are destined for greatness but live in the darkroom of life.
4. You are born to excel.
5. In every child of destiny, there is an inborn urge propelling him to something of outstanding significance.
6. In every child of destiny, there is a drive to reach his full potential.
7. There is a difference between living long and living effectively.
8. You are born to contribute something to this life and you are unique.
9. It is a big tragedy if at the age of 30 and 40 you cannot give a good account of your life.
10. The greatest tragedy in life is a wasted life.
11. There is nothing more tragic than to forfeit your divine destiny.
12. You were born to be remarkable.
13. No one else in the world is like you. Your genetic make-up belongs only to you. Your fingerprints are so personal

that there are no other fingerprints like them in the whole world.

14. You can still become the man or woman you ought to be.
15. Be determined to fulfil your destiny.
16. Complete your deliverance. It will make you truly free.

PROCESS OF SELF-DISCOVERY

The process of self-discovery is one in which a person is guided through self-questioning and self-examination of one's thoughts, words, and actions, to reach conclusions regarding who they truly are. Through the process, you gain a deeper understanding of yourself, your character, values and purpose in life. You will also become more aware of your potential, who you should walk and work with, in order to fulfil your divine purpose. Beloved, knowing yourself is one of the wisest steps to take in life. When you discover who you are, you will be free. That is why the Bible affirms that *"Ye shall know the truth and the truth shall make you free"* (John 8:32).

TOOLS FOR SELF-DISCOVERY

As a believer, there are several biblically tested and proven tools you can use to successfully discover your correct identity. Some of these tools are as follows:

1. **The Word of God:** God's word is a potent and effective tool for self-discovery.

    > James 1:22-25 *But be ye doers of the word, and not hearers only, deceiving your own selves. For if any be a hearer of the word, and not a doer, he is like unto a man beholding his natural face in a glass: For he beholdeth himself, and goeth his way, and straightway forgetteth what manner of man he was. But whoso looketh into the perfect law of liberty, and continueth therein, he being not a forgetful hearer, but a doer of the work, this man shall be blessed in his deed.*

God's word is a true reflection of who you are.

I encourage you to use God's word as a mirror to truly understand yourself. You need to find out how you are faring and where you need to grow in the things of God. You also need to examine yourself and your actions (1 Cor. 11:28; 2 Cor. 13:5; Gal. 6:4) in the light of the word.

Through self-discovery, you can find a deeper connection between whom you are and whom you want to be. This happens when you allow God's word to take the right place in your life. God's word will reveal your true identity and heritage in Christ to you. Read it; memorise it; meditate on it day and night. Let it dwell in you richly! I counsel you to make God's word your necessary spiritual food and esteem it more than gold.

2. **Holy Ghost-Inspired Prayer:** Similarly, praying Holy-Ghost-vomited and targeted prayers of inquiry will make heaven release beneficial information about who you are, what your divine destiny is, the potential, gifts and talents that God has blessed you with as well as how you can accomplish your divine mission in life or fulfil your destiny. One of the mysteries of prayer is that it unlocks and unveils God's mysteries to His children.

3. **Divine Revelation:** Dreams, visions and revelations from God constitute powerful means of discovering one's correct identity and purpose in life. Jacob had an eye-opening and life-changing dream at Bethel. Joseph had a dream that showed a correct picture of whom he

was and who he would become. An essential condition for having divine dreams or heavenly visions is to be holy within and without as well as to live in complete obedience to God. God's secrets are with the righteous!

4. **Divine Encounter:** Whenever God wants to do a special work or effect a supernatural change in the affairs of men, He would intervene directly or send His angels to man. It was through encounters like this that Mary got to know her true identity and her special assignment to bring the Son of God into the world. It was through a divine encounter with God's angel that Zechariah learnt about the blueprint of the life and destiny of John the Baptist. It was also through a divine encounter with Jesus that Peter and Paul knew their assignments and purposes on earth. Do you want to know who you are? Pray fervently to God to give you a special and eye-opening encounter that will make an undeniable change in your life.

5. **Befriend the Holy Spirit:** I advise you to befriend the Holy Spirit and be completely yielded to Him. He is the author of the Scriptures, the unveiler of mysteries,

secrets, deep truths and eternal revelations. He will give you an insight into the mysteries and secrets of life. He will make your identity and heritage in Christ fully known to you.

Beloved, getting baptised in the Holy Spirit and the fire of God will open your understanding to the profitable word of God, make your prayer life effective and fruitful, give you life-changing revelations from heaven and birth divine encounters in your life.

Prayer Points

1. O God arise and show me who I am, in the name of Jesus.

2. O God arise and show me beneficial secrets about my life, in the name of Jesus.

3. Powers blocking me from knowing who I am, die violently, in the name of Jesus.

4. Negative destiny adjusters troubling my life, scatter unto desolation, in the name of Jesus.

5. Any power killing my divine identity, be killed by the slapping angels of God, in the name of Jesus.

6. Any servant or slave occupying the horse of my destiny, somersault and be removed, in the name of Jesus.

7. Powers assigned to terminate my glory, destroy yourselves, in the name of Jesus.

Chapter Two

THE ALL-IMPORTANT QUESTIONS YOU MUST ANSWER

The world is a deep place and there are profound items of information in it. These items of information, like precious mineral resources, cannot be found on the surface of the earth, but deep inside it. To access eye-opening, liberating and life-changing information from heaven, you must ask the right and probing questions. There are several questions that the inquisitive mind asks in the school of the mysteries of life. The answers to these questions will give you divine direction and the ability to succeed in life. The 8 all-important questions are as follows:

1.   Where am I from?

2.   Why am I here?

3.   What do I have?

4.   What can I do?

5.   Who do I work with?

6.   Where am I going? Now that I am here, where am I going?

7.   What kind of legacy am I going to leave behind?

However, the deepest and the most serious of these questions in the school of the mystery of life is:

8.   Who am I?

Beloved, an unexamined life is not worth living. Let us examine each of the questions one after the other. Getting a deeper understanding of each question as well as the right answer will give your life, destiny, marriage and ministry the quantum leap you have always desired.

1.   WHERE ARE YOU FROM?

The question of where you came from is one you and everyone should find the right answer to. People who live in ignorance of their true origin usually live in ways that are inconsistent with what God intends for them. People who have the wrong notion of their origin do not live in obedience to God and His word, neither do they live purpose-driven and eternity-in-view lives. You need to know where you came from, who to live for, your purpose in life, how to fulfil it, who to journey with, and where you are going when you leave the earth.

The enemy does not want you to fulfil your destiny in life and make heaven. That is why he fights terribly to prevent you from knowing vital truths about yourself: who you are, where you are from, your purpose and where you are going. Scientists have come up with numerous theories about the origin and evolution of man. These theories have all been proved to be wrong. They are lies and deceits of the devil to mislead people and keep them from fulfilling their divine purposes. The moment a person lives on the wrong premise of where he came from, his life will be wrongly directed and positioned. The consequence of this is that the person will fail in life and miss heaven. That will not be your portion, in the mighty name of Jesus.

Similarly, Charles Darwin's theory of evolution as well as other theories propounded by scientists, in an attempt to explain the origin of man, did not attribute man's origin exclusively to God. Hence, they have been faulted and flawed even among scientists themselves. However, the Bible did not leave believers clueless about the origin of man. The word of

God affirms that God is the Creator of all things and the Perfect Manager of the whole universe. The work of creation, including the making of man, was the central focus of the first three chapters of Genesis, the first Book of the Bible. The following Bible passages reveal the true origin of man and his citizenship:

Genesis 1: 26-31 And God said, Let us make man in our image, after our likeness: and let them have dominion over the fish of the sea, and over the fowl of the air, and over the cattle, and over all the earth, and over every creeping thing that creepeth upon the earth. So God created man in his own image, in the image of God created he him; male and female created he them. And God blessed them, and God said unto them, Be fruitful, and multiply, and replenish the earth, and subdue it: and have dominion over the fish of the sea, and over the fowl of the air, and over every living thing that moveth upon the earth. And God said, Behold, I have given you every herb bearing seed, which is upon the face of all the earth, and every tree, in the which is the fruit of a tree yielding seed; to you it shall be for meat. And to every beast of the earth, and to every fowl of the air, and to every thing that creepeth upon the earth, wherein there is life, I have given every green herb for meat: and it was so. And

God saw every thing that he had made, and, behold, it was very good. And the evening and the morning were the sixth day.

John 1: 1-5 In the beginning was the Word, and the Word was with God, and the Word was God. The same was in the beginning with God. <u>All things were made by him; and without him was not any thing made that was made.</u> In him was life; and the life was the light of men. And the light shineth in darkness; and the darkness comprehended it not.

Colossians: 1:16-17 For by Him all things were created that are in heaven and that are on earth, visible and invisible, whether thrones or dominions or[a]principalities or [b]powers. All things were created through Him and for Him. And He is before all things, and in Him all things consist.

The foregoing scriptural passages firmly and convincingly establish the truth that man originated from God, his Maker and Potter. Man did not evolve from apes or any other source that some scientists have erroneously claimed. He is God's masterpiece of creation. He is made to worship and serve

God. Man cannot fulfil this vital purpose of His creation if he attributes his origin and creation to anyone other than the Almighty God. Knowing the truth that you came from God, that you should live to worship Him and that you will return to Him is paramount. Unfortunately, the devil does not want you to know and live by these truths. He does not want you to acknowledge that God created you and that you owe Him worship, allegiance and obedience.

He invaded the Garden of Eden and destroyed the relationship between the couple, Adam and Eve, and God. The couple knew God created them, and they had intimacy with God. The devil was envious of that. Similarly, the enemy's incessant and terrible attack on Job was simply to destroy Job's relationship with God. He wanted Job to deny God and lose the intimacy he was enjoying with Him. The enemy wants to have the worship and glory that are due to God.

Having the correct and scriptural notion of where you came from will help you to achieve the following:

1.   Have and grow a beneficial relationship with God.

2.   Live Christ-like, abundant and fulfilled life.

3.   Live a purpose-driven life

4.   Be heaven-focussed

5.   Identify and fulfil your calling and ministry

Beloved, you are a citizen of heaven walking on planet earth. You are the crowning glory of God's creation. He made you fearfully and wonderfully. You are not an accident but a deliberate miracle of God sent to earth to dispense His grace and enforce His dominion. God owns your life and everything about you, and to Him you will return to give account.

YOUR BACKGROUND AND ANCESTRY

Apart from being certain about your heavenly citizenship or origin, you must also make deep enquiry about your background, your foundation and your roots. In addition to all these, you must know your family pattern.

Some of the salient questions that will help to unravel the mystery surrounding your ancestry, your birth and your destiny transformation include:

1.   Who are your ancestors?
2.   Where do they hail from?

3.   What was their occupation?
4.   Who did they serve (God or idols)?
5.   Are there ancestral strongholds to confront and conquer?
6.   Are there evil family patterns to pray aggressively about?
7.   Are there sicknesses and diseases that run in the family?
8.   Are there particular challenges that are common with male members but not found in female members of the family, and vice versa?
9.   Does your family have taboos, culture and traditions?
10.   Is there any evidence of collective captivity, slavery, polygamy, alcoholism, etc in the family?

Dearly beloved, you need to find answers to all these questions. When you get correct information on where you hail from spiritually and physically, you will successfully free yourself from bondage, possess your divine inheritance and enjoy all-round fulfilment.

Finally, knowing your true origin will enable you to know, appropriate and enjoy the authority and blessings freely given to all genuine children of God. As a believer, if you do not know where you came from or your citizenship (heaven) and the rights and privileges that are attached to being born again, the enemy will keep short-changing and harassing you.

Similarly, knowing where you hail from spiritually will enable you to pattern your life in line with the values and expectations of your place of origin and return at the end of your sojourn on earth. Physically, it will enable you to obtain deliverance from evil collective captivity, ancestral yokes, evil family pattern and flow, parental mistakes and deficits, and so on. Therefore, I encourage you to get the right answer to the question of where you came from and let the answer bless your life tremendously.

2.   WHY AM I HERE?

Discovering and fulfilling your divine purpose is the greatest achievement that you can record in life. The truth is that it will also determine whether you spend your eternity in heaven or hell.

Many people live and die without making any meaningful mark in life. The reason is that they never found out their purpose and never lived to fulfil it. Such lives usually lack meaningful goals, direction and focus. Besides, they often achieve very little or nothing. Beloved, you must live with a God-given and God-driven purpose.

Purpose is the reason for which something is done or created, or for which something exists. In Ecclesiastes 3:1, the Bible says, *"To every thing there is a season, and a time to every purpose under the heavens."*

God is our Maker, and He alone determines our purpose, not our parents, pastors, bosses and political leaders, and so on. The decision of what our purpose should be is not for us to make; we must find it out from God and obey it to the letter. I have searched through the Bible diligently several times. I am yet to find one person who knew God's purpose for his or her life and devoted everything to fulfilling the purpose and did not succeed or leave a great legacy behind in life.

The Bible affirms that Jeremiah knew who he was and he fulfilled his destiny.

> Jeremiah 1:5-12 *Before I formed thee in the belly I knew thee; and before thou camest forth out of the womb I sanctified thee, and I ordained thee a prophet unto the nations. Then said I, Ah, Lord GOD! behold, I cannot speak: for I am a child. But the LORD said unto me, Say not, I am a child: for thou shalt go to all that I shall send thee, and whatsoever I command thee thou shalt speak. Be not afraid of their faces: for I am with thee to deliver thee, saith the LORD. Then the LORD put forth his hand, and touched my mouth. And the LORD said unto me, Behold, I have put my words in thy mouth. See, I have this day set*

> *thee over the nations and over the kingdoms, to root out, and*
> *to pull down, and to destroy, and to throw down, to build,*
> *and to plant. Moreover the word of the* LORD *came unto*
> *me, saying, Jeremiah, what seest thou? And I said, I see a*
> *rod of an almond tree. Then said the* LORD *unto me, Thou*
> *hast well seen: for I will hasten my word to perform it.*

Similarly, John the Baptist demonstrated clearly that he knew
his divine purpose. He was also resolutely committed to its
fulfilment. He said that he was not that Light, but was sent to
bear witness of that Light that all men might believe (John
1:8). Apart from bearing witness of the Light, he asserted that
he came to prepare the hearts of the people to receive Jesus
and to herald the arrival of the Messiah.

> *John 1:19-30 And this is the record of John, when the Jews*
> *sent priests and Levites from Jerusalem to ask him, Who art*
> *thou? And he confessed, and denied not; but confessed, I am*
> *not the Christ. And they asked him, What then? Art thou*
> *Elias? And he saith, I am not. Art thou that prophet? And*
> *he answered, No. Then said they unto him, Who art thou?*
> *that we may give an answer to them that sent us. What*
> *sayest thou of thyself? He said, I am the voice of one crying*
> *in the wilderness, Make straight the way of the Lord, as*
> *said the prophet Esaias. And they which were sent were of*

> *the Pharisees. And they asked him, and said unto him, Why baptizest thou then, if thou be not that Christ, nor Elias, neither that prophet? John answered them, saying, I baptize with water: but there standeth one among you, whom ye know not;* ²⁷ *He it is, who coming after me is preferred before me, whose shoe's latchet I am not worthy to unloose. These things were done in Bethabara beyond Jordan, where John was baptizing. The next day John seeth Jesus coming unto him, and saith, Behold the Lamb of God, which taketh away the sin of the world. This is he of whom I said, After me cometh a man which is preferred before me: for he was before me.*

The truth is that every Christian's purpose is the same as that of John the Baptist: be a witness for Jesus; draw attention to Jesus; proclaim Him as Saviour.

Jesus Christ, our Royal Master, also knew why He was on earth. On different occasions, He made clear statements about His purpose. He was also resolutely committed to the fulfilment of His purpose.

The Bible reveals that the divine purpose of Jesus on earth was to solve the sin problem and save mankind from eternal damnation.

> Matthew 1:21 *And she shall bring forth a son, and thou shalt call his name JESUS: for he shall save his people from their sins.*

Also, on the purpose and assignment of Jesus on earth, John 18:37 says, *"Pilate therefore said unto him, Art thou a king then? Jesus answered, Thou sayest that I am a king. To this end was I born, and for this cause came I into the world, that I should bear witness unto the truth. Every one that is of the truth heareth my voice."*

Beloved, you serve a God of purpose! He has a good purpose for your life. You are here for an assignment. It is your responsibility to find it out.

When a person does not know his purpose in life, he is likely to devote his entire life to things outside that purpose. Such a person will end up struggling, frustrated, and a failure, fishing and catching nothing in the ocean of life. That is the secret of profitless hard work, non-achievement and poverty that characterise the lives of many people today.

Beloved, it is a tragedy for one not to know why he is here on earth and what assignment he is here to do. Many lack this vital information and have ended up doing the wrong occupation or being in the wrong career. Some have ended up getting married to the wrong spouse, living for the wrong purpose or values and pursuing wrong dreams. At the end of the day, many of such people fail and live in regrets.

You need to discover your divine purpose and assignment early in life. You should also commit everything you have to fulfilling your purpose as early in life as you can. Moses did not know his divine purpose until he was 80 years old. You should not wait that long.

What do you need to do to discover your purpose? First, you should give your life to Jesus. Accept Him as your Personal Lord and Saviour. The moment you do that, God will begin to reveal deep secrets about who you are and your purpose in life to you. Second, you must be an avid reader and doer of the word of God. The Bible says that the entrance of His word gives light and it gives understanding to the simple. God's word will bring you inspiration, illumination and direction. Third, you should live a holy and righteous lifestyle. With these, as well as complete and consistent obedience to God, heaven will reveal your purpose on earth and in Christ to you. Also, you need to be a friend of the Holy Spirit and be baptised in the Holy Ghost with the evidence of speaking in tongues. Lastly, you should be very prayerful. The effectual fervent prayer of the righteous believer avails much.

I pray that as Jesus, Paul, Peter and other Bible heroes knew and fulfilled their divine purposes, you will also know and fulfil yours, in the mighty name of Jesus.

3. WHAT DO I HAVE?

Having established the fact that you need to discover your divine purpose and do everything to fulfil it, the next step is to discover and uncover your potential, endowments, gifts and talents. God has blessed every individual with gifts and talents. Your gift or talent is your natural ability. They are those divine hidden treasures that have been prepared ahead of you, to get you into the full picture of what God has designed you to be. Without discovering and putting them to use, your purpose in life may not be fully realised.

Some gifts are physical while some are spiritual. You are supposed to use both of them to fulfil your destiny, serve God and man as well as leave a glorious legacy behind when you depart this planet. God gave Esther the gifts of a good look. She was a ravishing beauty with exceptional brain and an amiable personality. God also gave her favour with Himself and all men. God gave her those gifts not just for her benefits but to serve Him and to benefit others. It is your responsibility to use your God-given gifts correctly, judiciously and in ways that glorify God. Esther did this. In addition to the gifts earlier mentioned, God gave her the position of queen and wife to the greatest man in the kingdom. She used her position to serve God by putting her life on the line, and she ended up saving her people (the Jews) from the plot of destruction masterminded by Haman. God gave David the ability to use his slingshot to kill Goliath. God turned the rod of Moses into a supernatural weapon and a gift that demystified the magicians of Egypt, brought plagues upon the land and later parted the Red Sea.

Joseph and Daniel were gifted in dream and dream interpretation. Similarly, God gave Bezaleel the son of Uri and Aholiab the son of Ahisamach (Exodus 31:1-6 and Exodus 35:30-35) special abilities to do the work of artistry ingenuously to build His temple.

Beloved, all good and perfect gifts are from God (James 1:17). They are given in different measures (Ephesians 4:7). They are precious and should not be neglected (1 Timothy 4:14). Also, always remember that God has given you His gifts to accompany you and be useful in your life's journey as well as for the fulfilment of your divine assignment and purpose. That is why the Bible says that the gifts and calling of God are irrevocable (Romans 11:29).

What physical and spiritual gifts do you have? Have you identified them? It is your responsibility to put them to gainful use; serve God with them and build His kingdom. You should also use them to benefit your own life and others. God has given you every gift to help you succeed in your divine assignment, career and destiny. Remember also that you will give account to the Owner of the gifts on how you used the gifts He has given to you.

You and I were created in the image of God with a supply of talents, gifts and abilities that we are to use in building His Kingdom here on earth and bringing glory to Him. It is disheartening that many people do not know what their gifts and talents are. Many have died without discovering what they have in terms of potential, gifts and talents. As a result, such people left the earth not fulfilling their divine purposes. In case you do not know your gifts and talents, help is available for you. The things you are good at. The things you enjoy doing and that make you feel accomplished and fulfilled are your God-given talents and abilities. This is true, whether you are using your gift to serve God in church, your career and in other areas or not.

Beloved, I encourage you to take the matter of knowing your gift to God in prayer. Tell Him to show you the gifts He has endowed you with. Take an inventory of those gifts (physical and spiritual) by writing them down. You can also look inward and ask yourself what you are good at, what you enjoy doing and what gives you a sense of fulfilment when you do it? Once the Lord helps you to know your gifts and talents, pray to Him to teach you how best to use them to glorify Him and serve others.

4.   WHAT CAN I DO?

We established earlier that the reason God gave you gifts and talents is that you might serve Him and others with them. It is your responsibility to ensure that you do not bury, despise, lose, under-utilise or fail to use your gifts and talents to build God's kingdom and bring glory to Him. They have been given to you in trust, and you will give account to God on how you use them.

God has endowed each of us with divine abilities, skills, gifts and talents to achieve the utmost for our destinies. The Apostle Paul calls it "Treasure in earthen vessel" (2 Cor. 4:7). Your gifts and talents are the divine tools for handling your responsibilities and duties in life. Starting with Adam in the book of Genesis, God created a garden and equipped it accordingly. He put Adam there and gave him the responsibility to "keep and to dress it" (Gen. 2:15). Thus we saw the first man involved in horticulture. That was a divine assignment for the first man, according to God's purpose.

God gave Moses the rod, a divine tool for him in the work of deliverance of the Israelites from bondage in Egypt. To the ordinary person, it was just a rod; but in the mind of God, it was more than a wooden object. It was the Rod of God to display His wonders before the Egyptians and to bring deliverance to God's people. Also, God gave Bezaleel the son of Uri special abilities to do the designs of the Tabernacle. His gift, talent and assignment were not the same as Moses' and Aaron's. Bezaleel used His gifts to serve God and earned a good name in the Bible. God knows our abilities and what each of us can do to achieve the utmost for His glory.

Beloved, failure to discover and use God's gifts to serve and glorify Him often ends in tragedy and regret. God gave Samson unusual anointing and strength. He made him a judge in Israel. Though Samson was supposed to represent God and deliver His children, the Israelites, from the unbelieving Philistines, he failed God by constantly breaking divine covenants and defiling himself before his holy God. He lost his anointing and strength, dying shamefully with his enemies. Saul, the Benjamite, also got the throne of Israel on a platter of gold. It was a gift that heaven graciously bestowed on him. The gift rewrote the history of his lowly family and brought them from obscurity to fame. However, King Saul lost this gift and privilege because his heart was not right with God – he was a disobedient servant. The consequence was that God took the kingdom from him and gave it to David, a man after His heart. Do you know that Judas' inclusion among the disciples of Jesus was a gift and blessing heaven conferred on him? What did Judas do with what he was given? He wasted it. The spirit of mammon and betrayal got the better part of him, and he died miserably.

Beloved, a man can receive nothing except it is given to him from heaven. In the same vein, heaven expects you to use your gift and talent wisely and productively to serve God and others. If you do not, there are grave consequences as we read in the instances of Samson, King Saul and Judas Iscariot. Therefore, I encourage you to seek God's face and get His direction on how to use His gifts and talents to best serve Him and benefit others.

Can you sing and play musical instruments like David? Discover your potential; use it to serve God and bless other people. Remember, the Bible says the gift of a man shall make a way for him and make him stand among great men (Prov. 18:16). When you use your gifts and talents to serve God and others, heaven will open the door of greatness and elevation for you. It was these gifts that took David, the shepherd boy, to the palace. He became the musician who played godly and anointed music to chase away evil spirits from King Saul. Can you see the power of music and its divine therapeutic effect on man? This can only be done through God, not by human ability. Similarly, the sling in David's hand brought down Goliath, the boastful giant. By strength shall no man prevail! What is in you? What is in your hand? God wants you to use it to achieve spectacular results.

Are you gifted in writing? Get your pen ready as that of a ready writer and use it to dispel the Good News of salvation. Have you been blessed with a good voice? Use it to sing to the glory of your Lord and Master. The blind minstrel, Fanny Crosby, despite her disabilities, wrote over 9,000 hymns. Be a Dorcas and a Lydia in the ministry of hospitality. Be an encourager like Barnabas, the son of consolation. The list is endless! The secret to your greatness is a treasure inside of you waiting to be discovered! As you do these, God shall be glorified in your life, in Jesus' name.

Beloved, when you use your God-given gifts and talents to build His kingdom, glorify Him and serve others, He will protect those gifts and talents from being destroyed or stolen by the enemy. He will also give you more and make your life a bigger bundle of testimonies. Therefore, if you have not been serving God and blessing others with your gifts and talents, start to do so today. If you have been doing so, begin to do more from now. Heaven will give you pleasant surprises, in the name of Jesus.

5.   WHO DO I WALK WITH?

In Prov.13:20, the Bible states that the companion of wise people shall be wiser, but the companion of fools shall be destroyed by his folly. This simply tells us that the company you keep has a great role to play in your life, and it can make or mar your divine fulfilment. That is, the association you keep, the friends you walk and work with, your acquaintances and all would greatly determine the level of your success in life. Your relationships and interpersonal skills are key to becoming who God created you to be (Ps1:1).

The same is the message of 1Cor. 15:33. Your friends will make or mar your life. Even the popular saying, "show me your friend and I will tell you who you are" is very much applicable here. It is an obvious fact that there will be a level of influence upon your life by the company you keep. This influence may be positive or negative, and it goes vice versa.

To become what God has destined you to become, you must keep the right company. Matt. 7:17-20 says that a good tree cannot bear bad fruits, neither can a bad tree bring forth good fruits; rather, by their fruits, we shall know them. These fruits are the by-products of your relationships, either good or bad.

However, the journey of life cannot be walked alone. God did not create anyone in a vacuum. We are to relate with God vertically, and horizontally with our fellow men. It is like the symbol of the Cross!

1 John.4:20 tells us that you cannot claim to love God whom you don't see, but hate your brother who is right beside you. We are all created in the express image of God. Therefore, we must live peaceably with all men. However, wisdom teaches us to refrain from men of negative reputation and conduct. In Prov.1:10-19, the preacher kept giving a sound warning to his son to desist from walking with the wrong group of friends. Their way leads to death and destruction. It goes to confirm, therefore, that no man can be in the wrong association and yet fulfil divine purpose.

Let us consider a good example. God instructed the children of Israel, through Moses, not to follow the idolatrous way of the nations whose land they possessed through God. Failure to comply with these divine instructions would cause them to disobey God and go the way of these heathen countries. It happened! God was displeased with His chosen people, and He gave them over to the hands of their enemies to be afflicted as He had said. The wrong company separates a man from God and easily leads to sin and iniquity (Exodus 23:23-33).

God had to separate Samuel from the children of Eli, as close as they were, living together. It was for a divine purpose: so that His word concerning the priesthood and the lineage of Eli would come to pass. God changed the baton, and Samuel got the divine mandate to continue as a priest and prophet unto God.

David had a faithful and trustworthy friend in Jonathan, who saved him from the death threats and attempts to kill him by King Saul, his father. We can also see Rehoboam, the son of Solomon, who sought counsel from his peers, but rejected the right counsel of the elders. He embraced the wrong counsel and, unknown to him, the purpose of God to tear away the kingdom from him as a result of his father's sins was accomplished.

In 2 Cor. 6:14-18, God gave a strong word for the intentional separation of His children from the wrong association. He said, *"Come out from among them!"* There is absolutely no valuable relationship between light and darkness. Why then should a Christian be found in the company of unbelievers? The new wine and old wine cannot be mixed in the same wineskin, else there will be an explosion. If you are really for God, then you should endeavour to walk with your kind (the children of light), and become an example for others to follow, a godly role model, and a pacesetter.

Beloved, there are some persons you must not meet in life if you must achieve your divine purpose. At the same time, there are people you should not miss! These are destiny helpers- people that have been divinely ordained to play a definite role in your life towards fulfilling God's will for your life. I pray that you shall not miss your destiny helpers, in Jesus' name. May heaven connect you to the right persons and disconnect you from destiny aborters, in the name of Jesus.

Being in the wrong company will make you an enemy of God and a friend of the world (James 4:4, 1John 2:15-17). Such a person shall have no part in God's kingdom. Why are you embracing ungodliness? You can still make a turn. Now is the day of salvation; tomorrow may be too late. How can you be a child of God and yet be rubbing minds with the enemies of God? You cannot sit on the fence; you are either for God or against Him. Stop giving excuses! Avoid compromise, it destroys! Your relationships speak! As written in Mathew 5:13-16, you are called to be the light and salt of the world, standing out and distinct from negative influences that can truncate and destroy divine promises upon your life.

When you walk with the right company, you will:

1. Become a friend of God.
2. Be divinely connected.
3. Be listed among the believers and God will be pleased with you.
4. Ask, seek and knock, and God will answer you.
5. Have divine confidence that whatever you ask, you will receive.
6. Receive power to know the mind of God concerning your life and situations around you (Ps. 25:14)
7. Be divinely guided and led through the journey of life (Ps. 32:8).

Do you want to end life a fulfilled man or woman? Then you must walk with the right company. The Bible counsels us "not to be unequally yoked..." Imagine two animals yoked together for farming purposes; neither of the two can go faster than the other. To achieve the purpose for which they were yoked, both must go in the same direction and at the same pace per time.

The same applies to us humans. It simply means that you cannot go too far from the company you are yoked with. Your speed is determined by the kind of people you are yoked with. If you keep company with crawlers, you will experience slow progress. Conversely, if you walk with flyers, you will be a high flyer and an uncommon achiever.

Beloved, it is time you looked inwards and around you.

- What values are your friends and acquaintances adding to your life?
- Or is their company draining your virtues?
- Are you the only one-eyed man among the blind? Remember, the Bible says that the blind cannot lead the blind; both will fall into a ditch.
- Are you challenged to be innovative and expand your horizons?
- Or you are among those who are satisfied with average and remain in their comfort zone?
- Are you in the company of the dead or the living? (Prov. 21:16)

Are you among the lazy and the slothful ones? Come out and be diligent and you will stand before kings and not before mere men, as stated in Prov. 22:29.

The dead are those who have no relationship with God. They lack wisdom and every trait of godliness. Their lives and activities are an abomination unto God. But the living are those who have come to know and accept Jesus Christ as Lord and Saviour. He is the Way, the Truth and Life! He is the Light. None that is found in Him shall walk in darkness. In Him is life and that life is the light unto all men (John 1: 4).

In case you need a change, you should do the following:

1. Repent and ask God for forgiveness for moving with the wrong company.

2. Prayerfully ask for the wisdom to retrace your steps and separate yourself to God and to the right company.

3. Read and study God's word (Josh1:8).

4. Pray fervently and pray always

5. Resist temptations to walk with the wrong people or do what they do.

6. Continue steadfastly in faith, serving the Lord.

7.   Be diligent and resourceful.

8.   Be a Godly role model, one that will draw others to
        Christ and not the contrary.

9.   Be a true soldier of God that is ready to wage a good
        warfare. Your victory is ever secured in Christ.

6.   WHERE AM I GOING, NOW THAT I AM HERE?

This is a pertinent question everyone should ask and find a
genuine answer to. We have established that you did not
originate from ape. Rather, you are God's glorious creation and
masterpiece. You are a citizen of heaven and you have a
marvelous heritage in Christ. Since the question of where you
came from is important, the one on where you are going should
equally be treated with utmost importance. In 1 Corinthians
15:19, the Bible says, *"If in this life only we have hope in Christ,
we are of all men most miserable."*
Unfortunately, many people live their lives as if this world is their
home and all will end here. They do not live with eternity in view.
They love the world and things of the world. They have lost sight
of the fact that we need to use this life to prepare for our eternity
in heaven.

As believers, our hope in Christ should transcend this life. We should enjoy His salvation, atoning sacrifice, forgiveness and justification. We should receive eternal life and the grace to reign with Him in heaven as well as the glory of the hereafter. We should not hope in Christ only for the things of this life. If we do, Apostle Paul says we should be pitied.

Beloved, now that you are here on planet earth, where are you going? This question reveals an interesting truth. That is, you are on a journey. This world is not your destination. You have come to this world to carry out an assignment. When the time given to you by God to spend on earth is up, you will depart from this world. That is why the Bible says that it is appointed for man to die once, and after that, there is judgement (Hebrews 9:27). So, the truth of the Scripture we must all live by is that there is life, death, judgement and eternal life in heaven or hell, depending on who you serve and live for while on earth. There is continued life after death. Another interesting point is that just as you did not determine when to come into this world, you may not be able to determine when your exit from it will be. However, you can determine whether you want to spend eternity in heaven or hell by the things you do here and the ways you live your life.

The following are some of the essential steps you should take to spend your eternity in heaven:

1. **You must be born again:** Jesus said that except you are born again, you cannot enter into the kingdom of God (John 3:3). Nicodemus was well known among the Sanhedrin. He was a successful man by human standard, but to Jesus and heaven, he was not qualified to enter heaven because he was not regenerated. He went to Jesus and asked what he could do to make heaven. Jesus' answer to him was that he must be born of the Spirit. Beloved, if you want to spend eternity in heaven, you must be born again and live for Christ consistently throughout your lifetime.

2. **You must hate sin and iniquity:** Sin, iniquity and the works of the flesh are the greatest hindrances to making heaven. They are also the evil magnets that draw people to hell.

God hates sin and iniquity with perfect hatred. It was sin that sent Adam and Eve out of the Garden of Eden. Iniquity was found in Lucifer, and it turned the arch-angel to a fallen angel, a rebel and an arch-enemy of man.

You must also pray the works of the flesh out of your life. You must walk in the Spirit and be God-driven. You must also pray the fruit of the Spirit into your life and manifest Christlikeness spiritually and physically.

3. **You must make holiness and righteousness your lifestyle:** The Bible says that without holiness, it is impossible to see God. The Most High is holy. He is upright and there is no unrighteous in Him. If you want to spend eternity in heaven, you must avoid the filthiness of the spirit, the soul and the body. Be God-conscious and heaven-conscious always. Stay with God and stay in faith in all situations and at all times. The Bible says that all unrighteousness is sin. Always steer clear of anything ungodly. I pray that God will keep you from falling and present you blameless before His throne, in the name of Jesus.

4. **You must be obedient:** To the obedient, walking with God will be profitable and rewarding here on earth and in eternity. Obedience is better than sacrifice, and hearkening is better than the fat of rams (1 Sam. 15:22). Beloved, if you desire to spend your eternity in heaven, your walk with God must be characterised by complete, prompt and unquestioning obedience.

5.   **You must love and live by God's word:** The word of
        God is essential in pointing you to heaven and helping
        you to get there. When you are an avid reader of God's
        word and allow it to dwell richly in you, the devil will not
        be able to deceive and short-change you. As Jesus
        answered and defeated him by quoting the word of God,
        you will also confidently pull out your sword of the Spirit
        and defeat the enemy. Therefore, I encourage you to
        make God's word a weapon and tool in your journey in
        life as well as your compass in your heaven-bound
        journey.

6.   **You must serve God with your life and all you have:**
        When you dedicate your life and all that God has given
        you to serving Him and advancing His kingdom, you are
        simply making yourself a candidate of heaven. Jesus lived
        a life of utmost service and sacrifice. If you want to make
        heaven, your life must be sold out to God on the altar of
        sacrifice and service, just as the heroes of faith in
        Hebrews 11 did. Paul was so sure he fulfilled its condition
        that he declared, *"I have fought the good work of faith,
        completed my course and the crown of righteousness
        awaits me"* (2 Tim. 4:7-8).

7.   **You must be very prayerful:** Prayer is a powerful weapon in the life of every believer. Prayer helps you to have constant intimacy with God, keep His presence and continue to serve Him. Prayer releases angelic intervention and help. Prayer unleashes the grace that will move you away from temptation and sin as well as the broad way and move you to righteousness and the narrow way. When you pray fervently and constantly, heaven will purge you of everything that pertains to hell and perdition and endow you with the grace and blessings of heaven. Prayer will draw you to the throne of grace and heaven. Pray without ceasing!

7.   WHAT LEGACY AM I LEAVING BEHIND?

What remains to be done for a man or woman who has lived a fulfilled life, having observed every leading of the Holy Spirit? Such a person, having achieved his life's purpose, only needs to show the world the history of how he fared while here. The same goes for someone who lived and passed through life without leaving any trace of positive influence, nor produced his kind in whatever way. This is where the issue of legacy comes in.

The big question is, what legacy are you leaving behind? What shall be said of you when you would have left this world? What impact do you intend to make on humanity as a whole? Would you depart from this earth without leaving your footprints boldly on the sands of time? All these and more are what should preoccupy your mind, not at the end of life, but even as you are journeying through life, seeking to know and do the will of God. Think about it!

We read about biblical characters, men and women who did exploits for God, affected humanity positively and the world would not forget that they came, lived and made their marks. Certainly, you do not pray to die unfulfilled, unsung and uncelebrated. This is why you should begin to prepare the evening of your lifetime from the morning. Anyone that intends to leave a godly legacy must have been working towards it and doing all that would bring it to bear.

What is a legacy? It can simply be defined as a gift, possession, wealth or materials that have been passed down from one person to another. It could be from parents to their children or ancestors to the generations after them. Even the Bible records in Proverbs 13:22 that a good man leaves an inheritance to his children's children. If so, then it means a bad man can also leave a bad legacy for his children. No wonder we see cases of negative generational inheritances. As a result, the present generation suffers consequences of things they are not originally involved in nor guilty of. I pray that you shall not suffer for the trouble you did not create, in Jesus' name.

This tells us that a legacy has a generational perspective. That is, your legacy lives beyond you, whether it is positive or negative. It tells of how well you have lived and the residue of what you are passing on or handling over to others. It could be the reminiscences of war and inter-tribal or family disputes. It could be an overflow of bad character and an ungodly reputation. It could be the consequences of sin and iniquity. For instance, Gehazi left a legacy of leprosy for his children because of his greed and covetousness. He earned a curse that ran through generations after him, as recorded in 2 Kings 5:27. Also, due to their carelessness and unbridled tongue, the Jews brought the consequences of bloodshed upon the heads of their children (Matt. 27:25).

But as a child of God, it is expected of you that you leave a godly legacy that reflects who you are in the Lord and speaks of the richness of divine accomplishments and positive impact that would not only be seen on your immediate family but also the entire human race.

As Christians, we often claim Abraham's blessings because we believe we are children of Abraham by faith. But can you recall that Abraham lived a life of obedience at a time when such was uncommon among men? This was counted as righteousness for God's sake; he became a friend of God. What a godly reputation! Can God be that confident in you? Ps.112:1-6 also explains the blessedness of a man that obeys the commandments of the Lord and walks according to it. The generation of such a man shall be blessed.

Are you leaving behind a godly legacy for your children and others or a curse? The Bible says a man that troubles his own family shall reap the wind (Prov. 11:29).

The Rechabites commanded their generations to abstain from drinking wine, and they remained committed to the end (Jer.35:5-6). Not for any reason were they ready to desecrate this godly vow. They remained faithful to God and their fathers.

In 2 Tim.1:5, Paul reminded Timothy of the godly legacy of knowing Christ, which his grandmother, Lois, and his mother, Eunice, bestowed on him. What legacy could be better, richer and eternal, if not that of unfeigned, genuine and sincere faith in God through Christ? Even, Paul, the apostle of Christ, poured out himself to his various followers as Jesus did to the disciples (Acts 1:8).

Paul, with confidence, told Timothy to pass on the godly teachings he got from him to others (2 Tim.2:2). He was an unequal spiritual mentor who emulated Christ, walked in His footsteps and encouraged his followers to do the same. He called Timothy, "my son". He was a father indeed!

In conclusion, beloved, for you to leave behind you a godly legacy, you must start now. Be a friend of Jesus. Accept Him as your Lord and Saviour. Surrender your life to Him. When He is in control, things will fall into place, even beyond your imagination. Planning is of man, but the execution is of the Lord. By strength shall no man prevail! This simply means that without Christ leading and guiding you by His Spirit, you can pass through life without a definite trace of existence, not to talk of living behind you, trails of the positive impact that will speak to generations after you.

Be ready to pray yourself into divine arrangement and fulfilment. He leads, you follow; certainly, there will be obvious footprints on the sands of time, proving your significant impact. It is a godly legacy that is beyond words.

Prayer Points

1.   I shall not pass through this life without a positive impact, in the name of Jesus.

2.   Divine grace to be a positive influence, come upon me now, in the name of Jesus.

3.   Father Lord, glorify Yourself in my life and let others see You in me, in the name of Jesus.

4.   Father, make me a carrier of Your glory and power, in the name of Jesus.

5.   By Your mercy, O God, my generation shall not inherit evil, in the name of Jesus.

6.   Arise, O God and let generations confess through me that You are God, in the name of Jesus.

7.   The power of God to be a positive influencer, possess me now, in the name of Jesus.

Chapter Three

WHO AM I?

Have you ever asked yourself this question? Did you receive an answer, or you just took it for granted that everything is okay and you are fine?

> John 1:19 *"And this is the record of John when the Jews sent priest and Levites from Jerusalem to ask him, who art thou?"*

The Pharisees and Sadducees wanted John to answer the question WHO AM I? He confessed and declared to them: "I am not the Christ." They asked him who then, art thou, Elijah? And he said, "I am not." They further probed, "Art thou that Prophet? And he answered, "No." Then said they unto him, "WHO ART THOU? That we may give an answer to them that sent us? What sayest thou of thyself?" And he said, "I AM THE VOICE of one crying in the wilderness: make strait the way of the Lord as said by prophet Isaiah."

So, you can see that John the Baptist had the information about his true identity. They asked him, "Who are you? Are you Jesus?" He said, "No!" Are you Elijah?" He said, "No, I am not." Are you that prophet they said would come in the last days? He also said, "No." Finally they asked, "Then who are you?" He answered, "I am the voice and a forerunner to somebody who is coming after me."

Do you know who you are? Have you asked heaven to show you who you really are? A correct definition of who you are will yield the following results:

1.   Lead to a correct evaluation of your ability.
2.   Help you to know how to live and take care of your life.
3.   Help you to know the kind of friends you should have and those you should not.
4.   Show you the pattern of life that you should follow.

God told Jeremiah, *"I knew you when you were in your mother's womb and I have ordained you a prophet from your mother's womb."* So, it would have been a disaster for Jeremiah to come to the world and not know that he was a prophet. His whole life would have been a tragedy. That is because from the word go, he got it wrong by not knowing his true identity.

LOOK UP TO GOD

Beloved, you need to pray seriously if you see yourself achieving something great in the dream, but you do not see it happening in real life. It is because you do not really know who you are. You need to pray to discover your correct identity and God's purpose for your life. A wrong definition of your life will lead you to an incorrect assessment of your personality and destiny, but the correct and exact definition of yourself can only be received from your Manufacturer who is the Almighty God. No one can explain or interpret a product better than the one who made it. God is the creator of all things, and the correct information about each of His creatures can only be obtained from Him.

As you read this chapter, I decree by the decree of heaven that:

- Powers blocking you from knowing who you are shall die violently, in the name of Jesus.
- All those negative destiny adjusters troubling your life shall scatter unto desolation, in the name of Jesus.
- Any power killing your divine identity shall be killed by the slapping angels of God, in the name of Jesus.

- Any servant or slave occupying the horse of your destiny shall somersault and be removed, in the name of Jesus.
- Powers assigned to terminate your glory shall destroy themselves, in the name of Jesus.
- The carefully designed spiritual blindness, to make you ignorant of your identity, shall be wiped away by the blood of Jesus, in the name of Jesus.

KNOW THYSELF

It is time for you to know your real self in life. God did not create anybody as a feather weight, but heavy weight. If you desire and ask, God will show you beneficial secrets that will positively change your life. However, the principle of the Scripture is very simple: the person who asks, will receive. If you do not ask, heaven will be looking at you.

Therefore, you are not what your enemies say you are. You are not what your parents say you are. You are not what your background says you are. You are not what your feelings say you are. You are not what your government and leaders say that you are. The only Person, who can tell you who you are, is the Almighty God. It is only from Him that you can get the correct definition of yourself.

I pray that this book shall signal the beginning of unending laughter in your life, in the name of Jesus.

> *Psalm 100:3 Know ye that the Lord, He is God. It is He that has made us and not we ourselves, we are His people and the sheep of His pasture.*

God made us. Hence, He is the One who knows us best. Take note of this truth. You cannot know yourself through native doctors, witch doctors, prophets, positive thinking, astrology (by looking at what the horoscope claims that your star says) or by somebody reading your palms. You cannot know yourself through all the demonic deception with which people are being deceived. Even our ancient parents, who used to go to witchdoctors to know the future of their children, were manipulated by the devil because they sought help in his territory and from his agents.

God made you for a purpose. The biggest enemy you are going to face in your life is yourself. The greatest tragedy in life is trying to be who you are not and doing what you are not supposed to do. You say, "I want to become a lawyer." When you are asked to give your reason, you replied, "I like the uniform lawyers wear." Someone said, "I want to become a soldier." Why? He responded, "I like the gun that soldiers carry." That is not how it works. You must have cogent reason with a divine backing before making the choice of a career. Trying to be who you are not will lead to an unequalled disaster.

Since God ordained Jeremiah as a prophet from the womb, he would have been a failure in life if he had come into the world and said, "I want to be a pilot." No matter how noble and lucrative the profession may be, he wouldn't have succeeded. His plane would have crashed and he would have lacked fulfilment in that career because he was not supposed to be there. This is the secret of the failure and frustration that many people are passing through today. A stone may remain in the river for two hundred years; it will never become a crocodile. Many of our challenges in life arise from the fact that we do not know ourselves; consequently, we operate in wrong positions while we expect great results. What a disappointment this would bring!

YOU ARE UNIQUE

We sometimes ignore our true virtue and concentrate on another person's virtue. Many people, rather than praying to discover their true identity, uniqueness or purpose, waste precious time and resources trying to be someone else. Beloved, you are unique. You are God's masterpiece. You will be surprised that you could be more endowed and more blessed than the individual you focus on imitating or desire to be like. Henceforth, I advise you not to ignore your true virtue. Rather, pray to God until you discover who you are and your true virtue. This will guide and help you to fulfil your destiny.

It is a tragedy that most people live their entire lives as complete strangers to their true selves. Let me give you some examples from the Scriptures.

Anyone looking at Moses in the desert would have seen a shepherd. Truly, he would have died a shepherd, but as far as heaven is concerned, Moses was a law maker and a deliverer.

Similarly, those who saw David, while taking care of his father's flock, would have seen a shepherd boy who also played an instrument of music. However, his real identity, according to heaven's record included: David was a champion, a king, a psalmist and a prophet. In fact, the Bible further reveals a man with seven kinds of anointing, namely: the prophetic anointing, kingly anointing, warrior anointing, priestly anointing, worship anointing, prayer anointing and deliverance anointing. What a divine investment, all in one person! Can you see how a person can be diverted from his real self or correct identity? To be so spiritually endowed and loaded yet undefined is nothing but spiritual and physical calamity!

There was a prophet in Elisha, but he focused on farming. If he had not answered the call of God, there would have been trouble in his life because he was created to be a prophet, not a farmer.

There was a Messianic prophet in Isaiah, but he was busy prophesying in the king's palace. There was an apostle, a prophet, a teacher, an evangelist and a pastor in Paul the Apostle. But he didn't know; he was busy killing the Christians in his time. He eventually wrote 13 books of the New Testament when he discovered his true self. Those things were inside him and would have died with him if he had not been saved by the Lord.

There was an Apostle in Peter, but he was a fisherman. It was later that Jesus said, "Peter you are catching fish now, but I will make you a fisher of men." He would have died a fisherman, and nobody would have seen his name in the Bible.

There was an Israel in Jacob, but he didn't know. For many years, he lived a fake life as a cheat and supplanter until he encountered God. His name changed from Jacob to Israel; his personality changed too.   So, your current appearance or situation is not the final plan of heaven for your life. Whatever you are now is a comma, not a full stop. However, I want you to note that in the School of Victory, information is the greatest asset. Information transforms a man. Lack of information deforms a man. When you lack spiritual information, you are an accident waiting to happen. You must get the beneficial information that will correctly position your life and destiny for supernatural acceleration, favour, great blessings and all-round fulfilment.

DIGGING DEEP

Spiritual treasures are not found on the surface, just as you don't find gold, silver, crude oil on the surface. They lie in the deep belly of the earth or sea. The Bible says that deep calleth to the deep (Psalm 42:7). If you want spiritual information about your life, you must dig deep and pray deep prayers. When things are very precious, people look after them and keep them very well. If, as you are reading this book, you have 1million dollars in your bag, I am sure you will put it between your legs and hold it tight. You will also watch it carefully.

God prospers us by instructions. He is a secret keeper. God Himself has secrets. When you have access to God's secrets, you will become an uncommon success. God knows all things and He is willing to reveal beneficial secrets about your life to you. There are secrets you need to know about your life so that you can move forward. That is why some of the greatest destiny prayer points in this planet are:

- God, arise and show me the secrets of my life, in the name of Jesus.
- God, arise and show me who I am, in the name of Jesus.
- God, arise and show me beneficial secrets about my life, in the name of Jesus.

ELOQUENT TESTIMONIES

In the early 90's, an American got hold of one of our books and came across these prayer points. He found them strange, but he prayed them. He did not know how to pray MFM prayers very well. All he just did was to sit down and repeat, O God, arise and show me the secrets of my life. He would drink some tea, rest a little bit and continue. After some time, he started saying the prayer point constantly. He told me that anytime he prayed to a level, he would find himself on top of a tortoise, riding it as a horse. Immediately he stopped praying, it would disappear, only to appear again when he continued to pray. He went to his Pastor to explain this regular vision. His Pastor looked at him and said, "I think you need to see a psychiatric doctor; I don't think you are well. How else would one explain the strange vision you have seen again and again? When you prayed other prayer points, did you see the same vision?" He said, "No, Pastor. It began when I prayed about the secret of my life."

This man's dreams continued like that until we had a crusade in America. He then he saw me and narrated his vision to me. I explained to him that God was showing him the secret of his life. I told him that he would not get far in life riding a tortoise and that he needed to get off the tortoise.

A brother prayed the same prayers here at the headquarters. He had a master's degree but wasn't making any progress. He was always broke and couldn't pay his house rent. He cried to heavens for three nights. On the third night, he saw a pot. The pot did not mean anything to him. He continued the prayer: O God, arise and show me the secret of my life, in the name of Jesus. All he saw was a pot. When he came to see me, he said, "Sir, anytime I pray this prayer point, I see a pot." I told him that he would need to go to his village, talk to his parents and find out whether they made or got a pot for him.

The brother travelled to his parents who were now very old and had not seen him for years. They were glad to see him. They said, "The man from Lagos, you are welcome." He sat them down and asked, "Daddy and Mummy, do I have a pot?" They said, "Yes. All our children have pots." He said, "Ok, what did you do with the pots?" They said, "We put the hairs we shaved from your heads for the first time as a baby inside the pot and buried it inside the compound." He inquired further, "Did you do it for all of us?" They said, "Yes." And all the three children in the family were not doing well at all. He now became very clever with them and asked, "Can you show me where the pots are?" They said, "Yes come and see." He saw the three pots buried in the ground. He asked, "Which of them is my own?" His parents pointed to one. After this, they all returned to the living room. When he was sure that his parents were sitting inside and relaxed, he ran back to the place uprooted the pot, fled and brought the pot back to Lagos.

When the man brought the pot, his hair was still inside. Those of you that know about deliverance know that your hair represents your glory. However, it is unfortunate that the hair had been buried and covenanted to the earth.

- O God, arise and show me the secret of my life, in the name of Jesus.
- O God, arise and show me who I am, in the name of Jesus.

A thirty-nine year old sister prayed this prayer and had a dream. She saw herself at a wedding ceremony with her late daddy as her groom. Surprised, she said, "Daddy, you can't be my husband. What are you doing here?" Her late father's reply made her even more surprised. He told the sister, "Since your mother died when you were young, I have converted you to my wife and my mother." For the first time she saw why things were hard for her and why getting a suitor had been very difficult. The truth is that without any doubt, she needed to pray more. When prayer gets to a level, deep secrets will be made known. The more you pray, the more you discover. The more you discover, the more you recover, and the more you recover, the quicker you will fulfil your destiny.

I encourage you to pray day and night: O God, arise and show me the secrets of my life. It is not too late to become and to achieve what God created you to do.

PRAYER UNLOCKS THE DOOR OF MYSTERIES

Deep prayers unlock deep secrets. It is time you make up your mind to cry to the heavens to know who you really are. The Bible says you shall know the truth. As you know and apply that truth, it shall set you free! What a tragedy to have lived up to 20, 25, 30 years without knowing who you are. If from the womb, all God has ordained for you to come and do on earth is to give birth to a prophet, unknown to you that prophet is going to be your only child. Unfortunately, in your ignorance, you started to engage in your fornication while in the secondary school, got pregnant and aborted the glorious baby. Where will you start from now? This is why we need prayers.

This kind of prayer is not what you pray and your mind will be roaming around, and your body will not know that you are praying. It is not the passive and docile kind of prayer; it is not religious prayer or weak and feather-weight Christians' prayer. It is a desperate cry to heaven that you want to know who you are. Father, show it to me, let me know who I am.

As many as are destiny-conscious and will like things to happen should pray the following prayer points:

Prayer Points

1. O God, arise and show me who I am, in the name of Jesus.

2. O God, arise and show me the secrets of my life, in the name of Jesus.

3. Powers assigned to re-invent my destiny for evil, before I finish this prayer, die, in the name of Jesus.

4. Lay your hand on your face: Satanic veil hiding my identity, catch fire, in the name of Jesus.

5. Heavens of divine information, open unto me by fire, in the name of Jesus.

6. My Father, give me the grace and wisdom to use divine information profitably, in the name of Jesus.

7. Powers that hate my progress, destroy yourselves, in the name of Jesus.

Chapter Four

DISCOVERING YOUR POTENTIAL

There is a rich, valuable, potent and untapped resource locked away within you. It is called your potential. God has endowed you with gifts and talents. You must discover, unveil and use them to bless the Church and the world.

Someone said that the cemetery is the wealthiest place on planet earth. I agree with the person. It is filled with unfulfilled dreams, undiscovered potential, untapped talents, unused gifts, truncated visions, unexecuted projects, unfulfilled purposes and unharnessed endowments. The reason there are numerous individuals who are unfulfilled as well as destinies that end up as failures is that such people neither discovered nor used their potential and talents.

Your potential is not supposed to remain a potential forever. You are expected to deploy it as a veritable tool to achieve your life's purpose. It is disheartening that thousands of people bury their talents (when they fail to use them or allow them to lie fallow and dormant for life). Many people waste their talents. Some allow the enemy to steal and pervert their talents while several others abuse theirs by using them to serve the devil rather than God.

A lot of believers will not fulfil their divine purposes until they discover and maximally use their potential and talents. The enemy has terribly wicked plans to destroy the youths. He does not want them to discover their potential nor fulfil their divine purposes in Christ.

Beloved, the only way for you to take your place in destiny and attain the glorious status that God has bequeathed to you as His child is to discover your potential and talents. These are special physical and spiritual abilities that God has given you to help you to get to the place of fulfilment or your Promised Land. God has given you those talents or potential for a purpose: to serve God and others, glorify Him, build His kingdom and achieve your life's purpose. It is your responsibility to discover the potential that God has buried within you as well as to maximally use it to achieve your divine purpose and succeed in life.

AVOID AN UNEXAMINED LIFE

Someone said that an unexamined life is not worth living. I agree with the person. As stated in the preceding chapters, you must ask yourself some salient questions if you want to be all God has created you to be. Some of the questions border on your potential, gifts and talents as well as how you should use them to fulfil your life's assignment.

- Why were you born?
- What can you do?
- What potential or talents do you have?
- What are the purposes of your potential?
- Do you believe in your true potential?
- What are the keys to fulfilling your potential?
- How do you use your potential maximally?

Your ability to answer these questions correctly will give you fulfilment in life and destiny.

DISCOVER, DEVELOP AND DEPLOY

Your potential is a priceless treasure like gold hidden within, but you have to get it out. It is your responsibility to do three things about your potential. First, you must discover your potential, gifts and talents. Second, you must develop them and make them more productive. Third, you must deploy them and make them profitable. I advise you to focus on doing these three things to create the life you desire.

Knowing what you are good at and what you want to do in life will make your life more satisfying and fulfilling. Beloved, in order to discover, develop and deploy your potential, I advise that you do the following:

1. Identify what you love to do (what you do effortlessly).
2. What is that thing that you do uniquely that people commend you for?
3. Listen to others. Find out what others say about you and learn from it.
4. What is that thing you enjoy doing without being paid?
5. Pray enquiry prayers.
6. Befriend the Holy Spirit. He will reveal your potential to you, help you to discover it and teach you how best to use it.
7. With what do you influence people easily?

You can be more than who you are if you discover your potential. The power to be more, greater and to attract all-round fulfilment lies within you. It is like a seed that has the potential to become a tree, a bird that has the potential to be a flock, a sheep that has the potential to become a flock, a cow has the potential to become a herd, a boy that has the potential to become a man, a girl that has the potential to become a woman, and a family that has the potential to become a generation. That is why you should not allow your potential to die untapped and unused.

YOUR POTENTIAL WILL MAKE A WAY FOR YOU

For you to maximally utilise your potential, you have to fight your greatest fears. You must believe in yourself. I advise you to focus on discovering your own potential to create the life you desire.

In discovering and using your potential to glorify God lies the key to your greatness and destiny fulfilment. Moses changed from being a fugitive and shepherd to an outstanding leader, deliverer and prophet when he discovered and used his potential to accomplish his divine purpose. When Gideon discovered that the seed of valour was in him, he deployed it to serve God's purpose and he entered God's hall of fame. When Peter discovered his potential to fish for souls and win them to God, he became a foremost apostle and fulfilled his destiny in Christ. I encourage you to prayerfully discover, develop and deploy your potential, gifts and talents as well. Heaven will increase and bless them, and your joy will be full.

WHY YOU NEED TO DISCOVER YOUR POTENTIAL

When it comes to fulfilling your purpose in life, ignorance will not be a sufficient excuse for failure. It is your responsibility to discover your God-given purpose, your potential and to ensure that you fulfil your divine assignment with the potential and talents that God has given you. This is the secret of success and greatness in life. God has not created anyone a failure. Rather, people become failure in life when they do not know who they are, why they are here on earth and what potential lies within them to reach their goal in life.

Your potential and talents are given to you to make you win the battles of life. They are given to you to make you productive and fruitful. They are also given to you to make you excel and prosper in life. The Bible says that the gifts of a man will make a room for him and make him stand before kings (Proverbs 18:16). When you discover, develop and deploy your potential, you will not be unfruitful in life, neither will you wander aimlessly or be stranded in the journey of life. Also, with your potential and God-given talents, you will fulfil your divine vision, make impacts on others and be a blessing to the household of God.

A WORD FOR THE YOUTH

There is a period in man's existence that is called the morning of life. The devil waits at this juncture, when many young people are inexperienced, exuberant and careless to derail them from God's agenda and truncate their glorious destinies. That is why I specifically want to advise the youth.

> Ecclesiastes 12:1 *Remember now thy Creator in the days of thy youth, while the evil days come not, nor the years draw nigh, when thou shalt say, I have no pleasure in them;*

The best time to begin with God is early in the morning of life. It is important to have a correct idea of life while you are young. The morning of life is the best time to find answers to who you are, where you are from, what your purpose on earth is, what potential and talents you have, what you are supposed to do with them, who you should work and walk with and where you are going at the end of your sojourn on earth. However, if you are reading this and you are already advanced in age, do not despair because God is never late, and He can do all things.

Many young people have no clue of how God expects them to live. Some have an idea but they refuse to pursue their divine agenda. For a lot of young people, their idea of how to live is out of tune with the Almighty.

Youth is not the time to sow bad seeds, neither is it the time to occupy your life with sinful pleasures. It is not the time to run the race of vanity. It is not the time to explore the dark side of life. It is not the time to be crazy about the fashion of the world that encourages sexual perversion. It is also not the time to exhibit sexual agenda or to engage in unholy and destructive relationships.

Beloved, youth is the time for 23 things:

1.   **Time to find God:** The best time to find and serve God passionately is your youthful days or years. In Ecclesiastes 12:1, the Bible says, *"Remember now thy*

Creator in the days of thy youth. "The same Scripture explains that it is wise to do so before the evil days come.

2. **Time to be in tune with God:** It is highly beneficial to know God early and walk with Him in righteousness. Samuel knew God early and his life and ministry were exemplary.

3. **Time to buy the future with the currency of the present:** When you spend the time of your youth serving God, you will be securing for yourself a glorious and impactful future. The seeds of divine service and commitment to God's Kingdom that you sow will earn you a great harvest.

4. **Time to start knocking the rough edges off your life:** It is wise to use the days of your youth to identify challenges in your root or foundation and bombard them with prayers until your desired change manifest.

5. **Time to plan how to beat the best and be the best:** The time of your youth is the time to discover, develop and deploy your potential, gifts and talents. It is the time to pursue self-improvement as well as divine guidance that will lead to a life of excellence and the fulfilment of your purpose in life.

6.   **Time to discover the termite in your root and fight it
      to a standstill:** The time of your youth is the best time
      to encounter God and receive the power of the Holy
      Spirit. With the power and help of the Holy Spirit, you
      can detect and destroy the termite or any other
      stranger that the enemy has introduced into your life.

7.   **Time to discover what is worth living for in life:** Many
      people were 50 or 60 years old before they discovered
      what their purposes in life were. They had wasted
      quality time in pursuing an agenda that is contrary to
      God's plan for them. They realised that life would have
      been more fruitful if they had discovered their purpose
      earlier. Therefore, the time of your youth is the best
      time to find out what is worth living for in life and
      actualising it.

8.   **Time to yield to the call to give God the best part of
      your existence:** Perhaps, you are fortunate like Samuel
      to get the call of God. Have you been ignoring the
      call? I beg you not to. You will not serve God in vain.
      He rewards those who diligently seek and serve Him.
      I, therefore, implore you to yield to God's call and
      commit your entire life to serving Him perfectly.

9.   **Time to set the stage for a future without tears:** Many
      of the mistakes that put many adults in bondage and

put their destiny vehicle in permanent reverse gear were committed in their youthful days, full of lustful and sinful pursuits. I want you to learn from the mistakes of such adults and not repeat them. When you live for God as a youngster and seek His kingdom passionately, you will not have any cause to shed tears or live in regret in the future.

10.   **Time to use the first half of your life so well and prevent making the second half miserable:** The life of a man can be likened to a football match that has first half and second half. The first half of your life is the time of your youth. If you use the first half wisely and are on the Lord's side, the second half will not be miserable for you. Rather, it will be full of success and testimonies.

11.   **Time to avoid coping with painful memory of badly spent youth later:** Those who live according to God's word and will consistently from their youths do not live with painful memory in their adult lives.

12.   **Time to avoid handing over your youth to the enemy:** Through sin and iniquities, sexual escapades, abortion, cultism and other vices common among the youths nowadays, many have handed their youth and future to the devil. Such people need the mercy of God to get

delivered. You should avoid anything that can make the devil harvest you soul or make you his prey.

13. **Time to prevent your manhood from becoming a struggle and regret:** The Bible says that any person that lacks self-control is like a city broken down and without walls. Sexual looseness has sent many young men and women to their early graves. Sexual sins, rape, incest, and so on are at an alarming increase. You must pray to God and receive the fruit of self-control. You should dare to be different. Sex is exclusively for marriage. Do not allow anyone to deceive you. Your body is the temple of the Holy Spirit. You must present it to God as a living sacrifice, holy and acceptable to Him.

14. **Time to spend and be spent for God:** God has deposited potential in you. He expects you to use your potential to serve Him and others, win souls for Him and bless His Kingdom. He does not expect you to return to Him with the same potential, gifts and talents unused. You must be a profitable servant. The time of your youth should be committed totally to serving God.

15. **Time to hatch the egg of your destiny:** Your destiny is the purpose you are here on earth. It is also the

assignment God wants you to accomplish. The time of your youth should be devoted to discovering and actualising your divine purpose.

16. **Time to lay the foundation for an impactful future:** There is no super-structure without base. Every great edifice stands on a foundation. The best time to build a good foundation for your life, a foundation built on Christ, are the days of your youth. A life that is built on total dependence on Jesus Christ, His word, name and blood as well as His Holy Spirit is secure.

17. **Time to take preventive tablets against an old age of sorrow:** The days of your youth is the right time to take divine inoculation and guard yourself from spiritual arrows that the enemy uses to trouble people in their old age. Your spiritual inoculation includes making God's word dwell in you richly. God's word is life and health or medicine to those that find it. A life of holiness and prayer constitutes another spiritual inoculation. Beloved, be wise and use the days of your youth in God's will and service.

18. **Time to begin your climb on the ladder of having a good life:** Samuel and David began their climb on the ladder of good life and destiny fulfilment as youths. They were able to do because they committed their

lives to serving Jehovah early enough. I advise you to emulate these Bible heroes.

19.   **The most acceptable time with God:** God has special and favourable plans for youths. He wants you to fellowship with Him intimately from the days of your youth and grow the relationship. He wants His purpose for your life to be fulfilled. It is your responsibility to cooperate with Him.

20.   **The most advantageous time to serve God:** The strength God gave you and the time He made available to you as a youngster are meant to be used to serve Him. The time of your youth is the best period of your life to worship God and contribute to the advancement of His Kingdom.

21.   **Time to ally with God in the battle against the forces of darkness:** God is in the business of recruiting loyal Christian soldiers. The call, "Who shall we send? Who will go for us?" is still ringing. Dare to be a loyal Christian soldier from the days of your youth. Your reward will surely be great.

22.   **Time to fully understand the song "Take my life and let it be":** Personal consecration is a must for every youth that wants to make a positive difference in this generation. You should make a quality decision to give

your life to Jesus. As the song writer wrote, tell God to take your life and all, and let them be consecrated to Him forever.

23. **Time to sort out your destiny:** Destiny fulfilment is an agenda that the enemy fiercely opposes in the life of every man. The time of your youth should be devoted to getting closer and closer to God as well as pushing the devil out of your life through the power of God's word and prayer.

Dearly beloved youth, understand, appreciate and use your current stage of life wisely. Use the opportunities God has made available for you to secure a glorious future for yourself. Avoid the mistakes others make out of ignorance and folly. Do not truncate your destiny or bury your glory in the time of your youth. Do not give the devil a foothold or legal ground in your life. Many who did are still finding it difficult to get their liberation many years after.

This is the acceptable time for taking your place in destiny. Samuel started out with God early in life. He was an outstanding prophet in Israel. Now is the summer of life. The weather is relatively favourable. You have strength and zeal. Now you can go the second mile. Dedicate the days of your youth to finding purpose, serving God and fulfilling your purpose in Him.

Always be in the epicentre of God's will. Make Him your all in all. Trust Him with all your heart always. Do not ever depart from Him. When you leave God out of the picture of your life in your youth and put Him in the picture later, you start life behind schedule. Remember that whatever is started behind schedule does not, in most cases, go according to plan.

Wisdom is the principal thing. Make a resolve to live in the fear of God and to do His will always. I pray that the agenda of the enemy to turn youths all over the world to endangered, perverted and wasted species will not prosper in your life, in the name of Jesus.

Prayer Points

1. Powers assigned to attack and kill my potential, die, in the name of Jesus.

2. I unlock my potential and command it to manifest, in the name of Jesus.

3. Power to be more, achieve more and become more, fall upon me, in the name of Jesus.

4. Powers that do not want me to discover, develop and deploy my potential for God, die, in the name of Jesus.

5. Holy Spirit, breathe upon my potential and talents. Make them productive for You, in the name of Jesus.

6. I refuse to bury my talents and potential, in the name of Jesus.

7. My potential and talents, arise, make room for me at the top, in the name of Jesus.

Chapter Five

WHEN YOU DON'T KNOW WHO YOU ARE

Every life has certain secrets it must discover and use. Those secrets are with God, who makes them known to specific people who meet His conditions. It is your responsibility to search out, know and use the information heaven has for you to pilot your life and destiny to fulfilment. If you do not have the information, you will not know who you are. If you don't know who you are, it will be very difficult to succeed in life. Beloved, God's will is for you to know your correct identity and fulfil your purpose in life.

Psalm 25:14 The *secret of the Lord is with them that fear him and He will show them His covenants.*

Life is a mystery. A mystery is coded information, undisclosed information, unrevealed and cryptic information, a deep matter, something shrouded in secrecy and something that goes beyond normal human understanding. A mystery is an undisclosed thing that is hidden.

Life has problems; life has secrets. There are hidden dimensions of yourself that you may not be aware of. There is a hidden part of your life that, even at your present age, you have not been able to unlock, because every human life involves a mystery. As a matter of fact, there is a mystery about your life that you need to know. There is a personal mystery you need to discover so that you can unlock your destiny. Do you want to reach your personal goal in life and achieve your dreams? You need to unlock your personal mystery. The principle of the Scripture is very simple: Ask and it shall be given unto you; seek and you shall find; knock and the door shall be opened. Whosoever asks receives. However, if you do not ask, you will not receive anything.

Beloved, God reveals secrets to His people. Going through life without your personal mystery or unlocking who you are, will limit your potential. It will make your life to be without impact. Going through life without knowing that deep secret about yourself will make servants to take hold of your horse and ride it while you trek. I pray that will not be your portion, in the name of Jesus.

IGNORANCE KILLS

It is ignorance of these secrets that makes you to choose a pattern that your life should not follow. You start passing examinations nobody asked you to take. It makes a man to fish and catch nothing in the ocean of life. It makes you a material for testing new weapons. The enemy will keep using you to test new equipment and new weapons. Most importantly, it could make a man to die before his time. It could also make him a permanent slave. When you see people who are slaves to prophets, pastors, herbalists and witch doctors, it maybe that there are secrets about their lives they do not know, hence they visit wrong places endlessly for solution.

By design, some people are not supposed to put a drop of alcohol in their mouth till they die. Some are not supposed to smoke till they die. Some women are not supposed to be deflowered before they get married, but because they do not know this personal secret about their lives, they break the rule. Consequently, they open doorways to satan to afflict them, life becomes unpleasant for them, strange battles bombard them and prayer becomes very difficult for them. For example, the angel of God told the parents of Samson, *"You are going to have a child. But you yourself, don't drink alcohol; avoid anything that can defile or contaminate you. The baby you are going to have is going to be God's vessel."*

So, God already gave Samson's parents instructions; those are the mysteries we need to take note of and use to our advantage. If his parents had broken that law, they would have wasted Samson and truncate his assignment as well as his destiny. If Samson himself, who had also been told that he was a Nazarite and should not take alcohol, had started drinking alcohol, there would have been a problem. This is why you need to know the mysteries about your life and pray seriously. The wisdom of God is hidden; therefore, you need to ask Him to grant you access to it.

Job 29:4 *As I was in the days of my youth when the secrets of God was in my tabernacle.*

The Patriarch called Job walked with God and enjoyed a special privilege with Him: the Bible affirms that he had the secrets of God in his tabernacle. It means that he was able to access God's mysteries. As a New Testament believer, God desires that you know His secrets. That is why the Bible says that it is given to you (believer) to know the mysteries of the Kingdom of God (Matthew 13:11). Beloved, God's desire is that you enforce His dominion, dispense His grace and reign in life. All these can only happen if you know your personal secrets or mysteries as well as the mysteries of God's Kingdom.

Someone said, "Why worry when you can pray." Prayer is the surest route to discovering your correct identity and knowing beneficial secrets about your life. If you are willing to pray the right, word-based and targeted prayers like the life-changing ones on this subject, you will see the glory of God. The Bible affirms that the effectual fervent prayer of a righteous man avails much (James 5:16b). The more you pray, the closer you get to God and the more your faith increases, the more the secrets you know and the more glorious your spiritual and physical lives become.

I advise you to cry out in desperate, heaven-opening and secrets-unfolding prayers like these:

1.   Father, show me my personal mystery, in the name of Jesus.
2.   Father, show my house to my house, in the name of Jesus.
3.   Father, show me to myself, in the name of Jesus.
4.   Father, show me the secrets of my life, in the name of Jesus.

5.   Father, show me beneficial secrets that will catapult my destiny, in the name of Jesus.

GET AND APPLY THE SECRET

You need access to God's mysteries. His secrets have to be in your tabernacle. You need access to the mystery of the word, the mystery of the kingdom of God and the mystery of your life. Business has secrets; marriage has secrets, and every profession has secrets. There is valuable information you need from God. When you tap into that information, your destiny will explode. There is no reason for anyone to be poor, if he can tap into that mystery. You may be trading now, but when you pray to know secrets, the Lord may say, "Daughter, this is not the business that will give you prosperity. "Start selling peanuts." Did you say peanuts? I am already a real estate agent." God will say, "No, start selling peanuts!"

Immediately you get that code from heaven and you engage it, you will be surprised at the kind of breakthrough you are going to have. That is why you need to pray at this juncture:

O God, arise and show me the secrets of my life, by the power in the blood of Jesus, in the name of Jesus.

NEEDLESS PAIN

People suffer needles pain when they do not know who they are. Princes who do not know who they are will live as paupers and servants. This is because ignorance kills.

The devil is happy and comfortable when people do not know their correct identity. One of the strategies he uses is to make people blind to their status, opportunities, rights, etc. Ignorance and spiritual blindness are his trusted weapons. Knowing the secrets of your life and who you are will take you from the valley of life to its mountain-top. It will change you from a victim to a victor. You will live a purpose-driven life and record worthwhile achievements where others fail. Besides, knowing your correct identity will position you for success and shorten your journey to destiny fulfilment.

Beloved, it is disheartening that some people get vital information about who they are and their divine purpose but do not put the information to good use. The truth is that a person, who gets to know the secrets of his life but does not utilise it, is not better than the person who does not know the secret of his life at all. Therefore, taking the right action to translate the information heaven gives you to all-round fulfilment is very important.

DIVINE INFORMATION TRANSFORMS

When you tap into information from heaven, your destiny will explode. This truth reminds me of a woman who went to God and prayed some prayers asking that God should show her beneficial secrets about her life. She was the Vice Principal of a school, but her poverty was abject and so embarrassing. Before the end of the month, she would have borrowed money from school teachers. She got to a level that she became fed up with the situation, and she prayed.

As she prayed, the Lord visited her and said, "Daughter, what is this at the back of your house?" She said, "Lord, it is marshy ground." The Lord said, "Daughter, resign from your job; begin to plant and sell vegetables." Her reaction was, "Vegetables? I bind that voice." The Lord said to her, "You can't bind me. Do you want to die in poverty? Henceforth, plant and sell vegetables." She said, "This can't be true. I have a master's degree, but I am to sell vegetable?"

However, she listened and converted the back of her house to a vegetable farm. Beloved, when she started it, it got to an embarrassing level that people would come to the market and wait for her to bring her own vegetable. Though the other vegetable sellers had arrived and were ready to sell, the buyers would tell them, "No, we are waiting for Mummy Sunday." It is after she had finished selling that others would now begin to sell. The day she didn't come to the market, other vegetable sellers would be very happy. I am praying for you at this point; the secrets that will catapult your destiny, receive that revelation, in the name of Jesus.

The right information from heaven will set the pace for your distinction. Many Pastors may not tell you this gospel truth. If you are always struggling in your career, business, finance, family, academics, then something has not been revealed to you. You may be running around the place, trying to catch a husband who is sleeping with women around; madam there is something you do not know. You are running to control your husband. The man is just running like butterfly all over the place. There are secrets you do not know. When you get hold of those secrets, you will prevail against your challenging and perplexing problem. God's hidden wisdom is the answer to every problem. Once you make contact with that heavenly wisdom, you become an extraordinary person. This implies that success has secrets; business has secrets; marriage has secrets. The secrets you need are with God. However, not everybody, but a few people have discovered those hidden beneficial secrets. I counsel you to strive and seek to discover these secrets and put them to use. Success is yours, in the name of Jesus.

FASTING AND PRAYER: BELIEVER'S MOUNTAIN-MOVING KEY

This kind of information is something the devil does not want anybody to know. That is why the words of Jesus became very relevant: *"This kind goeth not except by praying and fasting"* (Matthew 17:21). There are certain items of information you cannot get unless you fast and pray. There are some demons that cannot be expelled until you apply fasting and prayer.

There are some things that need one hour of continuous, unbroken prayer before they can even shift. Some require two hours; some three hours; others seven hours; or even seven days before they can shift. Ice cream prayers, I mean, weak and powerless prayers will not shift them nor produce the desired result. Microwave prayers, prayers done in a hurry, will not shift them either. You need solid, concentrated, acidic, constant, bombarding and rugged prayers to move them.

If you look back at your family and you found out that there is practically nobody you know that is financially prosperous and you found yourself towing the same line, there is a secret you need to know. The family may actually have a hidden wealth that you do not know yet. There are some families, in the book of heaven, the instruction is that for all the members to prosper, they only need to sell salt. That is the family's prosperity code, but one of the family members is a medical doctor, another one is bricklayer and all of them are poor. There is need for serious prayers.

A brother came crying to me many years ago. He said, "Daddy, there are seven of us in my family. Six of us are born again. One of us is a native doctor. Sir, why is it that it is only the unbelieving native doctor among us that has money, while we are poor." I said, "Okay. Is the man a full time native doctor?" He replied, "No! He also sells palm oil." What happened is that the native doctor has demonically enquired to know the business of the family that will bring success and huge blessings, but the believers who are supposed to have the secrets of God did not know. They were doing what they should not do. No wonder the Bible says that the children of darkness are wiser in their generation than the children of light (Luke 16:8).

A lady prayed this prayer of inquiry into the secret of her life because she got fed up with her situation one day. She said, "I can't go on like this. Nothing is moving and nothing is working." So, for three days she abstained from food and water. God showed her a revelation. She saw some white men, almost ten of them. They were dressed in black. She didn't understand. She asked herself, "Who are these people? I'm a black lady. Who are these white men?" She was so confused, but she continued the prayer.

One night, when the prayer got to the correct level, an angel stood before her and said, "My daughter, well done. Did you see those white men with black attires? Your grandfather mistakingly caused trouble between these two white families and that mistake that your grandfather made caused the two white families to fight and kill themselves. This is why you have been like this. You need to pray atonement prayer to free yourself from this captivity. How would she have known this if she was just praying ordinary prayers?

The Bible says that by knowledge shall the righteous be delivered. The truth you know and apply will set you free. The other time, a young man prayed. Things were not working. After few days of prayer and fasting, he heard a strange voice: "Son, your father is your grandfather." He now began to ask questions until they told him a deep family secret. The father of his father slept with the wife of his son and they gave birth to him. And so his life was upside down. The family knew the secrets and they kept quiet. What a tragedy?

All the secrets you need to know that will move you to the next level, receive those secrets now, in the name of Jesus.

BIBLICAL EXAMPLES: JEREMIAH

In Jeremiah 1:4 *Then the word of the Lord came unto me, saying before I formed thee in the belly, I knew thee and before thou camest forth out of the womb, I santify thee and I ordain thee a prophet unto the nation's.*

It is quite amazing that from the womb and before he was born, Jeremiah had been sanctified, anointed, ordained in the mother's womb as a prophet. If after Jeremiah was born, he had become a farmer, he would have failed. If he did not know how to pray to unlock his mystery, he would have strolled unsuccessful and unsung to an unknown grave. So, Jeremiah would have lived an unfulfilled life if he had chosen to do any other thing outside what God ordained him to do. However, he may be fortunate one day and somebody says, "Mr

Jeremiah, God said you are a prophet. Don't do the work you are doing again. It won't work. Your work is that of a prophet."

So, the secret of the life of Jeremiah is that he has been ordained by the Bible College of heaven as a prophet from the womb. Strange, but it is true.

BIBLICAL EXAMPLES: JOHN THE BAPTIST

Luke 1:13-17   But the angel said unto him, fear not Zechariah for thy prayer is heard and thy wife Elizabeth shall bear thee a son and thou shall call his name John, and thou shall have joy and gladness and many shall rejoice at his birth. For he shall be great in the sight of the Lord and shall drink neither wine nor strong drink, he shall be filled with the Holy Ghost even from his mother's womb and many of the children of Israel shall be turned to the Lord there God. And it shall go before him in the spirit and power of Elijah, to turn the heart of the Father's to the children and disobedient to the wisdom of the just, to make ready a people prepared for the Lord.

That was the mystery of John the Baptist. If after he was born, he had become something outside what heaven had written about him in the Scripture, he would have become a huge failure. That is why when some people went to John the Baptist and asked, "Who are you? What sayest thou about thyself? Are you Elijah?" He said, "No!" Are you that Prophet? He answered, "No!" He said, "I am the voice crying in the wilderness, make strait the path of the Lord" (John 1:23).

Many people are born great, but they die unknown. Some others are born warriors but they die as slaves. A lot of people are born as millionaires, but they die as paupers. Several others are born as heads, but they die as tails. Some are born as world changers, but they die in frustration. Many are born as runners, but they die as crawlers. We have people that are born as eagles, but they die as chicken. Many are born as champions, but they die as losers. You have to choose and determine to be one of the eagles and the champions, not otherwise.

God knew Jeremiah when he was in his mother's womb. God sanctioned him and ordained him to be a prophet. If that baby was killed through abortion, then it would not have been Jeremiah alone that was killed. Jeremiah's mother would not have known that it was a potentially mighty man that was aborted, but since Jeremiah was in God's agenda, God would have felt the loss. The Almighty would have said, "Ah! I ordained a person a prophet and this man and woman aborted the pregnancy!" Heaven would feel the loss. God would deal with the person who aborted the pregnancy for wasting a heavenly resource.

Can you see why some people have trouble and deliverance ground is not able to help? It is because the problem is not just about demons. You are supposed to go to the east and you are going to the west, walking in opposite direction confusingly. God knew you before you were formed and he has a plan for your life. There is a secret you need to know to be fully accomplished in that divine plan.

In case you are not born again, you need to surrender your life to Jesus. Why not open your mouth and confess this: 'Father, in the name of Jesus, I come before you now, Lord Jesus come into my life, take control of my life, in Jesus' name.' The grace of salvation you just received will make the Holy Spirit to begin to dwell in your heart. The same Holy Spirit will reveal all the beneficial secrets you need to know about your life to you. Have faith in God and pray to Him.

The following prayers that you are about to pray are called veil-removing prayers. The enemy has put veils on the faces of many people. Beloved, he does not want you to know who you really are. He does not want you to know your beneficial secrets. Shout the following prayers, the way blind Bartimaeus shouted. Every satanic veil shielding you from knowing your beneficial secrets shall be consumed by fire, in the name of Jesus.

Prayer Points

1. O God, arise and open my eyes, in the name of Jesus.

2. Holy Ghost, decode my life. Decode me so that I will understand who I am, in the name of Jesus.

3. O God of turnaround, turn my life around, in the name of Jesus.

4. Powers that want me to live in ignorance of who I am and die a failure, you are liar, die, in the name of Jesus.

5. Any evil veil hindering me from knowing the mysteries of my existence, catch fire and burn to ashes, in the name of Jesus.

6. Blood of Jesus, walk through the last ten generations of my life and destroy every ancestral mistake, in the name of Jesus.

7. I receive the grace to utilise the information that heaven gives to me beneficially, in the name of Jesus.

Chapter Six

WHY YOU SHOULD KNOW WHO YOU ARE

I have been encouraging you to pray the following very deep destiny-fulfilling prayers:

- Father, show me the secrets of my life, in the name of Jesus
- Father, show who I am, in the name of Jesus
- Father, show me to me, in the name of Jesus.
- Father, show my house to my house, in the name of Jesus.

To get the best results and testimonies from the foregoing prayers, I advise that you pray them fervently, continuously (not once, but for days, weeks and months). Pray them day and night; pray them in vigils; pray them with fasting. They will produce great results and testimonies.

The Lord spoke concerning Jeremiah in Jeremiah 1:4 *Then the word of the Lord came unto me, saying before I formed thee in the belly, I knew thee.*

This biblical information about Jeremiah is pregnant with meaning. It means that before your father went to talk to your mother about marriage, God knew about you. *"Before I formed thee in the belly, I knew thee and before thou camest forth out of the belly, I sanctify thee and I ordain thee a prophet unto the nations. "* If Jeremiah did not know that he was a prophet and he heard a message like this and began to pray, "O Lord, show me who I am. Show me the secrets of my life." The word would have come to him one day as he continued to enquire: "Jeremiah, you are a prophet. You have been ordained from the womb." That is how the secret would have been made known to him.

Luke 1:13-17, the Bible records this concerning John the Baptist.

> *But the angel said unto him fear not Zechariah for thy prayers is heard, for thy wife Elizabeth shall bear thee a son and thou shall call his name John. And thou shall have joy and gladness and many shall rejoice at his birth.*

That was a great revelation from the heavenly visitor. It unveiled the destiny plan, the blueprint of the life of John the Baptist, even before he was born, that he shall:

1.   Be great in the sight of the Lord;

2.   Drink neither strong wine nor strong drink;

3.   Filled with the Holy Ghost, even from his mother's womb (It means that a child inside the womb can be filled with the Holy Spirit before he is born);

4.   Through him, many of the children of Israel shall be turned to their God;

5.   Go before the Lord in the spirit and power of Elijah, to turn the hearts of the Fathers to the children and the disobedient to the wisdom of the just, to make ready a people prepared for the Lord.

I want you to take note of the fact that when John the Baptist was born, he was not ignorant of his correct identity. He knew who he was and did not live contrary to the destiny blueprint that God gave him. This explains why he revealed his true identity when some people went to him and asked, "Who are you?" His answer to them was quite revealing.

Similarly, divine information from heaven was given to Gideon and Saul of Tarsus. By this information, these Bible heroes guided their lives to please God and fulfilled their destinies. You should borrow a leaf from them. Do not live your life based on guess-work or uncertainty. That is what many people are doing and have wasted many precious years on things heaven did not send them to do. As a believer, you have the

Holy Spirit. Pray to God and get definite directives before you take any step. That is when you will be sure that your results and achievements will be fulfilling. Today, the irony is that many people want God to bless what they are doing contrary to His will.

MANY ARE CALLED, FEW ARE CHOSEN

The Great Apostle Babalola used to train pastors and prophets. They did not have the kind of Bible College that we have now. Rather, they had what the Bible calls the School of the Prophet, where the master will sit down, students will sit around him and he will teach them, face to face. So, the Great Apostle had such a class. He had thirty-six students at that time, and taught them for two weeks or a little more.

One day, by the third week, the people gathered as usual. "Good morning, Daddy. Good morning, Papa," they chorused, as they greeted him. He did not answer any of them. He took his pen and just started writing, not looking up nor responding to those who greeted him. The students were surprised; they sat down looking at him. He wrote for close to two hours.

When he had finished writing, he looked up and said, "Everybody listen to me carefully." Then he began to call their names one by one. "Joshua, you are not a pastor; you are not a prophet; you are a police man. Carry your bag and get out of here." He mentioned the next person, "Brother Oke-nla, you are not a pastor, neither are you a prophet. You are a farmer. Carry your bag and go." That was how they left, one by one. Out of 36, he read out thirty-three names that were not pastors and prophets. He told them to leave, remaining only three. Look at that percentage, only three out of thirty-six men got their destinies right. The other 33 men did not get it right. May be they just like the title or they believed that being a pastor or a prophet was an avenue of making money, just as many people are doing pastoral work presently because of money.

The 33 people that were told their correct identities and occupations protested. They said to the Great Apostle, "Daddy, no, God told me. He spoke to me." Apostle Babalola did not utter a word. He had told them the message from heaven. So, it was only those three, he continued to train. Beloved, by the time he finished training those three men, the devil knew that he was in trouble.

I pray for you at this juncture that, any power that wants to push you into the wrong journey of life and negatively change your divine pattern, no matter how far it has travelled with you, I command such power to release you now, in the name of Jesus.

STRANGE BUT TRUE LIFE STORIES

When I came back from England after my P.hD., I started a gospel church in Makoko (an area in the Mainland, Lagos State, Nigeria). It was a tough terrain at that time. It was the first Pentecostal church in that place. Before then, no Pentecostal church could stay. It was the headquarters of white garment churches. It was there that the incident I want to share with you happened.

There was a very brilliant lady who, occasionally, would become insane. She had been taken to the hospital and given drugs on many occasions. Each time, it took her two months to recover. This kept going on in her life, and she was moving in and out of the hospital. On meeting her, I gave her a prayer point: "O Lord, show me the secrets of my life".

She prayed this prayer point aggressively. Later, she came to tell me her experience while praying: "Sir, when I prayed, a man stood before me and said, "I am going to give you four options. Tell me which one you are going to pick now: cow, goat, dog and leaf, which one will you pick?" She said her response was, "Leaf," and the vision cleared. When she narrated this to me, I understood her challenge. A leaf on a tree is usually blown here and there by the wind. A leaf is often controlled and driven by another thing, rather than being in control of itself. So, the truth is that the enemy had converted her destiny to that of a leaf.

Again, can you pause and pray this prayer with fire in your spirit and voice:

Powers assigned to re-invent my destiny for evil, die, in the name of Jesus.

Let me share another interesting story with you, to further buttress my point. A woman in our church brought her daughter for prayers. It was a strange situation. This lady had her first born, a baby girl. There was no problem in getting her delivered of the baby girl. The pregnancy was without stress and she had a safe delivery. Then she became pregnant again. This time it was a boy. Immediately she got to the maternity ward and she was being delivered of the baby, the nurses and midwives said, "Push!" She did and immediately the head of the boy came out of her womb. An unseen force entered into that room, cut off the head of the baby and it was rolling on the floor. The doctor and the nurses fled. It was strange! So they told her not to come to their hospital again. She cried and cried, what an incident! How can she explain this mysterious occurrence?

She forgot about that one. She got pregnant again. Again, it was a girl. There was no problem with the pregnancy and the delivery was safe like the first one. Everything went well. This lady got pregnant for the third time. This time it was a boy. Exactly the same thing that happened to the first baby boy happened in the clinic. His head was cut off by an unseen power that rushed into the room like a wind. This was the incident that made her mother to bring her to Church. Her mother was a member of Mountain of Fire and Miracles Ministries, but the lady was not a member. I told her, "Okay, you are going to work hard. We need to first of all understand why this is happening. This same prayer was given to her: Lord, show me the secrets of my Life. Show me who I am.

The lady started to pray this prayer. Then, all of a sudden, in the dream, she came across a tall man, dressed in dark regalia, who said, "Listen, there is no negotiation. You have to pick one, either male or female. You can't have both. It is either this or the other. Do you want male? We will have to kill all the female you have now; then you will start having male." At that point, she woke up. What a deep secret! What kind of wickedness is this?

That is the secret of the unseen power that has been terminating the lives of her male children. You should not be complacent or comfortable with evil terminators and disgracing powers, rather you must be ready to stop them before they stop you. The enemy understands only one language and that is violence; if you must say "enough is enough" to evil control in your life.

Pray this prayer with thunder in your voice again:

- Powers assigned to force me to accept evil, you are a liar, die, in the name of Jesus.

STICK TO GOD'S PLAN AND PURPOSE

God knew Jeremiah when he was in his mother's belly. God sanctioned him, and ordained him to be a prophet. As I pointed out earlier on, if by any abortion Jeremiah was killed, it would not have been Jeremiah alone that was killed; thousands of other destinies would have been killed indirectly.

Jeremiah's mother would not have known the kind of person that was aborted, but God would know and heaven would be unhappy. His mother may not have known that he was a potentially mighty prophet of God, but he was in God's agenda and God would have felt a loss.

So, God knew you and me before we were formed. He has a plan for every life. The plan could be fulfilled or aborted, depending on you and other factors. Everybody is unique in God's plan. Should you feel so frustrated and you take your own life, you would have killed the future prophet you are supposed to be. Should you feel so frustrated today as to destroy yourself, you would have destroyed the prophetic programme to manifest tomorrow. Then it will not be only you that died or just one man or woman that died, a whole divine mission would have been terminated. A whole life time project would have been aborted and the Almighty God would be seriously disappointed. Should the enemy move into a life earlier to destroy that life, or the forces of wickedness divert and abort that divine schedule, it will not be just one life that was wasted. No! A mission, a vision and a programme of heaven would have died, and by extension, all the destinies attached to it too would have died with it. God does not embark on a useless enterprise. The devil and his cohorts may collude to pollute God's intentions, but it is your duty to ensure that what God wants you to do, you are able do it successfully.

God has a purpose for every life that He has allowed to come into this world. The purpose may be delayed like that of Abraham. It may be under threat like Nehemiah's project to build the walls of Jerusalem, but there is still a purpose which cannot be killed, unless you allow it. It means that nobody can kill your destiny without your permission! This is a very serious matter and I want you to understand it. There is a prayer God taught me that I have been praying for years and with all the violence you can gather, I want you to pray that prayer:

- Powers assigned to rubbish my destiny, you are liars, die, in the name of Jesus.

You must refuse to be rubbished. You must not allow your destiny to be reduced to rags.

John the Baptist had a name and a ministry, even before he was born. His blueprint was made available before his mother even conceived him. It shows you how God plans our lives. That is why the question of what purpose you have been born to accomplish must be answered as early as possible in your life. You need to cry to the Lord: "Show me my divine blue prints."

The big question is this: "Do you know your own"? What is written in the records of heaven concerning you before you were even born? Is that why things are not working the way they should work? Is that not why you find things difficult in your current profession or occupation because those things are not the things you should be doing anyway? Why are you sitting for another man's examination when you do not even know the questions?" These and more are questions you should ask yourself under the searchlight of God.

John the Baptist had a ministry to God and to men. He was to prepare the way of the Lord. The parents had a role to play for him to fulfil his ministry. There were things he was not to do in his life. Those things were not consistent with the greatness he was called to attain. For example, he was not supposed to drink wine or strong drink. You do not mix wine or alcohol with the Holy Spirit. This is a serious matter. It means that the plan of God for your life, as it is written in the record of heaven, could be that you will be a great woman and will do wonders, but you must never attach fake hair to your head, never put incision on your body. If your ignorant parents bought you your first wig and put incision on your head, thereby breaking the rule of God for your greatness and existence, they would have done you a great harm. This is why we need prayers.

This is also why I often say that the two things many people need are mercy and prayer, because they have been distorted so much from the divine pattern they came with. They were born into a deficit from the beginning and divine intervention and restoration are necessary. Such people need to cry to the heavens in prayer and ask for the mercy of God. Only through this would they begin to experience divine intervention in their lives.

Again pause and pray this with fire in your voice:

- Power of restoration, overshadow my life, in the name of Jesus.

SAMSON'S BITTER LESSON

Samson learnt the lesson of sticking to God's plan and purpose in a bitter way. He did not use the divine information about his life wisely. He handled the treasure heaven gave him with levity and carelessness. He failed God and died unfulfilled.

Now, imagine how many people's destinies would have been truncated at John the Baptist if his mother had failed in their part of the deal, or if John the Baptist had killed himself or had drunk wine. Can you see how many would have perished? Do you now realise how many people perished because the man of God sent to them did not reach them?

Beloved, be careful what you do to yourself. Don't let modern gospel deceive you. When we say, "Don't do this; don't do that", some people feel that we are too strict. You might be about to kill a Jeremiah before he manifests in your life. Then it will not be just a Jeremiah that was killed, a whole plan of God would have been destroyed. A whole gift of God to mankind would have been destroyed in transit.

Many destinies are in a transition period and the owners must be careful what they do. God gave a man a plan. You are coming to the world but for you to succeed, you can only marry only one wife and you cannot sleep with any woman until you marry her. That was the plan consistent with the greatness of the man. The devil knew that plan. So, from the university, he became the handsome man. He just found girlfriends all over the place and was boasting that girls were following him, not knowing that practically, he was just killing his greatness. This is a serious matter, and I want you to understand that a lot of young men have destroyed themselves technically. Unknown to them, they have sacrificed their greatness in the place of pleasure.

SIGNS OF THE END TIMES

About twenty years ago, I was at one of the Universities in the South West of Nigeria for a student crusade. As the crusade was going to end that day, there was a word of knowledge: "There are three ladies here. You have been sent to this campus to destroy lives. You need to come out now so that I can pray with you. If you don't, seven days after this crusade, all three of you will die." The place was as silent as the grave. I counted till seven, no one came out. We closed the service and I left. That was on Sunday evening.

By Monday morning, when I got to the church office, three ladies from the university were waiting for me. They said they wanted to see me. They also said that I was in their campus the previous day. They came in and said, "Excuse me sir. Do you remember the word of knowledge?" I don't remember those things mostly. They now told me and I said, "Yes, I remember now." They said, "We are the ladies." I asked them, "But why didn't you come out the time it was announced that you should come out." They said, "We were ashamed and we also feared that the students may lynch us if we come out like that." I probed further, "So what do you want to do now?" They said, "We want to repent and go for deliverance." I said that was fine. They said, "But Sir, we need to hand this small pot over to you." One of them put her hand in the bag and brought out a small black pot with black liquid inside it. I asked, "What is this?" They said, "That is the semen of men. We have been collecting this in the campus. Anybody whose sperm is here is finished."

So, if any man attended the University at that time and had slept with any of these ladies, his sperm would be inside the pot, unknown to him. It could be the reason life has been hard and unpleasant for such a man and it is only the prayer of restoration that can help him.

BE CAREFUL

Many destinies are in transition. The owners must be careful what they do with it. A little mistake and the internal Jeremiah will die. There is something only you can do in this life. There is a problem that only you can solve; no one else can solve it. There are some assignments which God has set aside for you.

Everything God created was created to solve a problem. When God created light, it was to solve the problem of darkness. When God created water, it was to solve the problem of hunger and thirst. There is an appointed place for you in life. You must seek to know it.

There are two ladies in the Bible, one was called Leah and one was called Rachel. Rachel was extremely beautiful; Leah was ugly and not regarded. Leah was looked down on. She was called terrible names. She and Rachel were Jacob's wives, but Leah was not loved and honoured. Out of the same ugly and dishonoured Leah came the ten pillars of Israel. Supposing Leah had killed herself out of frustration or she allowed the enemy to kill her or she just gave up because of the way people were reacting to her, looking at her and calling her an ugly woman, the ten pillars of Israel would have gone into extinction. Never look down on yourself. A greater you is inside, waiting to manifest. Pray to God for that manifestation and it shall come to pass.

YOU MUST BE SAVED

Beloved, you have read the awesome testimonies of those who prayed the eye-opening prayers. It is your turn to access information from heaven that will completely bring you deliverance and new songs. However, this can only happen if you are born again. In case you have not surrendered your life to Jesus, do so very quickly now by praying: Father, in the name of Jesus, I come before you now. Lord Jesus, come into my life. Take control of my life, in Jesus' name.

There is more prayer work to do. Let the prayer: "O Lord, show me who I am" continue. Don't stop until you begin to receive revelations and beneficial information from heaven.

For clarifications and further help on the things you see and hear but do not understand, you can write to me and explain what heaven has told you or shown to you. You can also seek direction from reliable Christian counselees and ministers of God.

You need to pray the following prayers in the Gethsemane way, where Jesus prayed, sweated and His sweat was like blood. As you pray these faithfully, you will receive uncommon testimonies. God will open your eyes and ears and let you experience His touch, in the name of Jesus.

Prayer Points

1. Covenants behind the battle confronting me, break by the blood of Jesus, in the name of Jesus.

2. Wicked problems assigned to waste my days, backfire, in the name of Jesus.

3. O Lord, if I am the one fighting my destiny, deliver me now, in the name of Jesus.

4. Battles assigned to damage my happiness, you are a liar, die, in the name of Jesus.

5. Pray this three hot times: The file of my life in the graveyard, catch fire, in the name of Jesus.

6. Shadow of death assigned against my star, expire, in the name of Jesus.

7. O God, if I have missed my way, correct me now, in the name of Jesus.

Chapter Seven

DISCOVERY LEADS TO RECOVERY

A lot of people who had the opportunity to pray these destiny- changing prayers have written letters from different parts of the world to share with us the awesome and life-changing revelations they received from the Lord.

Let me recount one of these experiences to you. This person saw a strange figure presenting her with a basket of snails, and that creature said: "Well, this is why your life has been sluggish." I pray for you, dear reader, that the enemy tormenting your life with sluggish progress shall be destroyed, in the name of Jesus. Can you imagine that? Snails are naturally slow-moving animals. This simply explains the hidden work of the enemy in that person's life.

Beloved, it is one thing to discover that you have lost valuable things; it is another thing to recover all that you have lost. That is why we usually say that discovery leads to recovery. Let us see what the Bible says.

> James 1:17 *Every good gifts and every perfect gifts is from above and cometh down from the Father of light, in whom there is no variableness neither there is shadow of turning.*

All good and perfect gifts come from above.

It is telling us that forever God is focussed. He does not lie. He will do what He says He will do.

> In John 3:27 *John answered and said, a man can receive nothing except it be given him from heaven.*

From the Bible passage, we see two ways people can get gifts:

1.   Gifts can be obtained from above, which is from heaven.

2.   Gifts can be obtained from beneath.

The bottom line of these two scriptures is that God gives gifts to all men. Every man has proper gifts from God. You have your own as well. Gifts come from above. At the same time, gifts can come from below. That is, those gifts that are earthly and not from God or such gifts are from this earth below. You could be in a very good position, but God's hand is not in it. Something could be a very good idea, but it is not God's idea.

A man can fill his house with gifts from below, so that he cannot collect his gifts from above, because his hands are already occupied with worldly things.

The question now is this: Do you have your gifts from above in your hand? Has the enemies stolen those gifts from you? Has the enemy replaced those gifts? Gifts from above have no sorrow attached to them. Gifts from above are the gifts that endure and last. This is why we still have to continue praying this key and solid destiny-transforming prayer points. You should not be tired or weary. It takes time, effort and patience to achieve great things. The same applies to discovering your divine destiny and all that is attached to it.

1.   O Lord, show me who I am, in the name of Jesus.

2.   O Lord, show me the beneficial secrets about my life, in the name of Jesus.

3.   O Lord, show me to me, in the name of Jesus.

4.   O Lord, show my house to my house, in the name of Jesus.

5.   O Lord, let Your secrets be in my tabernacle, in the name of Jesus.

It is important that you continue to pray these prayers till you get to the point of recovery. I want you to understand that the more you pray, the more you discover, and the more you discover, the more you recover.

AMAZING TESTIMONIES

There was a handsome man. He had a nice house, a very lucrative job, a nice car, but no marriage. The ladies were just not interested in his face, money and everything about him. It appeared as if he was smelly to them. This challenge pushed him into the prayer I have been advocating that we should be praying: "O Lord, show me the secrets of my life."

This man had a revelation. An angelic figure stood before him and said, "Wait and see." Immediately, a short creature came out of his stomach and grew into an adult woman. A second creature came out of him and also grew into an adult woman. After this, the third, fourth and fifth creatures also came out. When all the five had come out, they faced him and said, "We are your wives; so you are already married." For the first time, the brother knew a deep secret about his life.

The truth is that once these deep secrets are known, prayer becomes a simple matter. That is because you can now sharp shoot your arrow of prayers instead of the general prayers. I pray for you, dear reader. If you have got involved in any secret covenant, consciously or unconsciously, that is detaining your future and destiny, I break those covenants in the name of Jesus.

Whosoever asks will receive; whosoever seeks shall find; whosoever knocks, the door shall be opened. When you ask to know, then you get knowledge and knowledge is power. Information will empower a man and lack of information will deform him. There is information from heaven that many need to know. There are secrets from heaven that you need to understand so that life can run smoothly for you.

I remember the story of Brother Mirror. Whenever I call this man Brother Mirror, he will just laugh. Only this brother and I know why I call him Brother Mirror. The brother had gone to marry a beautiful lady somewhere. For the engagement and introduction, he took all the items he should take along. However, the family of the woman said they did not want any of them. So, they did not take the items. The father-in-law to be said, "The only thing is this. I am going to give you this parcel. Just put it under your bed. That is all; no need for dowry'. The brother was happy, but since the day the brother put this parcel under his bed, anytime he closed his eyes to sleep, he would find himself roaming around the cemetery till daybreak. Then he would wake up tired, and things were turning upside down.

It was at that level that he came for counselling and prayers. Then he started praying: "O Lord, show me the secrets of my life, in the name of Jesus." As he continued to pray, he heard a voice, "Mirror!" When he kept silent, the voice would be silent. Once he started praying again, he would hear, "Mirror!" And that was the voice he heard repeatedly for almost one week, until he came to see me. I said, "Mirror?" Tell me about your marriage." He said, "Sir, I married from a very nice family. My in-laws did not take anything from me. They just gave me a parcel to put under my bed. I asked, "Is the parcel still there?" He said, "Yes!" I told him, "Go and bring it." He brought the parcel, wrapped like a present. I said, "Open it." When he opened it, it was a mirror. So, with this mirror, they subjected him to slavery, and every night he did hard labour in the cemetery. It is time to pray violent prayers again:

Raise your right hand to the heavens and declare these with boiling anger:

1. Powers assigned to make me a slave, you are a liar, die in the name of Jesus.
2. Powers saying that I will not go far, your time is up, die, in the name of Jesus.

One of the reasons that I am emphasising this kind of prayers is that if God did not ask you to do something, and you end up doing it, and you invite Him to bless it, He will ask you if He ever told you to go there: "Did I ask you to do this?" So, it is good for you to pray sharp-shooting prayers and know where you are going.

THE QUESTION YOU MUST ANSWER

So, who am I? How do I see myself? How does God see me? What does God think about me? These are questions that require deep thinking, deep meditation and fervent prayers. The answers to these questions will positively affect all areas of your life, including your work, your career, who you marry, who you relate with, how you respond to life situations, and ultimately, where you will spend eternity.

Your life is not what others think about you. Your life is not what you look like, or what you see in the mirror when you look at yourself. Your life is not your talents and abilities. It is not what your family says about you. Your life is what God has deposited into you.

Nobody is a mistake; nobody is an accident. God is a giver of life and never makes mistakes. So beloved, you are not a mistake. You are intentionally made by God. So the question of who you are is one you should answer as quickly as possible, because many people did not know who they are as well as how and why they came into existence early enough. Let us consider some cases:

JACOB AND BORROWED IDENTITY

Physically, Jacob was doing well. He was a good business man and he had a good family. He had servants or employees. It appeared that everything was going well for him, but the reality was that he knew that he was not in a place of blessing. If you read the story in Genesis 25, the name Jacob means he who grabs the heels. If somebody were to pray to find out why Jacob was in trouble and discover the secret of the problem of Jacob, he would be taken back to when Jacob was in the womb. The person would discover how Jacob's mother found out that there were twins in her womb and they were fighting each other. So, she went to a prophet who said, "Two nations are in your womb; two people are within you. One will be stronger than the other, and the older will serve the younger." That was a deep secret about Jacob.

Unfortunately, Jacob stole the identity of Esau, the person that that the prophecy said Jacob was going to be greater than. Therefore, when Isaac, their father asked, "Who am I speaking to?" Jacob told a lie and said, "I am Esau." No one can get far with a borrowed identity. So when the battle started and Jacob began to wrestle with the angel, he got to a point where he had to face reality and the angel asked him, "What is your name?" This time, he told the truth, "I am Jacob." The angel told him, "That name is your problem; let me change it now." I pray that if there is any evil name you are bearing in the spirit world that you don't even know about, I cancel such names now, in the name of Jesus.

SAMSON

Judges 13 contains an interesting account of divine information that heaven provided about an unborn child. It reveals that Israel was suffering from the attacks and deprivation of their enemies, and God decided to raise a deliverer for them. Hence, God sent an angel to Mrs Manoah and gave her some instructions: "You are going to have a child who will deliver his people. Madam, don't eat anything unclean. Don't drink wine. Don't touch strong drink." This is a very serious matter. Whether the prophecy is going to be fulfilled or not has to do with the obedience of that woman. God's programme for Israel's deliverance had been placed in the hands of the woman.   This means that the child can be defiled from the womb. If that happens, it also means that the child can be born contrary to prophecy. This is one of the reasons you have to pray fervently. Some people who were not supposed to drink alcohol have drunk several gallons of it. Some of those who were not supposed to have incisions on their bodies already have them. Some people came with a white destiny, but they are using charm or fetish things. As a believer, you were not supposed to touch any of these defiling things, but you have already touched them ignorantly. This is why prayer is needed.

The child Samson would have been born outside his prophetic coverage if his mother did not obey. Spiritual complications can arise through physical consumption of food. Even science tells us that food substances eaten by a pregnant woman can get to the child through the placenta.   These include salt, water, sugar, medications and drugs taken by the mother. They eventually get to the child. That is why if your mother is a witch, don't deceive yourself. Go for deliverance, because you are already a witch yourself. If she is drinking blood and eating flesh, you have already taken part of it in the womb. So, if a mother is taking spiritually unclean food, the child too will be defiled, even from the womb.

BATTLES FROM THE WOMB

Many challenges that people face in adulthood are traceable to the time they were still babies in their mothers' wombs. Problems and battles that began in the womb are often neglected or ignorantly glossed over by many Pastors. The result is that the enemy will continue to enslave and torment the victim. He thrives in people's ignorance.

Why am I delving into this area? It is to help you ask the appropriate questions that will dig up and unravel the mystery behind your battles as well as help you get permanent solutions to them from the Lord. Some of the questions you need to ask, the information you need to get from heaven may take you back to the womb.

Many things have gone wrong with many people while in womb, but how would you know what went wrong if you do not ask questions. Many of our mothers ate all kinds of things when they were pregnant. Perhaps you know that your mother, during pregnancy, drank concoctions, satanic holy water, and ate demonic food, oranges, bean cakes, all kinds of things from witchcraft parties, took snuff and drank alcohol. These things could be the foundation of what you are going through now.

Through food, so many mothers had their children initiated into witchcraft and unclean spirits. This now explains the foundation of blind witchcraft. Such a person is a witch, but he does not know. The eating of spiritually poisonous food can cause trouble. The consequence of some can lie dormant for years, only to appear later at adult life. It means that there are so many things deposited into somebody as a child which will not manifest until several years later.

Can a spirit possess a child from the womb? Yes! The Holy Spirit can possess a child from the womb. Unclean spirits can possess a child from the womb. I have seen cases of pregnancies disappearing and appearing within a particular time of the night, the baby is no longer in the womb. Around 4am, the baby comes back. Such a baby has been initiated before being born physically. How will this kind of child fulfil his or her destiny? That is why we need these prayers. We need to pray really hard.

PARENTAL MISTAKES

I remember the plight of a lady. She got married but had no child. The doctors checked but found nothing wrong with her. Medical reports showed that the woman and her husband were perfect health-wise. So, the couple did not know the cause of their childlessness. This problem went on for years until she too began to pray these kinds of prayers.

She prayed to a level and saw a bottle. The bottle was turned upside down. Anytime she prayed hard, she would see the bottle turned upside down. She didn't understand what the revelation meant until she came for counselling and prayers. I told her to go and ask her parents about the bottle 'Daddy, Mummy, when I was young, do you remember anything about any bottle?" The first time she and her husband went, her daddy did not remember anything. The second time, the man now remembered. The lady in question is very beautiful. So, the daddy was worried that men would get her pregnant in school. Therefore, he consulted a herbalist who gave him a bottle and said, "Go and hide this bottle somewhere. Turn it upside down and keep it there. As far as the bottle is there upside down, she may sleep with all kinds of men, but she will never be able to get pregnant. As nothing can stay inside a bottle turned upside down, the semen will be turned upside down." So he took the bottle home and did accordingly.

This lady went through her academic cadre up to the university, and later got married. The herbalist had told her daddy, "On her wedding day, go and turn the bottle the right way up. If not, she would not get pregnant." Probably, he had forgotten but with those prayers she prayed the father remembered and went to bring the bottle. I am praying for you, that all the secrets you need to know that will take you to the next level, they shall manifest now, in the name of Jesus.

Beloved, once more I implore you to pray the following destiny-changing prayers the Gethsemane way. God will use them to do great and mighty things in your life, in the name of Jesus.

Prayer Points

1. Power to discover the secrets of my life's battles and to recover from them, fall upon me now, in the name of Jesus.
2. Any battle that entered into my life from the womb of my mother, your time is up, jump out of my life and die, in the name of Jesus.
3. Blood of Jesus, deliver me from the consequences of my parents' mistakes, in the name of Jesus.
4. Handwriting of death on my forehead, blood of Jesus, wipe it away, in the name of Jesus.
5. Battles rising against the solution to my problems, die, in the name of Jesus.
6. Powers from the grave of my father's house, that said my glory will never speak, die, in the name of Jesus.
7. The key of my future in the hands of wicked elders, I recover you by fire, in the name of Jesus.

Chapter Eight

JOURNEY BACK TO THE WOMB (I)

Beloved, as I have stated again and again in the previous chapters, information empowers a man and lack of information deforms him. If you take this eye-opening teaching seriously, pray the prayers of enquiry and use the information you obtain correctly, it will definitely be the beginning of your unending laughter.

I have received so many letters from people who sat down to pray because they wanted information. These people paid the price, got the information they needed and experienced deliverance, transformation and all-round fulfilment.

Take, for example, the case of this sister. She said that anywhere she went people would love and welcome her with open hands. She would seem to be the darling of everybody. All of a sudden, things would change. Her employer would sack her and she would be going from place to place. This unpleasant experience continued until she had the opportunity to listen to the series of my message titled, "Who Am I".

The first week, she prayed after listening to the message. She listened to the next series of the message in the second week and prayed fervently too. As she prayed in the second week, the Lord took her to a place where a woman was being delivered of a baby, and the nurses were encouraging the woman to push. The baby came out. The mother who was delivered of the baby asked the nurses, "Is my baby male or female?" The nurses said, "Female." She replied, No! I don't want this one. I don't want this one. I don't want her." So the nurses asked her to shut up and the vision cleared. Then for the first time, she knew that since that day, the spirit of rejection had been following her. I pray that if there is the spirit of rejection attached to you, and following you from place to place, I separate you from that spirit, in the name of Jesus.

There is this case of another sister too. She noticed that even at the age of twenty five, all the men who approached her for marriage were fifty, sixty, sometimes seventy years old. One day she was even standing at the bus stop and an old man with a walking stick, walked up to her and said, "I want to marry you." That drove her into serious prayers.

Who Art Thou?   **163**

Also, she heard the message, "Who Am I?" The Lord told her to go and ask her mother how she was delivered." So she went, and her mother was able to remember what happened. There was a time her mother was very sick when she was pregnant of her. She was taken to a very old native doctor. The old man said, "I will heal you on one condition. When you give birth to the baby in your womb, I will marry her." The woman said, "Yes." However, before she gave birth to the child, the old native doctor died. That is what is responsible for what is happening to her now.

I pray again: Any unconscious covenant that wants to keep you in bondage and is attacking your future, I break it, in the name of Jesus.

KNOW YOUR ORIGIN AND THE SECRETS

God ordained Jeremiah from his mother's womb. God also ordained John the Baptist from his mother's womb. A lot of positive and negative things can happen to a person while in the womb as well as when he is a baby or a child. You need to find out what went wrong at these stages of your life. That could be where the secret of the battle you are facing now lies.

There are prayers to pray for you to send investigation down
to your roots.

1.   You need God to show you the secrets of any satanic
        investment in the foundation of your life.

2.   You need to ask the Lord to show you every hidden
        childhood poison. You need to pray to know the
        secrets.

3.   You need to also pray to know the secrets of every tree,
        not planted by the Father, growing in you since you are
        a child.

4.   You need to find out the secrets of any satanic seed
        growing in your foundation.

        The principle of Scripture is very simple: whosoever
        asks receives. If you do not ask, nothing will be shown;
        but if you ask, you will be shocked what heaven will say
        and reveal to you. You might say, "But Lord, why
        didn't you tell me these things all these years. The
        reason is that you never asked these questions. You
        need to pray these prayers until you are correctly
        positioned.

5.   You need to know the secret of every serpent and scorpion planted in your life, particularly if you are from a polygamous home.

6.   You need to find out about the glory killers entrenched in the foundation of your life.

7.   You need to ask for the secrets of any problem buried in your childhood to pollute your future.

      The enemy buried it there, but you don't know he did. It is like Jesus asking those people questions when he saw the small boy manifesting. "How long has this been troubling him?" The boy's parents said, "Since he was a child."

8.   You need to know the secrets of any childhood bondage battling with your adulthood.

SOME MYSTERIES ABOUT THE WOMB

Science, and more importantly the Bible, have made it clear to us that man's existence begins after conception and that a lot of good and bad things can happen in the womb. John Kelly and Thomas R. Verny also made this interesting finding in their co-authored book titled, *The Secret Life of the Unborn Child*. This book is an excellent resource on this subject.

What many people do not know is that whatever happens to a baby in the womb can have very strong positive or negative effect through adulthood and the person's life. Today, many people are wondering where their problem or battle originated from? If you are in this category, I advise you to enquire into what happened to you while in the womb.

Let us examine the scriptures

> Luke 1:41 *And it came to pass, that when Elizabeth heard the salutation of Mary the babe leaped in her womb and Elizabeth was filled with the Holy Ghost.*

Elizabeth heard the greeting of Mary, the mother of Jesus. The baby in the womb leaped for Joy. This tells us that babies can hear, feel and react to things going on externally while they are in the wombs.

> Luke 1:44 *For lo, as soon as the voice of thy salutation sounded in my ears, the babe leaped in my womb for joy.*

It means that the baby heard and leaped in the womb for joy.
This was a positive reaction. The contrary can be the case in
other instances

> Psalm 58:3 *The wicked are estranged from the womb,*
> *they go astray as soon as they are born, speaking lies.*

The foregoing Scriptures are deep and revealing. It means that
a person could be wicked from the womb. A person could be
a witch from the womb. A person could have a familiar spirit
from the womb. That is why the Bible says that they are
estranged from the womb. They go astray as soon as they are
born (Psalm 58:3). That is why some people find it very
difficult to give their lives to Jesus.

Those who studied science, as well as those who studied about
child bearing, pregnancy and things like that have been able
to show, through their studies, that babies in the womb can
know whether they are wanted or not. Unborn babies can
hear, feel and learn in the womb.

Similarly, the experience of a child in the womb can shape his
attitude and expectations. When there are deep and persistent
patterns of some terrible feelings in the mother, it affects the
unborn child. Even a father's feeling about his wife and the
unborn child can affect the pregnancy. If that womb is

friendly, the child may be predisposed to good health, happiness and normal development. But if the womb is unfriendly, the baby may be predisposed to bad health, nervousness, irritableness and arrested development.

Science has also proved that sound has an impact on the unborn child. Children in the womb can pick up any anger, quarrel, yelling, screaming, fighting between mother and father, and that will escort the child to real life. This is where many of us need very serious prayers.

That tells the voice of Mary carried an anointing and the anointing went into the baby in Elizabeth's womb. It connected with the baby positively. The voice of that holy woman had divine impact on the baby in the womb. Let us suppose the woman that visited Elizabeth that day was a witch from the coven or a satanic priest. That voice too would have had an evil or binding effect on the baby. So, voices heard in the womb have deep effects. Prayers prayed for a baby in the womb have deep effects. Curses issued on a baby in the womb also have deep effects. Most importantly, where your mother went when she was pregnant of you is very important.

I was at a university in Nigeria to minister to the young ones. I was talking about marriage to them. I asked all the sisters who were there if they would want to marry a man like their daddies. In other words, I said, "If you want the husband you want to marry to be somebody like your dad, stand up." Out of about two thousand students, only one sister stood up. Others did not want to marry someone whose behaviour was like their fathers'. It shows you the seriousness of this matter.

Jeremiah 1:5 *Before I formed thee in the belly I knew thee; and before thou camest forth out of the womb I sanctified thee, and I ordained thee a prophet unto the nations.*

This verse of the Scripture reveals the programme of God for Jeremiah. It also shows that a person can be anointed from the womb, highly favoured, blessed and marked for greatness from the womb. But, if the enemies had altered the programme of God from the womb, which is possible, then there is a problem indeed. This is why you need to pray very serious prayers and fervently too. I advise you to also pray in the hours of the night and before you sleep. This may be why things have not been going the way you want them to go.

Satanic reprogramming from the womb will lead to terrible repercussion for the future. If you do not know about it, you may not address it. That is why so many people grapple with a problem from the cradle to the grave. Our fore fathers did not serve the living God. They served the devil. Unknown to them there are many grave consequences for these idolatrous practices.

It means that when a woman is pregnant, if the kind of information she got were from the devil, the kind of things she ate and drank were from the devil, you can see where things went wrong.

MAN'S DEVELOPMENTAL STAGES

The first six years of life are the foundational years. By the time somebody is six, the structure of the character is formed. By the time the person is ten, the character is already set in concrete. It means that what we are supposed to pray against now might have been set in concrete, twenty, thirty or forty years ago. When people now become leaders with fractured foundation, they get those that they lead into trouble. So, we need prayers.

The following things happen when there are problems emanating from the womb:

1.   **Resistance to normal gentle prayers:** Problems that have their roots and origin in the womb would have developed tap roots and deeply entrenched themselves by the time they manifest later in life. Therefore, such deeply-rooted problems will not answer to normal, gentle prayers. The demons behind them will not shift except the fire of the Holy Spirit is unleashed against them through effectual, fervent and violent bombardment of prayers.

2.   **Deliverance failures:** One of the signs that a problem emanated from the womb is that the victim will constantly experience deliverance failure. That is, the person will not get the result he or she desires after going through deliverance once or twice. The person will have to repeat deliverance until the root cause of the problem from the womb is properly addressed and destroyed.

3.   **Constant dream harassments:** This is another manifestation of problems that are traceable to the womb. Most of the people who experience constant nightmares and bad dreams have prayerfully sought to know the cause and found that the seed of the problem was sown into their lives while they were still babies in their mothers' wombs.

4.   **Unexplainable hatred:** Many people are victims of
        unexplainable hatred and favour famine today. Such
        people have continued to wonder about what could be
        the cause of their problem. Everywhere they go,
        people will like and embrace them only for hatred to
        follow perpetually. This cycle continues even when
        they change their location. The truth is that many of
        such victims received the arrow of unexplainable
        hatred directly as babies in their mothers' wombs or
        indirectly through their mothers when she was carrying
        them in the womb for nine months.

5.   **Serious character disorder:** The problem of character
        flaw and disorder has robbed many people of great
        opportunities in life. This problem is also often
        traceable to the womb. Sometimes, it is the result of
        evil flow or evil inheritance from the mother to the
        baby or as a result of some sinful lifestyles like,
        drunkenness, lying, stealing and other vices that the
        parents, especially the mother, was committing while
        she was pregnant the baby. The grace of God and His
        anointing can deliver the victim with character
        disorder who also determines to turn a new leaf.

6.   **Spiritual blockage:** This is not a problem anyone
        should take lightly. Spiritual blockage has rendered

many of its victims stagnant, redundant, unproductive and unsuccessful. Perhaps, through some negative covenants parents, especially mothers enter into, they put their unborn children in bondage and invite demons that will constantly stand in their way and hinder their children's lives. Such victims need not despair because there is still deliverance, holiness and recovery of lost possessions on Mount Zion.

7.   **Sickness:** Mothers who go about eating concoctions and drinking all kinds of things given to them by just anyone are simply laying a terrible foundation for sickness and diseases for their unborn children. Science has shown that the mother shares everything she eats and drinks with the baby. So as a mother, you should eat only the things that will promote your baby's physical and spiritual wellbeing.

So far, we have abundantly proved that what parents do (good or bad) affect the baby in its formative years and is capable of flowing into adulthood. For example, when couples fight seriously during the woman's pregnancy, it leads to the baby having asthmatic attack. This is because of the effect of the quarrel of the parents on the baby in the womb. If your father was beating your mother in the pregnancy state, it would have an effect on you as a baby in the womb and most probably later in life.

I encourage you to shout this prayer, irrespective of what happened to you in the womb:

-       Blood of Jesus, arise in your cleansing power and wash my roots, in the name of Jesus.

WOMB SECRETS

Some items of information are essential for you to obtain in order to pray targeted and result-oriented prayers and to experience deep deliverance. Without these items of information, your deliverance is likely to be cosmetic, superficial and temporary. The best way to obtain these items of information is to walk back to the womb. The womb secrets will help you to tailor your prayers appropriately and obtain deep deliverance. Here, I will provide some of these vital items of information and give specific examples. They will make your prayers highly result-oriented. They are findings from spiritual and medical researches.

1.   **Children born but not wanted by one or both parents:** When a child is not wanted, but the child is

born, there are things that will begin to show up in his or her characteristics, pattern of attitude and behaviour after birth. The child that is not wanted will always be striving, always seeking to perform, and struggling to excel above others. The child will be struggling to earn the right to live. This kind of child may have inordinate desire towards the opposite sex. The child will also be followed by rejection. Such a child will get angry very quickly. Sometimes such a child grows into an adult and wishes that he/she dies. Sometimes, such a person frequently battles with sickness. Similarly, he or she could face problems with bonding with any of the parents. The person will not like the father or mother, or sometimes both of them. Sometimes, some of such persons just run away or avoid having any contact with the father or the mother. It is the effect of the fact that they were not wanted from the womb.

2. **Children born out of wedlock:** When children are conceived out of wedlock: no marriage, no engagement, no introduction, they usually exhibit some problematic traits that call for serious prayers and deliverance. Such children were just brought into the world carelessly. They have escaped from the covering

of the Almighty who has ordained that children can only be born inside wedlock. So such children, as far as God is concerned, will have some deep sense of shame. They will be struggling and they will have spiritual blockages. They need to pray very hard, because they were born when there is no cover of marriage. Such children are already born into deficit.

3. **Children that are born when their parents are too young:** In this case, the parents of the child are not really ready for marriage. The pregnancy and birth of the child are considered an accident and a mistake. So, if somebody was born out of fornication between two young people, of course, that child would have challenges. The child would have attacks and may not be able to do what others are doing. The child may be unruly, rebellious and very loose with the opposite sex. This is simply because he or she was born when the parents were not ready for parenting. The tragedy of our world now is that children are giving birth to children. When a thirteen or fourteen-year old boy is impregnating a fifteen or sixteen-year old girl, that is a tragedy.

4. **Children born by mothers with poor health:** When the mother of a child has very poor health and the child is born, the child will grow up with guilty feeling and sometimes go from one sickness to the other. Those are the effects of what happened while in the womb.

I have explained this to you with some illustrations, but your major information should be your prayer:

1. Lord, show me the secrets of my life, in the name of Jesus.
2. Lord, show me beneficial secrets about me, in the name of Jesus.
3. Lord, show my house to my house, in the name of Jesus.
4. -Lord, show me to me, in the name of Jesus.
5. Lord, show me every secret I need to know about my childhood, in the name of Jesus.
6. Lord, show me what I need to correct, in the name of Jesus.
7. Lord, show me beneficial secrets about my origin and birth, in the name of Jesus.

These are prayers you seriously need to pray regularly and unceasingly.

5.   **Children born of a gender different from what the parents wanted:** When a child is born and both parents consider the child as the wrong sex. They wanted a male and they got female. As a result, the parents did not rejoice but showed attitude of disappointment and rejection towards the newly born baby. The result or implication is that the child will have sexual identification problems. Sometimes that child will be involved in terrible sexual perversion. Sometimes such a child will have this defeatist attitude: "I was not wanted anyway." Then the spirit of rejection will follow. Some people call it bad luck, but it is actually the spirit of rejection.

Pray these revealing prayers fervently, militantly and with 'enough is enough' spirit. The reason for this warfare-approach is that we are about to deal with something planted when you did not know who you were.

Prayer Points

1. Satanic investments in the foundation of my life, your time is up, die, in the name of Jesus.

2. Every tree the Father has not planted, that is polluting my life, catch fire, in the name of Jesus.

3. Every satanic plantation in my foundation, die, in the name of Jesus.

4. Serpents and scorpions planted in my childhood, die, in the name of Jesus.

5. My Father, walk into my childhood days and purge my life, in the name of Jesus.

6. Powers planted in my childhood to trouble my future, die, in the name of Jesus.

7. Plantations of polygamous witchcraft in my foundation, what are you waiting for? die, in the name of Jesus.

Chapter Nine

JOURNEY BACK TO THE WOMB (II)

As I explained in the last chapter, both medical and spiritual studies have shown that a baby in the womb can hear what you say. Actually, from 6 to 8 weeks, the brain, the divine computer of the baby, begins to record things. Unborn babies can hear, feel and learn from the womb as earlier stated. An important thing to note is that any terrible experience or happening that is recorded while in the womb can affect them later in life.

I also highlighted some kinds of womb-related problems, their symptoms and consequences. I emphasised that part of deep deliverance is to walk back to the womb and come back again.

It is unfortunate that the words of the Scriptures have come to pass again, *"My people perish for lack of knowledge"* (Hosea 4:6). Also, Jesus said, *"You shall know the truth and the truth shall set you free"* (John 8:32). Beloved, it is the truth that you know, believe and apply that will set you free. Truth is very powerful, but it is useless to you when you do not know it. Many people are ignorant of all these things and the enemy is short-changing them.

Also, as these things happen to people, but they do not take them back to the roots or the womb, where the problems actually started from, they will pray and pray, but it will be surface prayers without desired results. I pray that the light of the Scriptures and the fire of the Holy Spirit will flood your spirit man and you will detect the origin and roots of your problems. When you address such problems appropriately by waging war against it, the power behind it will bow and flee, in the name of Jesus.

WOMB INJURIES

Beloved, there are other injuries that can happen in the womb that will affect the life of a person. We will continue our discourse here from where we stopped in the last chapter:

6.   **Children conceived and born when their parents were facing bad time financially:** Such children may experience hardship, poverty and financial challenges. Similarly, except people in this category pray very well,

they may become victims of profitless hard work and non-achievement.

7.   **Children that follow other conceptions that were lost:** This kind of children can be affected by such an incident. Such children may be insecure and exhibit the fear of death. Similarly, such children will demonstrate lack of confidence. They may become over-serious, always trying and trying to over-achieve. These are the consequence you will notice.

8.   **Children whose mothers had inordinate fear of delivery:** When such children are born, they may have fear or insecurity. The female among such children may also have the fear of child birth.

9.   **Children whose parents fought each other seriously during their pregnancy:** When there is serious fight and disagreement in the home during pregnancy, that child may be born being nervous, and he or she could become asthmatic.

10. **Children whose fathers died or left home before they were born:** Experience has shown that such children always exhibit the fear of being guilty; they have deep-

rooted anger, and they sometimes get very depressed or very rebellious.

11. **Children whose mothers lost a loved one and is in a state of grief during pregnancy:** In this instance, if the mother does not shake herself out of that grief, when that child is born, he or she may experience deep sadness, a melancholic spirit, depression, having the wish to die, fear of death and loneliness. All these things have effects on babies in the womb.

12. **Children who were sustained by dark powers in pregnancy:** A woman was having miscarriages. So, she sought for help from beggarly powers. They did some magic to keep the child in place. The child may be born alright, but that child may suffer constant spiritual attacks from the forces that kept him or her at that time.

13. **Children born after repeated attempts to give birth to them:** The consequence in this instance is that such children may be aggressive and have terrible hatred for any form of opposition.

14. **Children whose mothers were smoking and drinking alcohol:** Such a child may be born with severe anxiety

problems. Mother consumes alcohol because more of the chemical effects will be absorbed by the baby into the body and cause serious problems to the child when that child grows up. The child may now be born and becomes a drunkard and find it so difficult to break away from alcoholism.

I read the story of a baby that was born and that baby cried endlessly. The doctors could not diagnose what was wrong with the baby. It was somebody who knew that the mother of the baby was a drunkard that provided a solution to the baby's problem. The person said, "Can we try something? Though it is crazy, but we can try it. Put a drop of alcohol in the mouth of the baby." They put a drop of alcohol in the mouth of this baby. Strange but true the baby smiled and stopped crying. That means the baby had been getting dozed with alcohol in the womb. The baby is out now, she could not find any alcohol, and she started crying.

15. **Children whose delivery was painful or involved a breach:** The truth is that such children may have problem with learning and with anger.

16. **Children born with cord around their neck:** When a child is born with a cord around the neck, the child may be born and start having speech problems. Also, the child may be born talking to anybody anyhow, behaving like a criminal and exhibiting a lot of anti-social behaviours because of that cord that was around his or her neck.

17. **Children born out of wedlock:** All the conception out of wedlock is something filled with troubles, and it is something that should be avoided at all cost.

18. **Children conceived in anger or rape:** When such children are born, there may be fear of abandonment as well as sexual perversion in the life of that child.

19. **Children that come at the wrong time in the parents' life:** Such children may grow up having marital difficulties, poverty and all kinds of inconveniences.

20. **Children abandoned by both parents:** Such children may experience chronic poverty and deep sense of loneliness.

21.   **Children not wanted at all but born:** Children in this category may have rebellion, identity crisis and constantly quarrel or fight with people.

These are examples of things that happen to an unborn baby in the womb. This is why we are praying that the Lord Jesus should walk back into the womb and cause great deliverance to happen.

So, things happen in the womb and they affect people in real life. This is also why we need to pray more secrets-revealing prayers.

Let us see some deep revelations that changed the lives of people when they prayed these prayers. You can experience the same too in Jesus name.

GREAT REVELATION, GREAT DELIVERANCE

A sister said that she could not understand how her life was going. Everything was upside down: her work and career had problems; her marriage was also full of problems. This made her to take time to pray. The prayer point she focussed on was: O God arise, show me the secrets of my life, in the name of Jesus. After the prayers, she slept and a man came to her, dressed all in white and tall. The man said, "You want to know why you've been having troubles?" She said, "Yes." The man further said, "I will tell you now because you asked. If you had not asked, you would not have got any answer."

The angel asked her again, "Do you want to know why you are in trouble?" Again, she replied, "Yes." The angel of the Lord told her, "You are a bastard." He said it to her three times. When she woke up, she could not sleep again. Early in the next morning, she ran to her mother. She said, "Mummy, you know things are not going well. I prayed, and this is what I heard."

She said that to her surprise, her mummy just bowed down her head. Then she asked, "Mummy, what is the matter?" The mother responded and said, "It is true. Your father and I had a quarrel. So, I parked out of the house. While I was away, I had three male friends and I was sleeping with all the three of them. But then the family now settled the quarrel and brought your father and me back together. That was when I went back to my matrimonial home, not knowing I was already one month pregnant. The problem was that I couldn't tell who your father was among of those three men." Her mother added, "Certainly, the person whose name you bear now is not your father." It was a serious problem she discovered at the age of 37.

I pray that the secrets that will move you forward, the secrets that will turn your destiny around, the secret that will catapult your destiny to the next level, the God of Elijah shall arise and reveal them to you, in the name of Jesus!

There was this other interesting story that revealed the sovereignty and goodness of God in human affairs. There were three daughters from a family. The first one brought in somebody who wanted to marry her. A week to that marriage, the man ran mad, and then the lady too ran mad and died. The second daughter brought somebody home that she wanted to marry. The day of the wedding, the man did not show up. As a result, the second daughter ran mad and died. It remained one daughter in the family.

When this last daughter brought somebody home that she wanted to marry, she noticed that the parents broke down and cried. Then they told the man, "Why do you want to marry our daughter. You can't marry this lady." Then, they chased the man away.

That was her experience, and she now started praying. Unfortunately, her father had covenanted all the three girls in an evil covenant to increase his wealth and that covenant is that they cannot marry, and if they marry, they will die.

Any hidden covenant that you do not know about and is pursuing your life, I command it to be broken, in the name of Jesus.

There was a man who looked so well. In his place of work, people believe that he is very rich, not knowing that he had no money in his pocket. People were also begging him for money because of the way he looked. He looked wealthy and well fed, but he was suffering. It was this prayer he too prayed: O God, arise and show me the secrets of my life, in the name of Jesus.

Then he heard a voice that told him to go and check his praise name. In Yoruba land, there are some praise names that are given to people, a set of poetry that they read about people. The man had heard it sung to him over the years, but he never sat down to think about its meaning.

So, he looked at it and read it again. He now got to a place that read in Yoruba: 'Omo ajopo iya ma ru'. It means the one who gets fat and looks comfortable, but is suffering. That was what they wrote down for him. So physically, he looked prosperous, but he was suffering.

I pray once again, that hidden covenant assigned to truncate your destiny shall collapse today, in the name of Jesus.

THE ENEMY AND WOMEN

Sisters really need to pray hard because the devil and his demons have more than a common interest in them. The devil hates women with perfect hatred. He can go to any imaginable extent to carry out evil against them. Right from the Garden of Eden, he had begun to target the woman. In the plan of redemption that God put down, it was the seed of the woman, and not the man, that was to bruise the serpent's head. So, women give satan nightmares. That is why his agenda is to totally destroy them. Therefore, it is a tragedy when a woman befriends the devil.

A sister prayed this kind of secret-unveiling prayers I have been encouraging you to pray. This person had a strange case. Her body was always hot. All medical tests were negative. She started praying and all of a sudden, God opened her eyes. She saw a pot on a fire and a woman was standing by the pot. The woman was boiling something in the pot. Something prompted her to look at what was inside the pot. It was blood the woman was boiling. Then she heard the voice, "This is why your body is always hot." We need secrets to fight in this warfare. That is why you need to pray violently. Shout this loud and clear:

- O God, arise and reveal the secrets behind my battles to me, in the name of Jesus.
- My Father, by Your mercy, turn my prayer points to joy and testimony, in the name of Jesus.

From all the illustrations you have read so far, it is abundantly clear that things happen in the womb and they affect people in real life. It is also clear that the enemy does not spare anyone in carrying out his evil agenda. This is why we are praying these secrets-revealing prayers. I enjoin you to pray them militantly and activate your faith. The Lord will show you beneficial womb secrets that will move your life to the next level.

Again, salvation is important. Without being saved, these prayers will be mere recitations. You must surrender your life to Jesus; that is when you will have full-blown testimonies

In case you have not given your life to Jesus, I advise that you do so now, so that the prayers will bring forth desired results from the Lord. As you pray these Holy Ghost-vomited prayer points, you will have great revelations and mighty breakthroughs, in the name of Jesus.

Prayer Points

1.   My Father, walk back to my childhood and deliver my life, in the name of Jesus.

2.   Blood of Jesus, arise in your cleansing power and wash my root, in the name of Jesus.

3.   Every evil effect of anything I have swallowed or eaten as a child, die, in the name of Jesus.

5.   Any seed of wickedness planted in my childhood to trouble my future, Holy Ghost Fire, destroy it, in the name of Jesus.

6.   Poison of darkness in my foundation, dry up and die, in the name of Jesus.

7.   Powers that fought the childhood of my parents and are now fighting me, die, in the name of Jesus.

Chapter Ten

HOW TO KNOW YOUR CORRECT IDENTITY

There are essential keys for unveiling the mystery of your identity. God wants you to know who you are. He wants you to have access to divine information that will liberate you from the battles of life and make you all that He has created you to be. Conversely, the enemy wants you to live perpetually in ignorance of your true identity and the best that God has purposed for you. It is your responsibility to obtain the keys that will give you access to the secrets you need to know about yourself and use them for your good.

Here are the keys that will help you to know your correct identity and fulfil your purpose in life. I advise you to get and use them wisely:

1.   **Salvation:** This is the first and most important of all the keys that you can use to discover your identity and unravel all mysteries about your existence. You must surrender your life to Jesus and accept Him as your

personal Lord and Saviour. You must be born again. This change of your spiritual status will earn you the right to obtain and enjoy the heritage of saints (children of God). The Holy Spirit will begin to dwell in your heart and guide your life. You will begin to have access to God's revelations, information and secrets. Your prayer will rise to God with sweet-smelling savour. Beloved, if you are not born again already, go on your knees now and pray to Jesus to forgive you, come into your life and be your Lord and Saviour. When you are born of the Spirit, heaven will help you to reach your goal.

2. **The Word of God:** This is an important key to deploy in knowing your identity and your heritage in Christ. The word of God is life's best compass to show believers the way in life. God's word is spirit and life. It is a mirror that enables you to see yourself through the lens of God. It is the best safeguard against errors and mistakes as well as the antics of the devil. Jesus quoted the word and defeated the devil who wanted to deceive Him about His true identity as the Son of God. Though the tempter knew that Jesus is the Son of God, yet he told Jesus, *"If you are the Son of God, tell this*

stone to turn to bread." Jesus answered, "Man shall not live by bread alone but by every word that proceeds from the mouth of God." Again, he took Jesus to the pinnacle of the city and said, *"If you are the Son of God, cast yourself down. For it is written, He has given his angels charge over you. They will bear you up in their hands and you will not dash your foot against the stone."* Jesus answered him, *"Thou shall not tempt the Lord Your God."* The word of God is the sword of the Spirit and a veritable weapon to defeat the devil.

Also, the word of God gives light and dispels darkness or ignorance. The Bible says that the entrance of God's word gives light and it gives understanding to the simple. The power of God's word is capable of opening your spiritual eyes and unveiling the secrets of heaven to you. Therefore, I encourage you to study the word of God regularly to show yourself approved as a workman that needs not be ashamed, dividing the word correctly. Let God's word dwell in you richly. Memorise it, meditate on it day and night, and live by it constantly.

3.   **Prayer and Fasting:** Prayer and fasting have done
       marvellous things where other strategies have not
       yielded sufficient results. That is why Jesus said that
       "this kind does not go out except by prayer and
       fasting". What fasting does is that it helps to crucify
       the flesh. When the flesh is weak, the carnal part of
       man gives way to the Spirit. It is the strengthened and
       sharpened spirit that is aligned to God that receives
       beneficial spiritual signals and divine information. It is
       the disciplined and strengthened spirit man that can
       dig deep and uncover deep treasures of God's secrets.

       Beloved, if you want God's secrets to be available to
       you like Job, Abraham, Daniel and others, I advise you
       to pray and fast regularly. I also encourage you to live
       in holiness within and without and pray in the spirit
       constantly.

4.   **Unwavering faith:** Without faith it is impossible to
       please God, walk with Him and receive the best from
       Him. Faith is having courageous trust in the Almighty.
       It is to believe that God will do everything He has
       promised to do, no matter the obstacle that stands in
       the way. If you want to access mysteries of God's

kingdom as well as personal secrets about your own life and destiny, you must have unwavering faith in God, the Custodian of all secrets and the One who reveals His secrets to His children.

With faith in God, Daniel prayed and was able to know the dream of King Nebuchadnezzar as well as the interpretation. Beloved, when you demonstrate genuine faith in God, He will illuminate you and reveal all the secrets that will move your life forward and upward to you. The Bible affirms that if you believe, you will see the glory of God.

5. **Life of Holiness and Righteousness:** Anyone who desires to walk with God and have constant access to His secrets must live a holy and righteous life. Job, Noah, Abraham and even the apostles in the New Testament set themselves apart. That is why God saved them by His grace. If you want to know the mysteries of your existence and the secrets of your life, you must steer clear of sin and iniquity. You must separate yourself to God and present yourself to him as a living sacrifice, holy and acceptable. God is holy, and He requires that you should be holy unto Him.

Those who have right standing with God will always have His Spirit working wonders in their lives and supplying them with valuable information from heaven.

6. **Obedience:** This is another important key for accessing divine information. Anyone who lives in constant disobedience of God's commandment cannot enjoy the privilege of getting classified information from heaven. Beloved, I encourage you to be an obedient child of God. When your obedience to God is prompt, unquestioning and complete, then you will call upon Him and He will answer you and show you great and mighty things that you never knew before (Jeremiah 33:3).

7. **Divine Encounter:** This happens when the supernatural meets the natural. Each time this takes place, there is divine intervention, destiny change, answer to prayer, revelation, miracles and life-changing testimonies. It took a divine encounter at Peniel for Jacob to know who he was. It was through a divine encounter that Gideon discovered his correct identity and went on to fulfil his assignment. It was through divine encounter that Mary knew her identity, heritage

and assignment. It was through separate divine encounters with Jesus that Peter and Paul knew who they were and what God had brought them to the earth to accomplish.

Beloved, you need a divine encounter. One encounter is enough to give you the divine information your life needs and turn it around for good. Why not cry to heaven today: Father, give me a life-changing encounter, in the name of Jesus.

8. **Stay in God**: Beloved, if you want to stay constantly under open heaven and access God's information regularly, your heart must not only be right with Him, it must be connected and knitted to Him. God will not reveal His secrets to those who are one leg with Him and the other leg with the enemy. You must pant after Him as the deer pants after the water brooks. You must also love Him genuinely and trust Him absolutely. You must not be a doubter. The Bible says that a doubter is like the surging sea, driven and tossed by the wind. Those who are double-minded and unstable in the ways should not expect anything from God (James 1: 6-8). Therefore, no matter the negative things the

enemy brings your way, stay in God and keep trusting Him. He never fails. Anyone who has this characteristic will gain access to God's secrets and be fulfilled in life. God is faithful!

Prayer Points

1. My Father, give me the keys to access your secrets, in the name of Jesus.

2. Father, let Your word give me divine light and understanding, in the name of Jesus.

3. By Your mercy, O God, give me an encounter that will reveal beneficial secrets about my life to me and change my story to glory, in the name of Jesus.

4. O heaven of divine secrets, favour and breakthroughs, open unto me, in the name of Jesus.

5. Secrets that will give me supernatural acceleration and uncommon testimonies be revealed to me now, in the name of Jesus.

6. Angels of God, minister to me and give me divine information that will move my life forward, in the name of Jesus.

7. Strong man hiding the information that will change and rewrite my family history, somersault and die, in the name of Jesus.

Chapter Eleven

DEEP DELIVERANCE

The quest for knowledge about the secrets and mysteries of your life will birth deep deliverance for you. Deliverance is God's medicine bottle. Since Jesus came with the cardinal ministries to save, heal and deliver, mankind has never been the same again. The Son of God was manifested to destroy the works of the devil. The enemy and his demons have been subdued and their victims liberated. The ministry of deliverance is one of the greatest blessings Jesus Christ bequeathed to the Church.

Deliverance can be superficial, surface-level, cosmetic and ordinary. It can be great and deep. It can also be complete or incomplete. The best kind of deliverance is one that is complete and deep. Deep deliverance thrives on the accessibility and availability of correct and genuine information. It also thrives on grace and anointing.

SOME PROBLEMS THAT REQUIRE DEEP DELIVERANCE

The following are examples of problems that have deep and stubborn roots. They cannot be tackled by ordinary deliverance methods and sessions. They require a deep search and discovery of the secrets and powers at work. You will gain more understanding of what deep deliverance is as you read these examples:

1.   Problems that are deeply rooted and require the second touch of Jesus.

2.   Problems traceable to the womb, root or foundation.

3.   Problems that have to do with ancestral powers and yokes.

4.   Problems associated with spiritual blockages, spiritual blindness, spiritual blankness, no dream, no vision, no divine information.

5.   Deep sexual sin and perversion cases (change of sex, homosexualism, lesbianism, prostitution, same sex marriage, etc).

6.   Prolonged pregnancy (4 years, 8 years 10 years, etc), instead of the normal nine months.

7. Cases of disappeared pregnancy and organs of the body.

8. Cases of Babies travelling out of the womb and coming back.

9. Cases of people who hear strange voices.

10. People that have invisible load on their heads.

11. People that have personal rain falling on them (when it is not raining on others).

12. The rage of satanic birds screaming around.

13. People being pursued by the moon, sun and the stars.

14. Strange disappearance of some people's money, cloths, etc

15. Cases of strange odour and unexplainable hatred.

16. Cases of spiritual farming - total inability to read the Bible or pray. Such victims begin to feel sick immediately you start reading or praying.

17. Excessive tiredness are signs that you need deep deliverance

18. Strange occurrences in your environment. For example, you could have bush babies crying on your windows.

19. Sleep walking.

20. Demonic look alike

GET THE SECRETS

You need divine information to unravel the mysteries surrounding the deep deliverance cases highlighted above. The Bible assures us that God's secrets can be made available to you if you are His child who fear and obey Him, and if you are His prophet.

Beloved, the secret things belong to our all-knowing God.

Daniel 2:22 *He revealeth the deep and secret things: he knoweth what is in the darkness, and the light dwelleth with him.*

As a believer, you are a steward of the mysteries of the God

(1 Corinthians 4:1) When you seek and receive divine information about a problem, many of the mind-boggling questions you have will be answered: why, when, how, who, and the way out. The secrets that heaven reveals to you will enable you to get to the root of the problem and find great help and lasting solution. Lack of such beneficial and mystery-unravelling information is the reason that many captives of the mighty and prey of the terrible are still in bondage today.

DEEP DELIVERANCE CASES

A man of God cried uncontrollably day and night because his children (two boys and two girls) committed incest and the two sons impregnated their two sisters. He began to say, "I want to know what caused this." He began to pray. Suddenly, there was a flash back. He was taken to when he was young. His father married a lady. He raped his father's young wife. As he was forcefully sleeping with the lady, she issued a curse, "Your children will give you sorrow." This man of God had to repent before the Lord, and go through deliverance.

I pray for you that every legal ground the enemy has against you, let the blood of Jesus wipe them off, in the name of Jesus.

Esa was the youngest of his father. When he was going to school one day, he met a woman at the door with her two breasts touching the ground. The woman said, *"My husband, how are you doing?"* He ran inside to tell his father what happened. He said, *"Daddy, I saw a woman with two breasts touching the ground. She called me her husband."* Esa's father was sad. He said, *"That is our family spirit that didn't show herself to me, but has shown herself to you."* Now as at the age of 40, has divorced three times.

Again, the strange case of one woman also comes to mind. She had three girls. The fourth pregnancy was a boy. When it was time for her to be delivered of the baby boy in the hospital, the nurses and midwives told her, "Push." She did, and immediately the head of the baby came out, an unseen power standing in the labour room cut off the head of the baby. It was rolling on the floor. The nurses and midwives ran away because they could not see the hand that cut off the head of the baby.

This woman got pregnant again the fifth time. It was a boy again, and she went to the hospital to be delivered of the baby. The same thing happened again. As the head of the baby came out, it was cut off by an invisible evil hand.

Beloved, the three cases I narrated do not call for ordinary deliverance, but deep deliverance. The truth is that it is not everyone that can access the secrets behind deep problems like these. It is also not every minister that can handle deep deliverance cases. That is why I have stated repeatedly that those who seek deliverance or help from the enemy would only worsen their problems sink deeper into bondage. Jesus Christ is the Yoke Breaker and Mighty Deliverer.

DON'T GIVE UP

Life is a mystery and we cannot decide to be silent. It is possible to be born again, sanctified, Spirit-filled and you do not yet know who you are.

When you find people who are completely ignorant of their divine destiny, they will show traits such as feeling of being unneeded and unloved. They will exhibit lack of initiatives, lack of motivation, spirit of hopelessness and argumentative spirit. In addition, such people often harbour resentment. They are always intolerant, over-sensitive, moody and depressed. By God's arithmetic people in these situations are dead but living; they need deep deliverance. The good and cheering news is that there is deliverance in Mount Zion and Jesus is willing to help set the captives free. However, you must be willing and ready for it.

If you are having trouble, you need to know the source and the cause. Is it heredity? Is it environmental? Is it traceable to curses, evil covenants, spells, sin, carelessness or witchcraft attacks? You can pray to know the secret and the way out. God can also give you deep deliverance, if that is what your case requires. Most of the deep deliverance candidates have one thing in common: they have not discovered their correct identities. That is why the devil finds it easy to trouble them. I encourage you to give your life to Jesus Christ now. You cannot experience great deliverance if you are not born again. The salvation of your soul is the beginning of your deep and complete deliverance.

HEARING FROM GOD

The inability to hear directly from God has been one of the greatest undoing of many believers around the world. The enemy has used it to short-change, deceive and misguide a lot of people. Being able to hear from God is not only a mark of spiritual growth but also a pointer to a believer's spiritual maturity. It is unfortunate that a lot of people have missed out on their divine purposes and failed to attain the heights that heaven ordained for them because they are both spiritually blind and deaf.

Hearing God speak is a blessing we receive as His children. The voice of God gives us direction. When He speaks, we will receive an answer to something we have asked or a request we did not even know we needed. When God speaks to us, we gain clarity

God desires fellowship with us. Through His communication to us and ours to Him, the fellowship is established, strengthened and made rewarding to us. The Bible gave us an example of this in God's fellowship with Adam and Even in the Garden of Eden before the fall. The Almighty still desires that intimate relationship with us today.

Revelation 3:20 *Behold, I stand at the door, and knock: if any man hear my voice, and open the door, I will come in to him, and will sup with him, and he with me.*

John 10:3-5 *To him the porter openeth; and the sheep hear his voice: and he calleth his own sheep by name, and leadeth them out. And when he putteth forth his own sheep, he goeth before them, and the sheep follow him: for they know his voice. And a stranger will they not follow, but will flee from him: for they know not the voice of strangers.*

John 10:27-29 *My sheep hear my voice, and I know them, and they follow me: And I give unto them eternal life; and they shall never perish, neither shall any man pluck them out of my hand. My Father, which gave them me, is greater than all; and no man is able to pluck them out of my Father's hand.*

BENEFITS OF HEARING GOD

There are several advantages and privileges that those who can hear God's voice have over those who do not. Let us examine some of them:

First, hearing God's voice is indispensable to living a consistent and victorious mountain-top Christian life. The Book of Joshua chapters 6 and 7 will help to buttress this point. When Israel defeated and captured Jericho, and the wall of Jericho fell down, the victory was due to the fact that Joshua heard the voice of God, received the battle strategy from Him and followed it to the letter. The ability to hear from God gave Israel that resounding victory over their enemies and enabled them to possess their possession – the Promised Land. However, when Joshua heard and obeyed the voice of men rather than God's, he did not know that Achan had brought an accursed thing into the camp of God's children and had incurred God's wrath. They suffered an unimaginable defeat in the hands of the people of Ai.

> *Joshua 7:1-5 But the people of Israel broke faith in regard to the devoted things, for Achan the son of Carmi, son of Zabdi, son of Zerah, of the tribe of Judah, took some of the devoted things. And the anger of the LORD burned against the people of Israel. Joshua sent men from Jericho to Ai, which is near Beth-aven, east of Bethel, and said to them,*

"Go up and spy out the land." And the men went up and spied out Ai. And they returned to Joshua and said to him, "Do not have all the people go up, but let about two or three thousand men go up and attack Ai. Do not make the whole people toil up there, for they are few." So about three thousand men went up there from the people. And they fled before the men of Ai, and the men of Ai killed about thirty-six of their men and chased them before the gate as far as Shebarim and struck them at the descent. And the hearts of the people melted and became as water.

Those who hear from God enjoy divine leading and guidance. In Isaiah 30:2, the Bible assures, *"And thine ears shall hear a word behind thee, saying, This is the way, walk ye in it, when ye turn to the right hand, and when ye turn to the left."*

Those who hear God's voice will know the will of God and remain in it. God's word reveals the will of God to believers. Also, when we can hear and recognise God's voice, we will not be misled by strange and negative voices that enemy often uses to deceive his targets and victims.

When we can hear our Father's or Shepherd's voice, we have access to divine secrets and that puts our hearts and minds at rest, even when other people are troubled or panicky. God's voice is reassuring and peace-giving. This was the scenario in

Paul's life when he and several other passengers experienced a storm on the sea before they later got shipwrecked on the Island of Malta.

Paul heard the Lord's voice at the time of his conversion on the road to Damascus. This time, God spoke to him through His angel:

> *Acts 27:20-25 And when neither sun nor stars in many days appeared, and no small tempest lay on us, all hope that we should be saved was then taken away. But after long abstinence Paul stood forth in the midst of them, and said, Sirs, ye should have hearkened unto me, and not have loosed from Crete, and to have gained this harm and loss. And now I exhort you to be of good cheer: for there shall be no loss of any man's life among you, but of the ship. For there stood by me this night the angel of God, whose I am, and whom I serve, Saying, Fear not, Paul; thou must be brought before Caesar: and, lo, God hath given thee all them that sail with thee. Wherefore, sirs, be of good cheer: for I believe God, that it shall be even as it was told me.*

It is apparent here that what gave Paul peace in the midst of the storm and precarious situation was the voice of God he had heard. He became a source of encouragement to other passengers in the ship.

Those who hear the Shepherd's voice will enjoy everlasting life. This is Christ's reward to His sheep who hear Him and follow Him.

Also, those hear God's voice will enjoy everlasting protection. Jesus Himself said, *"They will never perish. Neither shall any man pluck them out of my hand."* Beloved, ensure you become blessed to the extent that you hear God clearly yourself everyday. You will not wander away from path of understanding or pitch your tent with fools, and you will not die untimely or miss heaven.

Faith is an indispensable element in our Christian walk. It comes by hearing and hearing by the word of God. Those who consistently hear from God will receive the grace that grows and strengthens their faith daily.

Finally, those who can hear from God will supernaturally experience deep deliverance from bondage, slavery and all troubles. Once the Great Deliverer speaks to you, you will know the escape route you are to take; the way out of your predicament will be opened for you.

I know several thousands of people who were supernaturally delivered from the battles fiercely confronting their lives the moment they heard from God. Heaven revealed the secrets behind their travails and taught them what to do to be liberated.

CONDITIONS FOR HEARING GOD'S VOICE

Do you desire to hear God's voice yourself and consistently too? If your answer is in the affirmative, here are some conditions you need to meet:

First, you must demonstrate genuine desire and willingness to hear God. This is the first key that will open the door for you to access the divine voice.

Second, you should pray and ask God to teach you to hear His voice. The promise of the Lord in the Scripture should propel you to make this important request from the Lord.

John 14:13-14 And whatsoever ye shall ask in my name, that will I do, that the Father may be glorified in the Son. If ye shall ask any thing in my name, I will do it.

John 16:23-24 *And in that day ye shall ask me nothing. Verily, verily, I say unto you, Whatsoever ye shall ask the Father in my name, he will give it you. Hitherto have ye asked nothing in my name: ask, and ye shall receive, that your joy may be full.*

Third, to hear God's voice, you should give listening ear to what God is saying to you. We often miss hearing God's voice because we are not paying attention. Do not let the noise of the world keep you from hearing the voice of God. You need to turn down the world's volume to hear God's voice.

It is one thing to be able to hear God's voice and it is another thing to be able to differentiate it from the enemy's. The ability to discern God's voice and obey it always as well as the grace to discern and reject the enemy's voice is something every believer should pray for and receive. When God's voice comes to you, the peace of God will flood your heart. Also, God's voice or word is usually in line with the Bible; it will never contradict it.

I pray that the grace to hear from God and access beneficial information that will transform your life and destiny shall be yours from today, in the name of Jesus. As you begin to hear

God clearly, your life will move forward and upward, and you will become a bigger bundle of testimonies, in the mighty name of Jesus.

Prayer Points

1. Goliath in my root, die, in the name of Jesus

2. Buried yoke and buried bondage afflicting my body, die, in the name of Jesus.

3. Spiritual embargo from my father's/mother's house, die, in the name of Jesus

4. Any childhood bondage that has escorted me to adult life, break, in the name of Jesus.

5. Plantation of darkness troubling my star, die, in the name of Jesus

6. Power of Herod tracing my star, what are you waiting for? Die, in the name of Jesus.

7. Glory killers entrenched in my foundation, you are a liar, die, in the name of Jesus.

Chapter Twelve

KEEP YOUR SECRETS SECRET

Beloved, so far, I have stressed that it is very important that you obtain genuine information from heaven about your correct identity (who you are), what your purpose in life is, the gifts and talents God has endowed you with, who should walk and work with, where you hail from and where you will spend your eternity. I have also taught you the keys and strategies you can deploy to access the vital information from heaven and how to use them wisely to experience all-round fulfilment. Remember that I also emphasised that a person who receives useful divine information and fails to use it is not better than another person who did not receive divine information at all.

These helpful hints will not be complete if I do not add the importance of wisely managing and safeguarding the beneficial secrets God gives to you. That is why this chapter is titled, "Keep Your Secrets Secret".

A secret is a piece of information that is covered or hidden. It is not accessible to everyone. You need an access code to reach, have and use it. This simple definition shows that secrets are meant to be guarded and treasured. Therefore, when God gives you invaluable information about your life, you must handle it wisely. The devil, his demons and human agents do not want you to succeed. Therefore, you should not give them access to the secrets heaven reveals to you.

God kept a top secret from the devil and that made Jesus to triumph over him. The Bible says that if the prince of this world and his demons had known that by killing Jesus, their defeat and doom would be sealed, they would not have killed the Son of God and King of glory (I Cor. 2:7-8). Beloved, the secrets heaven gives you are your winning keys. If you are careless with them heaven will be disappointed in you. This is because the enemy will use the secrets of your life you reveal to him to attack and short-change you.

SAMSON

Samson was a one-man riot squad. As a judge and deliverer. With the help of God, he terrorised and subdued the Philistines for years. Israel dominated their enemies and had peace. The Philistines wondered at the supernatural strength and abilities of Samson. They knew there was a secret behind it and were willing to part with any fortune to know Samson's secret. They gave the assignment to one of their daughters called Delilah. The lady pestered Samson until he carelessly revealed the secret of his anointing and exploits. I pray that any Delilah that the enemy has planted in your life shall die suddenly, in the name of Jesus.

Delilah, the treacherous and unfriendly friend, gave Samson strong drink and lull him to sleep. She then invited other Philistine enemies. They tied Samson and shaved the seven locks of hair on his head. Samson lost his strength, anointing and ministry. The enemies plucked his eyes and ridiculed him. In the end, he prayed, strength was restored to him and he died with thousands of his enemies. What was the mistake that led to Samson's tragic end? He did not keep his secret as a secret. The word of the Scripture in Proverbs 6:2 were fulfilled in the life of Samson: *"Thou art snared with the words of thy mouth, thou art taken with the words of thy mouth."*

Dearly beloved, has God revealed some important secrets about your life to you? Keep them to yourself and use :hem wisely. I pray that you will not be snared by the transgression of your lips, in the name of Jesus.

JOSEPH

In Genesis 37, the Bible affirms that Jacob loved Joseph more than all his children, because he was a child of his old age. He also made Joseph a coat of many colours. This made Joseph's brothers to be envious of him. One would have thought that Joseph, having seen their unfriendly and envious' reactions, would have been discrete about his life affairs. He was not. The Bible says he dreamt and told his brother how their sheaves stood round about his and bowed to it. This infuriated his brothers and made them to hate him more.

The same Joseph had a second dream and still would not keep it to himself. He told his brothers and his father, *"I had another dream. The sun, the moon and eleven stars made obeisance to me."* Joseph was not careful with the vital information heaven gave to him about his life. It could be because he was a teenager. The Bible says that what is written is for our learning. Joseph's age is not enough reason to be careless in handling divine information. Whether you are 17 or 40 or 80, God expects you to handle divine information maturely: keep your secret a secret!

The consequences of Joseph's flippant nature cost him 13 years in slavery and prison until God intervened, turned his life around and fulfilled his promise in his life. In Proverbs 25:2, the Bible says that it is the glory of God to conceal a thing: but the honour of God to search out a matter. The Bible also says that by the word of our mouth we shall be justified or condemned (Matthew 12:37). Beloved, I advise you not to make Joseph's mistake. Don't sell your destiny and future to your enemy by being loose with your mouth.

Don't be a tale-bearer. The Bible affirms that a tale bearer reveals secrets, but he that is of a faithful spirit conceals the matter. Avoid mouth diarrhoea! Don't let your tongue trap you.

BE WISE!

The Bible says that wisdom is profitable to direct. At a point in his earthly sojourn and ministry, Jesus instructed His disciples not to reveal His identity to anyone. He would sometimes perform a miracle and tell the receiver not to tell anybody about it. Why? The reason is that everything has its appropriate time and season.

In Shushan, Esther and Mordecai kept the fact that they were related by blood a secret for some time. David and Jonathan were bosom friends but they kept the relationship a secret.

These ones did so to enable God's purpose for their lives to be fulfilled. Haman would not have fallen and destroyed himself if he knew that Mordecai and the Jews he was plotting to destroy were related to Queen Esther. When you keep your secret a secret, you will have an edge over your enemies and triumph over them.

You do not need to keep telling people your secrets. When you draft a personal plan to pursue your divine purpose, keep it to yourself. Learn to talk less; learn to keep some issues of your life between you and God alone. It has been well said that the less your enemy knows about you, the better for you. Some people innocently and unknowingly share your secrets with your enemy.

Many people have died untimely. Some have been captured and ruined because they allowed the enemy undue access to the secrets of their lives. My question to you is this: How safe and secure are the pieces of information that heaven has made available to you? Don't be like those who use every available information platform to tell the world the secrets of their lives. Be wise. Keep your secret a secret!

WHAT TO DO WITH DIVINE SECRETS

The first thing you should do about divine information and secrets that heaven gives to you is to thank and praise God for providing them. It is important to make thanksgiving a lifestyle. Give God the sacrifice of thanksgiving daily, and He will increase His blessings upon your life.

The second thing you should do about divine secrets that heaven gives you is to store them in your heart, meditate on them and pray about them regularly. For some, your prayers may be to avert something bad from happening. At other times, your prayers will be required to make God hasten His word to perform it. The issue involved may be about you, your family, your church, your workplace, a neighbour of yours, your nation, or even the world at large. The Lord would like you to play the role of a prayer warrior or intercessor to the glory of His name.

Also, make constant positive confessions to yourself about the information heaven gave you. Prophesy concerning it in line with the word of God.

In conclusion, beloved, I want you to note that many believers who are not discrete with vital heavenly information about their lives have put their career, marriages, ministries, and so

on in trouble. A lot of such careless people are yet to recover
from the problems they brought upon themselves till today. I
pray that God will show such people mercy today, in the name
of Jesus. I implore you not to imitate them. Keep your secret
to yourself and heaven will entrust you with more.

Prayer Points

1. Let the blood of Jesus wipe off every beneficial secret about my life in the archive of demonic powers, in the name of Jesus.

2. O God, arise and make my enemies suffer from memory failure for my sake, in the name of Jesus.

3. My Father, forgive me for the carelessness I have entertained in releasing secrets about my life to the enemy, in the name of Jesus.

4. Power to watch over my tongue, fall upon me now, in the name of Jesus.

5. My mouth shall not put me into trouble consciously or unconsciously, in the name of Jesus.

6. Every unfriendly friend associating with me in order to tap into divine information about my life, be exposed and put to shame, in the name of Jesus.

7. O Lord, keep a watch over my tongue and guard the door of my lips by the power of the Holy Ghost, in the name of Jesus. (Ps. 141:3).

Chapter Thirteen

PRAYERS FOR SELF-DISCOVERY, RECOVERY AND DESTINY FULFILMENT

The power and wonders of prayer are yet to be fully understood and maximised by man. Prayer brings God's power to bear and turns precarious situations around. In this chapter, I enjoin you to pray the prayers presented to you section by section.

Each section of prayers, vomited by the Holy Ghost, is presented here to meet you at the point of your needs and do exceedingly above all you can ever ask or think.

You can pray all the sections, one after the other. Alternatively, you can select the ones that are relevant to your most pressing needs and concentrate on them.

Section 1-3 focusses on deliverance (deep deliverance, complete deliverance and power to overcome generational inheritance). Each of the three sections is a 21-day prayer watch. I advise you to pray the prayer points with great faith, concentration, persistence and violence.

Section 4 (A-D) focusses on prayers that unveil divine secrets and mysteries. As you pray them, God will open your spiritual eyes and give you unrestrained access to divine information that will turn your life and destiny around for good, in the name of Jesus.

Section 5 presents you prayers that provoke divine encounter. The discovery and recovery of Jacob's true identity and his destiny fulfilment are traceable to the encounter he had at Peniel. The same is true of Abraham, Moses, Peter, Paul and several others. As you pray these prayers, heaven will give you an unusual and life-changing encounter.

Section 6 is titled "Journey Back to the Womb". With these prayer points, you will be able to walk back to the womb, your foundation or root, repair any damage the enemy did to your life and destiny at that point and liberate yourself from their consequences presently and in your future.

Section 7, titled "Prayers to Correct Parental Mistakes", consists of prayer points that will birth great and unimaginable deliverance in your life.

Section 8, titled "Destiny Recovery and Repositioning Prayers" are anointed and power-packed to release angels of war to fight on your behalf and recover your lost destiny, virtues, breakthroughs and glory, in the name of Jesus.

You can declare a fast and pray in the day and night. You can also hold vigils to bombard the heavens with these prayer points. Any of these will help you to gain maximum rewards from the prayer programme in this life-changing book.

These prayer points, when prayed as led by the Holy Spirit and with unwavering faith, will be used by the God of all-possibilities, who answers by fire, to earn for you self-discovery, recovery and all-round fulfilment, in the name of Jesus.

Section One

DEEP DELIVERANCE

Confessions: Obadiah 1:17: But upon mount Zion shall be deliverance, and there shall be holiness; and the house of Jacob shall possess their possessions.

Day One

Praise and Worship

1. Every aggression against my star, die, in the name of Jesus.

2. My star, arise and shine to fall no more, in the name of Jesus.

3. Any power redirecting my star, die, in the name of Jesus.

4. My star, be invisible in the spirit realm to every dark observer, in the name of Jesus.

5. Blood of Jesus, make it impossible for the enemy to track down my star in the realms of the spirit, in the name of Jesus.

6. Unbroken curses troubling my star, break, in the name of Jesus.

7. I shall become a star in my generation, in the name of Jesus.

8. Every power troubling my star, be troubled, in the name of Jesus.

9. Every evil hand of the enemy upon my star, wither, in the name of Jesus.

10. Star hunters, pursuing my star, dry up, in the name of Jesus.

11. O wind of God, drive away every power of the ungodly rising against my destiny, in the name of Jesus.

12. Let the rage of the wicked against me be rendered impotent, in the name of Jesus.

13. Let the imagination of the wicked against me be neutralised, in the name of Jesus.

14. Every counsel of evil kings against me, be scattered, in the name of Jesus.

15. O God, arise and speak in great wrath against the enemy of my breakthroughs, in the name of Jesus.

16. I decree that anything God has not planted in my life should be uprooted now, in the name of Jesus.

17. I arrest any serpent of infirmity troubling my body, in the name of Jesus.

18. Destructive infirmities, hear the word of the Lord, die, in the name of Jesus.

19. I cut off the tentacles of internal disease spreading in my body, in the name of Jesus.

20. Power base of infirmity, dry up and die, in the name of Jesus.

21. Health arresters, be arrested by fire, in the name of Jesus.

Day Two

Praise and Worship

22. Every evil hand upon my star, wither, in the name of Jesus.

23. Every arrow of evil delay, fired into my star, die, in the name of Jesus.

24. Every arrow of backwardness, fired into my star, die, in the name of Jesus.

25. Chain of delay, holding my star, break, in the name of Jesus.

26. Glory of the later house, catch up with my star, in the name of Jesus.

27. My star, manifest by fire, in the name of Jesus.

28. My star shall arise and shine to fall no more, in the name of Jesus.

29. Every demonic blanket that has covered my star, I tear you and destroy you, in the name

30. My star must rise and shine clearly, in the name of Jesus.

31. Birds of darkness assigned to trouble my star, die, in the name of Jesus.

32. Every cord of darkness militating against my breakthroughs, die, in the name of Jesus.

33. Every band of the wicked that is arresting my progress, break, in the name of Jesus.

34. O God, arise and laugh my enemies to scorn, in the name of Jesus.

35. O God, arise and speak unto my enemies in Your wrath, in the name of Jesus.

36. O God, vex my stubborn oppressors in Your sore displeasure, in the name of Jesus.

37. By Your power of possibilities, O God, arise and manifest in my life, in the name of Jesus.

38. By Your binding powers, O God, arise, bind my tormentors, in the name of Jesus.

39. My Father, my Father, my Father, arise and let the world know that You are my God, in the name of Jesus.

40. I curse every satanically sponsored disease germ working against my life to die, in the name of Jesus.

41. O God arise and scatter every conspiracy working against my progress, in the name of Jesus.

42. My Father, arise in Your mighty power and disgrace my stubborn oppressors, in the name of Jesus. I release the stones of fire upon every Goliath of my father's house, in the name of Jesus.

Day Three

Praise and Worship

43. My star shall be honoured in the land of the living, in the name of Jesus.

44. My star, arise, and shine, no power shall stop you, in the name of Jesus.

45. Words of witchcraft attacking my star, fall down and die, in the name of Jesus.

46. Every cord of witchcraft troubling my star, break, in the name of Jesus.

47. Arrows fired into my star to demote me, die, in the name of Jesus.

48. Every assignment of dark hunters for my star, wither, in the name of Jesus.

49. Oh Lord, let the stars fight against every witchcraft bird, in the name of Jesus.

50. Thou evil sun, overshadowing my star, clear away, in the name of Jesus.

51. Every satanic arrow, fired against my star, fall down and die, in Jesus' name.

52. Every power of Herod, tracing my star, I bury you now, in the name of Jesus.

53. O Lord, break my enemies with Your rod of iron, in the name of Jesus.

54. O God, dash the power of stubborn pursuers in pieces like a potter's vessel, in the name of Jesus.

55. O God, arise with all Your weapons of war and fight my battle for me, in the name of Jesus.

56. O God, be my glory and the lifter of my head, in the name of Jesus.

57. My Father, be a shield for me in every situation, in the name of Jesus.

58. I charge my body with the fire of the Holy Ghost, in the name of Jesus.

59. Blood of Jesus, sanitize my body and make me whole, in the name of Jesus.

60. Eaters of flesh assigned against me fall down and die, in the name of Jesus.

61. My flesh, my blood, reject the voice of death, in the name of Jesus.

62. Any power feeding on my flesh, come out and die, in the name of Jesus. I revoke and nullify every witchcraft manipulation affecting my body, in the name of Jesus.

63. Any power assigned to eat me up, die, in the name of Jesus.

Day Four

Praise and Worship

64. Plantations of darkness troubling my star, roast by fire, in the name of Jesus.

65. Power to interpret the language of my star, come upon me now, in the name of Jesus.

66. Power to read the handwriting of my star in the heavenlies, fall upon me, in the name of Jesus.

67. O dragon tracing my star, I rebuke you, in the name of Jesus.

68. My star, appear, in the name of Jesus.

69. Powers, assigned to capture my star, loose your hold, in the name of Jesus.

70. By the power in the blood of Jesus, I break every witchcraft agenda to exchange and manipulate my star, in the name of Jesus.

71. O God, arise, cast Your fury upon agents of affliction troubling my star, in the name of Jesus.

72. I release confusion and backwardness upon every satanic programmer attacking my star, in the name of Jesus.

73.   Every cage formed to imprison my star, I smash you, in the name of Jesus.

74.   O God, hear my cry out of Your holy hill, in the name of Jesus.

75.   I will not be afraid of ten thousands of people that have set themselves against me, in the name of Jesus.

76.   O God, smite my enemies by the cheekbones, in the name of Jesus.

77.   My Father, break the teeth of the ungodly, in the name of Jesus.

78.   O Lord, hear my voice whenever I call, in the name of Jesus.

79.   Every demon termite eating my body, die by fire, in the name of Jesus.

80.   Every witchcraft poison in my body, dry up and die, in the name of Jesus.

81.   Every curse of consumption afflicting my life, break, in the name of Jesus.

82.   Every clearing pestilence, scatter, in the name of Jesus.

83.   Every satanic injection, working against my destiny, backfire, in the name of Jesus.

84.   Strangers from the grave, clear out of my body, in the name of Jesus.

Day Five

Praise and Worship

85. Every environmental witchcraft assigned to trouble my star, scatter unto desolation, in the name of Jesus.

86. Every witchcraft siren, assigned to confuse my star, die, in the name of Jesus.

87. Satanic command assigned to make my star wander, die, in the name of Jesus.

88. Every curse, evil covenants and enchantments militating against the star of my family, die, in the name of Jesus.

89. Every aggression against the star of my family, die, in the name of Jesus.

90. Coven cages, tracking down the stars of my family, break and backfire, in the name of Jesus.

91. Star hunters and observers of times, targeting my family star, receive blindness, in the name of Jesus.

92. Let my star be too hot for the enemy to handle, in the name of Jesus.

93. Every imagination against my star, be dismantled, in the name of Jesus.

94. Father, let every star hunter of my father's house be put to shame, in the name of Jesus.

95. O God, visit every power lying against me with destruction, in the name of Jesus.

96. Lead me, O Lord, in Thy righteousness, in the name of Jesus.

97. O Lord, make Your way plain before my face, in Jesus' name.

98. Let my enemies fall by their own counsel, in the name of Jesus.

99. Cast out my enemies in the multitude of their transgressions, in the name of Jesus.

100. I break the yoke of the invisible destroyers, in the name of Jesus.

101. My life, reject the strangers that smite unto death, in the name of Jesus.

102. Every venom of the serpent and scorpion eating up my flesh, dry up now, in the name of Jesus.

103. I bind and cast away every spirit of fear and worry, in the name of Jesus. Parasites, viruses, bacteria of infirmity, my body is not your candidate, die, in the name of Jesus.

104. Bewitchment of my flesh, blood and bones, terminate, in the name of Jesus.

105. Wasting powers, depart from my life, in the name of Jesus.

Day Six

Praise and Worship

106. Father, let every star hunter of my mother's house be put to shame, in the name of Jesus.

107. Everywhere I go let the star of my destiny arise and shine, in the name of Jesus.

108. Any area of weakness in my life giving access to the enemy to attack my star, Father, straighten me out, in the name of Jesus.

109. Every mountain of difficulty confronting my star, be levelled to the ground, in the name of Jesus.

110. Any evil observer of time assigned to monitor my star, receive blindness, in the name of Jesus.

111. O God, arise and let my star reject the voice of darkness, in the name of Jesus.

112. Father, let Your angels of war defend my star anywhere I go, in the name of Jesus.

113. Every infirmity assigned to bury my star, come out now, in the name of Jesus.

114. Every power of darkness surrounding my star, be scattered, in the name of Jesus.

115. Every power assigned to rubbish my star, lose your power, in the name of Jesus.

116. Every organised worker of iniquity, depart from me, in the name of Jesus.

117. Let all my enemies be ashamed and sore vexed, in Jesus' name.

118. Let sudden shame be the lot of all my oppressors, in Jesus' name

119. Every power planning to tear my soul like a lion, be dismantled, in the name of Jesus.

120. O God, command judgement on all my oppressors, in Jesus' name.

121. O God, arise and make me whole, in the name of Jesus.

122. My Father, arise in Your power and have mercy on me, in the name of Jesus.

123. Organs of my body, hear the word of the Lord, reject the voice of the grave, in the name of Jesus. I release the stones of fire upon every Goliath of my father's house, in the name of Jesus.

124. Thou Great Physician, send surgeons from heaven to work on me now, in the name of Jesus.

125. Agenda of infirmity for my life, die, in the name of Jesus.

126. Operating theatre of God, arise, admit me and work on me now, in the name of Jesus.

Day Seven

Praise and Worship

127. Plantations of darkness troubling my star, roast by fire, in the name of Jesus.

128. Power to interpret the language of my star, come upon me now, in the name of Jesus.

129. Every satanic arrow fired to divert my star, fall down and die, in the name of Jesus.

130. I refuse to be a wandering star, in the name of Jesus.

131. I bury every hunter of my star today, in the name of Jesus.

132. None shall pluck my stars out of my hands, in the name of Jesus.

133. None shall pluck my stars out of my head, in the name of Jesus.

134. Let every barrenness programmed into my star be deprogrammed, in the name of Jesus.

135. Every caged star, be released now, in the name of Jesus.

136. Every power troubling my star, die, in the name of Jesus.

137. Let the wickedness of the wicked come to an end, O Lord, in the name of Jesus.

138. O Lord, let Your anger boil against the wicked every day, in the name of Jesus.

139. O God, prepare the instruments of death against my enemies, in the name of Jesus.

140. O God, ordain Your arrows against my persecutors, in the name of Jesus.

141. Let every pit dug by the enemy become a grave for the enemy, in the name of Jesus.

142. Damage done unto my body by infirmities, be repaired by fire, in the name of Jesus.

143. Divine antibiotics, divine medication, bombard my body by fire, in the name of Jesus.

144. I withdraw every conscious and unconscious co-operation with any internal disorder, in the name of Jesus.

145. The battle of the terrible and the mighty against my health, expire, in the name of Jesus.

146. Thou great physician Jesus Christ, heal me now, in the name of Jesus.

147. Yokes of infirmity, break to pieces, in the name of Jesus.

Day Eight

Praise and Worship

148. Every organization of witchcraft working against my star, scatter, in the name of Jesus.

149. All satanic lions roaring to swallow up my star, die, in the name of Jesus.

150. I paralyse all aggression addressed to my star in the name of Jesus.

151. O God arise and invade my star and set it free, in the name of Jesus.

152. Any power bewitching my star, fall down and die, in the name of Jesus.

153. Every cloud of darkness covering my star shall melt away like cloud before the sun, in the name of Jesus.

154. Every evil manipulation of my star, die, in the name of Jesus.

155. You witchcraft hunters assigned against my star, fall down and die, in the name of Jesus.

156. Every witchcraft manipulation of my star, die, in the name of Jesus.

157. Any evil act carried out on the day of my naming ceremony that is now affecting the star of my life, be reversed and die, in the name of Jesus.

158. Let the mischief of my enemies return upon his own head, in the name of Jesus.

159. Let all weapons of my enemies backfire by thunder, in the name of Jesus.

160. O God, ordain strength for me and still the enemy and the avenger, in the name of Jesus.

161. When mine enemies are turned back, they shall perish out of Thy presence, in the name of Jesus.

162. O God, destroy the wicked and put out their name for ever and ever, in the name of Jesus.

163. Authority of infirmity scorpions over my life, terminate, in the name of Jesus.

164. Every cell in my body, hear the word of the Lord, reject evil commands, in the name of Jesus.

165. Let my bodily organs become too hot for any disease to handle, in the name of Jesus. Every wicked mouth opened to swallow my breakthroughs this month, dry up, in the name of Jesus.

166. Oh God, arise and empower the eagle of my breakthroughs to fly this month, in the name of Jesus.

167. Lord elevate me this month and do something in my life that will make men to celebrate me, in the name of Jesus.

168. I shall sing my song and dance my dance this year, in the name of Jesus.

Praise and Worship

Day Nine

169. Thou power in the heavenlies, release my captured star, in the name of Jesus.

170. Every dark power hunting for my star, fall down and die, in the name of Jesus.

171. Every satanic priest ministering against my breakthroughs, be disgraced, in the name of Jesus.

172. My season of unusual laughter and victory dance, manifest, in the name of Jesus.

173. Whatever has tied down by destiny, break loose from my life, in the name of Jesus.

174. Witches toying with my destiny, be wiped off, in the name of Jesus.

175. O Lord, reshuffle my environment to favour me, in the name of Jesus.

176. I will be a champion and not a casualty, in the name of Jesus.

177. If I have been disconnected from my destiny, O God arise and reconnect me, in the name of Jesus.

178. O Lord, whatever You have not positioned into my life, wipe them off, in the name of Jesus.

179. Let the enemy sink in the pit they have made, in the name of Jesus.

180. Let the feet of the enemy be taken in the net which he hid, in the name of Jesus.

181. Let the wicked be snared in the work of his own hands, in the name of Jesus.

182. Arise O Lord, let not man prevail, let the heathen be judged in Thy sight, in the name of Jesus.

183. Put the enemies in fear, O Lord, that the nations may know themselves to be but men, in the name of Jesus.

184. Blood of Jesus, pump out any stranger in my body, in the name of Jesus.

185. My body organs, reject the voice of early death, in the name of Jesus. Today, I position myself by fire for divine intervention, in the name of Jesus.

186. I drink the blood of Jesus. (Say this for 21 times)

187. Let God arise and let my infirmity be scattered, in the name of Jesus.

188. I bind and cast out every agent of weakness, in the name of Jesus.

189. O God, my Father, burst forth in my life by signs and wonders, in the name of Jesus.

Day Ten

Praise and Worship

190. O God, dismantle the poison in my foundation, in the name of Jesus.

191. Circumstances affecting my success, bow, in the name of Jesus.

192. O God arise, and give me a strong reason to celebrate and laugh this year, in the name of Jesus.

193. The enemy shall weep concerning my life this year, in the name of Jesus.

194. My Father, show me unusual secrets of my next level, in the name of Jesus.

195. Every month of this year shall be a disappointment to the enemy, in the name of Jesus.

196. My Father, distract my enemies with problems that are bigger than them, in the name of Jesus.

197. O God arise and invade my star and set it free, in the name of Jesus.

198. My adversaries, hear the word of the Lord, carry your loads, in the name of Jesus.

199. Every serpent assigned to bite my destiny, die, in the name of Jesus.

200. Let the wicked be taken in the devices they have imagined, in the name of Jesus.

201. Arise O Lord, lift up Thine arm in war, in the name of Jesus.

202. Break Thou the arm of the wicked and the evil man, in the name of Jesus.

203. Upon the wicked O Lord, rain snares, fire and brimstone and a horrible tempest, in the name of Jesus.

204. My enemies shall not rejoice over me, in the name of Jesus.

205. Resources of heaven, arise by fire, promote me, in the name of Jesus.

206. Any personality carrying the seed of wickedness against me, be exposed and disgraced, in the name of Jesus.

207. The enemy that came while I slept, be disgraced, in the name of Jesus.

208. You ladder of oppression, catch fire, in the name of Jesus.

209. You ladder of affliction, catch fire, in the name of Jesus.

210. You ladder of infirmity, catch fire, in the name of Jesus.

Praise and Worship

Day Eleven

211. O God arise and fight for me in the day and in the night, in the valley and on the mountain, in the name of Jesus.

212. Every power assigned to scatter my resources, dry up, in the name of Jesus.

213. Every power assigned to suppress my elevation, die, in the name of Jesus.

214. Every satanic panel set up against me, scatter, in the name of Jesus.

215. Rod of the wicked attacking my progress, break, in the name of Jesus.

216. Delayed breakthroughs, delayed promotions, manifest by fire, in the name of Jesus.

217. I disarm all vagabond problems, in the name of Jesus.

218. I disgrace all discouraging powers, in the name of Jesus.

219. O God arise and give my enemies leanness this year, in the name of Jesus.

220. My enemies will not rejoice over me this year, in the name of Jesus.

221. Keep me as the apple of Thy eye, hide me under the shadow of Thy wings, O Lord, in the name of Jesus.

222. Barricade me from the wicked that oppress me and from my deadly enemies who compass me about, in the name of Jesus.

223. Arise O Lord, disappoint my oppressors and cast them down, in the name of Jesus.

224. O Lord, deliver my soul from the wicked which is Thy sword, in the name of Jesus.

225. I will call upon the Lord, who is worthy to be praised, so shall I be saved from mine enemies, in the name of Jesus.

226. You ladder of failure at the edge of breakthroughs, catch fire, in the name of Jesus.

227. O God, arise and roar like a terrible lion, and devour my portion, in the name of Jesus.

228. Any power stealing my healing virtues, come out and die, in the name of Jesus.

229. Anointing that breaks the yoke, break every internal yoke and chains, in the name of Jesus.

230. Healing virtues from the King of kings, and the Lord of lords, saturate my body now, in the name of Jesus.

231. O Lord, save me and I shall be saved. Heal me and I shall be healed, in the name of Jesus.

232. O God of possibilities, make me whole, in the name of Jesus.

233. Let my body be electrified with the healing power of God, in the name of Jesus. Every King Uzziah sitting on the throne of God in my life, die, in the name of Jesus.

Day Twelve

Praise and Worship

234. Sorrow and tears, I uproot you from my life by fire, in the name of Jesus.

235. Any power assigned to sink the boat of my salvation, die, in the name of Jesus.

236. My Father, deliver me from costly mistakes, in the name of Jesus.

237. O God, arise and confound my enemies, in the name of Jesus.

238. O God of Elijah, arise and cancel all my afflictions, in the name of Jesus.

239. O God, arise by the thunder of Your power and let my story change, in the name of Jesus.

240. O God, arise in Your yoke-breaking power and break my yoke this day, in the name of Jesus.

241. O God of Abraham, arise and mesmerise my enemies, in the name of Jesus.

242. O God of Isaac, arise and multiply my laughter, in the name of Jesus.

243. O God of Israel, arise and promote me by fire, in the name of Jesus.

244. O God send out Your arrows and scatter the oppressors, in the name of Jesus.

245. O God, shoot out Your lightening and discomfit them, in the name of Jesus.

246. Let the smoke go out of Your nostrils and fire out of Your mouth to devour all plantations of darkness in my life, in the name of Jesus.

247. O God, thunder from heaven against all my oppressors, in the name of Jesus.

248. O Lord, at the blast of Your nostrils, disgrace every foundational bondage, in the name of Jesus.

249. Evil shoes of my parents will not size my feet, in the name of Jesus.

250. Serpents and scorpions assigned to put me to shame, die, in the name of Jesus.

251. Any witchdoctor assigned to terminate my life, die, in the name of Jesus.

252. Evil progress, hear the word of the Lord, die, in the name of Jesus.

253. Birds of darkness assigned to trouble my star, die, in the name of Jesus

254. Every power assigned to make God a liar in my life, die, in the name of Jesus.

255. O dragon power assigned against me, I bury you now, in the name of Jesus.

Praise and Worship

Day Thirteen

256. By Your binding powers, O God, arise, bind my tormentors, in the name of Jesus.

257. By Your power of possibilities, O God, arise and manifest in my life, in the name of Jesus.

258. My Father, my Father, my Father, arise and let the world know that You are my God, in the name of Jesus.

259. Every storm in my life, become calm by fire, in the name of Jesus.

260. (Mention your name), hear the word of the Lord, be still and know that God is God, in the name of Jesus.

261. O God arise and show me great mercy today, in the name of Jesus.

262. My Father, contend with whatever is contending with my peace, in the name of Jesus.

263. Every power assigned to make God a liar in my life, die, in the name of Jesus.

264. O dragon power assigned against me, I bury you now, in the name of Jesus.

265. Every evil mark stamped on me, dry up, in the name of Jesus.

266. O God, deliver me from my strong enemy which hated me for they are too strong for me, in the name of Jesus.

267. O God, bring down every high look that is downgrading my potentials, in the name of Jesus.

268. I receive power to run through satanic troop, in the name of Jesus.

269. I receive power to leap over every demonic wall of barrier, in the name of Jesus.

270. O Lord, teach my hands to war, in the name of Jesus.

271. Every evil mark stamped on me, dry up, in the name of Jesus.

272. Those that hate me shall be put to all-round shame, in the name of Jesus.

273. My light, hear the word of the Lord, shine brighter and brighter, in the name of Jesus.

274. I decree poverty upon my stubborn enemies, in the name of Jesus. This month, any power challenging God in my life must die, in the name of Jesus.

275. O heavens, arise and attack the powers of darkness inhabiting the garden of my family line, in the name of Jesus.

276. My Father, send Your angels to encamp about every member of my family and protect them, in the name of Jesus.

Praise and Worship

Day Fourteen

277. Those that hate me shall be put to all-round shame, in the name of Jesus.

278. My light, hear the word of the Lord, shine brighter and brighter, in the name of Jesus.

279. I decree poverty upon my stubborn enemies, in the name of Jesus. This month, any power challenging God in my life must die, in the name of Jesus.

280. Every occult pregnancy concerning my life this month, I abort you by fire, in the name of Jesus.

281. Oh heavens, declare your glory over my life, in the name of Jesus.

282. Every waster and emptier assigned to swallow me up, die, in the name of Jesus.

283. Sickness and infirmity shall not waste my life, in the name of Jesus.

284. Every arrangement to frustrate my breakthroughs, catch fire, in the name of Jesus.

285. Every priest of darkness divining against me, die, in the grave of fire, in the name of Jesus.

286. Every wicked mouth opened to swallow my breakthroughs this month, dry up, in the name of Jesus.

287. Let every bow of steel fashioned by the enemy be broken by my hands, in the name of Jesus.

288. I receive the power to pursue and overtake my enemies, in the name of Jesus.

289. My enemies are wounded, they are unable to rise; they are fallen under my feet, in the name of Jesus.

290. O God, subdue under me those that rose up against me, in the name of Jesus.

291. O God, arise and give me the neck of my enemies, that I might destroy them that hate me, in the name of Jesus.

292. Every generational sin and iniquity in my family line, be terminated by the blood of Jesus.

293. I bind with a chain every evil king reigning in my family, in the name of Jesus.

294. Every power in my root magnetising my progress backward, die, in the name of Jesus.

295. Foundational inheritance from my parents, come out, in the name of Jesus.

296. Ancestral wall built around my glory, be pulled down, in the name of Jesus.

297. Let the blood of Jesus go into the foundation of my family line to wash me and redeem me, in Jesus' name

Praise and Worship

Day Fifteen

298. O God, arise and empower the eagle of my breakthroughs to fly this month, in the name of Jesus.

299. Lord elevate me this month by fire, in the name of Jesus.

300. Do something in my life, O Lord, that will make men to celebrate me, in the name of Jesus.

301. I shall sing my song and dance my dance this year, in the name of Jesus.

302. Any power assigned to make me take foolish risks, die, in the name of Jesus.

303. Father, give me a new beginning, in the name of Jesus.

304. My Father, cause this year to be my year of Jubilee and rejoicing, in the name of Jesus.

305. Every curse of stagnation, break, in the name of Jesus.

306. O God, arise and fill my mouth with laughter, in the name of Jesus.

307. O God, arise and let my tears expire, in the name of Jesus.

308. O God, arise and let my shame expire, in the name of Jesus.

309. My enemies will cry, but there will be none to deliver them, in the name of Jesus.

310. I receive power to beat my aggressors to smallness as the dust before the wind, in the name of Jesus.

311. I cast out my pursuers as the dirt in the street, in Jesus' name.

312. By Your favour, O Lord, the people whom I have not known shall serve me, in the name of Jesus.

313. As soon as they hear of me, they shall obey me, the strangers shall submit themselves unto me, in the name of Jesus.

314. Every covenant, promise, oath, vow, dedication that my family line has made with demonic beings at various altars, I renounce you, in the name of Jesus.

315. I command future generations of my family line to be

released from every evil transaction that my ancestors have made, in the name of Jesus.

316. Oh earth, open and swallow every spiritual hired killer assigned against my family line, in the name of Jesus.

317. Every arrow that penetrated my life through my family line, be removed, in the name of Jesus.

318. Any ancestral power frustrating any area of my life in order to discourage me from following Christ, receive multiple destruction, in the name of Jesus.

319. Every ancestral chain of slavery binding my people from prospering in life, you are broken in my life by the hammer of God, in the name of Jesus.

Day Sixteen

Praise and Worship

320. O God, arise and turn my captors to my captivities, in the name of Jesus. Miracle, that surpasses explanation, manifest in my life now, in the name of Jesus.

321. O God, arise today, and let my situation change, in the name of Jesus.

322. Today, I position myself by fire for divine intervention, in the name of Jesus.

323. O God, my Father, burst forth in my life by signs and wonders, in the name of Jesus.

324. Resources of heaven, arise by fire, promote me, in the name of Jesus.

325. Any power that wants me to die like this, die, in the name of Jesus.

326. My Father, arise and let root of hardship in my life die now, in the name of Jesus.

327. O Red Sea of blockage, I cry against you, divide by fire, in the name of Jesus.

328. Every power holding tight to my instrument of advancement, die, in the name of Jesus.

329. I recover ten-fold all my wasted years, in the name of Jesus.

330. Any satanic threat to my existence, be uprooted, in the name of Jesus.

331. The dark strangers in my life shall fade away and be afraid out of their close places, in the name of Jesus.

332. O God, avenge me and subdue my adversaries under me, in the name of Jesus.

333. The Lord shall hear me in the day of trouble, the name of the God of Jacob shall defend me, in the name of Jesus.

334. O Lord, send me help from Your sanctuary and strengthen me out of Zion, in the name of Jesus.

335. My adversaries are brought down and fallen but I rise and stand upright, in the name of Jesus.

336. The height nobody has attained in my generation, I will reach it, in the name of Jesus.

337. I recover every good thing stolen by ancestral spirits from my forefathers, my immediate family and myself, in the name of Jesus.

338. Every ancestral embargo, be lifted, and let good things begin to break forth in my life and in my family, in the name of Jesus.

339. Every negative pattern, character, behaviour and habit flowing down from my family tree, I arrest you by the blood of Jesus.

340. Yokes, chains, fetters and bondage of my father's house, break, in the name of Jesus.

341. Thou cryptic demons and ancient dedications troubling my family line, vanish, in the name of Jesus.

Praise and Worship

Day Seventeen

342. My portion shall not be given to another, in the name of Jesus.

343. Sudden destruction will not be my lot, in the name of Jesus.

344. Every enchantment assigned for my downfall, die, in the name of Jesus.

345. Any personality carrying the seed of wickedness against me, be exposed and disgraced, in the name of Jesus.

346. The enemy that came while I slept, be disgraced, in the name of Jesus.

347. You ladder of oppression, catch fire, in the name of Jesus.

348. You ladder of affliction, catch fire, in the name of Jesus.

349. You ladder of infirmity, catch fire, in the name of Jesus.

350. You ladder of failure at the edge of breakthroughs, catch fire, in the name of Jesus.

351. O God, arise and roar like a terrible lion, and devour my portion, in the name of Jesus.

352. Vampire power, drinking the blood of my virtues, die, in the name of Jesus.

353. Let Thine hand find out all Thine enemies, let Thy right hand find out those that hate Thee, in the name of Jesus.

354. O God, make my adversaries as a fiery oven in the time of Thine anger, in the name of Jesus.

355. O God, arise and swallow up my enemies in Your wrath and let Your fire devour them, in the name of Jesus.

356. Let every seed and fruit of the enemy fashioned against my destiny be destroyed, in the name of Jesus.

357. Let the mischievous device of the enemy backfire, in the name of Jesus.

358. Every satanic animal living on my family tree, catch fire and die, in the name of Jesus.

359. Fiery darts of the wicked targeting my family line, backfire, in the name of Jesus.

360. Oh heavens over the prosperity of my family line, open by fire, in the name of Jesus.

361. I refuse to be an extension of any failure of my father's house, in the name of Jesus.

362. The iniquity that swallowed my parents will not swallow me, in the name of Jesus.

363. Family spirits power and supervising powers in charge of my father's house, die, in the name of Jesus.

Praise and Worship

Day Eighteen

364. Every location assigned to dislocate my life, clear away, in the name of Jesus.

365. Every Goliath boasting against my breakthroughs, die, in the name of Jesus.

366. My destiny, hear the word of the Lord, move to Your next level, in the name of Jesus.

367. Serpents and scorpions assigned to put me to shame, die, in the name of Jesus.

368. Any witchdoctor assigned to terminate my life, die, in the name of Jesus.

369. Evil progress, hear the word of the Lord, die, in the name of Jesus.

370. Birds of darkness assigned to trouble my star, die, in the name of Jesus.

371. Thou power of limitation, you are a liar, die, in the name of Jesus.

372. My glory, arise from the grave yard of backwardness, shine, in the name of Jesus.

373. Every arrow of confusion, be disgraced, in the name of Jesus.

374. O God, arise and make all my pursuers turn back, in the name of Jesus.

375. O Lord, let Your arrows pursue and locate every wicked power targeted against me, in the name of Jesus.

376. Do not be far from me, O Lord, be my help in the time of trouble, in the name of Jesus.

377. O Lord, make haste to help me, in the name of Jesus.

378. O Lord, deliver my soul from the sword and my destiny from the power of the dog, in the name of Jesus.

379. Foundational button pressed against my advancements, die, in the name of Jesus.

380. Strange animals in my roots, die, in the name of Jesus.

381. By the power in the blood of Jesus I renounce the gods that my ancestors or I have served, that have brought me into collective captivity, in the name of Jesus.

382. Thou power of collective demonisation in my family line, I destroy you, in the name of Jesus.

383. Every satanic odour coming out of the closet of my family, be neutralised, in the name of Jesus.

384. Every curse under which my family labour, be broken by the power in the blood of Jesus.

Praise and Worship

Day Nineteen

385. Every assembly of affliction, scatter, in the name of Jesus.

386. Blood of Jesus, cause confusion in the blood bank of witchcraft, in the name of Jesus.

387. I decree against serpents and scorpions. Let their poison die, in the name of Jesus.

388. The wind of impossibility shall not blow in my direction, in the name of Jesus.

389. You river of impossibility flowing near and around me, dry up now, in the name of Jesus.

390. I receive the strength of the Lord to leap over the wall of impossibility, in the name of Jesus.

391. Every Red Sea of impossibility, part, in the name of Jesus.

392. You angels of possibility and success, begin to minister unto me, in the name of Jesus.

393. With God on my side, no good thing shall be impossible for me, in the name of Jesus.

394. I will reach my goals before my enemies will know what is happening, in the name of Jesus.

395. O God, arise by the thunder of Your power and save me from the lion's mouth, in the name of Jesus.

396. Thou power of the valley of the shadow of death, release my destiny, in the name of Jesus.

397. O gates blocking my blessings, be lifted up, in the name of Jesus.

398. O Lord, keep my soul, let me not be ashamed and deliver me, in the name of Jesus.

399. Every drinker of blood and eater of flesh coming against me, die, in the name of Jesus.

400. Every covenant under which my family labours, be broken by the power in the blood of Jesus.

401. Dedications that speak against my family line, be broken, in the name of Jesus.

402. Every power altering the destiny of my family, be scattered, in the name of Jesus.

403. Every affliction in my family line, die, in the name of Jesus.

404. Every satanic investment in the heavenlies expected to manifest seasonal evil in my family, be crushed, in the name of Jesus.

405. My Father, lay a new foundation for my family line, in the name of Jesus.

Praise and Worship

Day Twenty

406. I shall fulfil my destiny, whether the enemy likes it or not, in the name of Jesus.

407. My steps shall be ordered by the Lord to fulfil my destiny, in the name of Jesus.

408. Let my disgrace be turned into grace, in the name of Jesus.

409. Let the dry bones of my destiny, come alive, in the name of Jesus.

410. Henceforth, I embark on a journey into destiny accomplishments in all ramifications, in the name of Jesus.

411. I cut off the spiritual umbilical cord through which evil flow into my destiny, in the name of Jesus.

412. No evil words from the sun, moon and stars will prosper in my life, in the name of Jesus.

413. Every evil word and chanting from prayer mats, evil forests, sacred trees, road junctions, marine environment and occult

prayer houses, be silenced, in the name of Jesus.

414. Father, thank You for a change in my situation, in the name of Jesus.

415. Every power, that needs to die for my testimony to manifest, die, in the name of Jesus.

416. Though a host should encamp against me, my heart shall not fear, in the name of Jesus.

417. Though war should rise against me, in this will I be confident, in the name of Jesus.

418. And now shall my head be lifted up above my enemies round about me, in the name of Jesus.

419. Deliver me not over unto the will of mine enemies, in the name of Jesus.

420. God shall destroy the camp of the enemy and their camp shall never be built up, in the name of Jesus.

421. Every power of the wicked avenger upon my family line, be destroyed, in the name of Jesus.

422. Blood of Jesus neutralise any evil thing inherited from the blood of my parents, in the name of Jesus.

423. By the blood of Jesus I deliver my family tree from serpent and scorpion, in the name of Jesus.

424. Every satanic termite operating inside my family tree, dry up and die, in the name of Jesus.

425. Blood of Jesus and Holy Ghost fire, purge the foundation of every member of my family, in the name of Jesus.

426. Architects and builders of affliction in my family line, scatter, in the name of Jesus.

Praise and Worship

Day Twenty-One

427. Every agenda of mocking powers for my life, backfire, in the name of Jesus.

428. By the power in the blood of Jesus, I receive miracles that will shock my friends and surprise my enemies, in the name of Jesus.

429. Dark authorities sponsoring continuous and repeated problems, scatter, in the name of Jesus.

430. By the power that divided the Red Sea, let my way open, in the name of Jesus.

431. By the power that stoned the head of Goliath, let my stubborn problems die, in the name of Jesus.

432. By the power that disgraced Sennacherib, let evil covens gathered against me catch fire, in the name of Jesus.

433. By the power that divided Jordan River, let my unusual breakthrough manifest, in the name of Jesus.

434. Every power mocking my prayers, receive double destruction, in the name of Jesus.

435. O God of Elijah arise, and make me a mysterious wonder, in the name of Jesus.

436. By the word of God, which cannot be broken, I move into my next level, in the name of Jesus.

437. O Lord, according to the deeds of the wicked, give them the works of their hands, in the name of Jesus.

438. O Lord, put off my sack cloth and gird me with gladness, in the name of Jesus.

439. Bow down Thine ear to me, O Lord, and deliver me speedily, in the name of Jesus.

440. Pull me out of the hidden net of the enemy, in Jesus' name.

441. My times are in Thy hand, deliver me from the hands of mine enemies and from that persecute me, in the name of Jesus.

442. Every negative powers like father like son, like mother like daughter, clear away by the power in the blood of Jesus.

443. In the name of Jesus, I ruin the power of every strong man assigned to trouble my blood line, in the name of Jesus.

444. Every agent of wickedness in my bloodline, I bind and cast you out with all your roots, in the name of Jesus.

445. Every curse, evil covenant and enchantment militating against the star of my family, die, in the name of Jesus.

446. Strongmen behind stubborn problems in my family line, die, in the name of Jesus.

447. Anything buried or planted in my family compound that is reactivating ancient demons, catch fire, in the name of Jesus.

Section Two

POWER AGAINST GENERATIONAL INHERITANCE

Watch One

Confessions: Psalm 68:1: Let God arise, let his enemies be scattered: let them also that hate him flee before him.

Isaiah 49:24-25: Shall the prey be taken from the mighty, or the lawful captive delivered? But thus saith the LORD, Even the captives of the mighty shall be taken away, and the prey of the terrible shall be delivered: for I will contend with him that contendeth with thee, and I will save thy children.

Job 5:12: He disappointeth the devices of the crafty, so that their hands cannot perform their enterprise.

Isa 54:17: No weapon that is formed against thee shall prosper; and every tongue that shall rise against thee in judgment thou shalt condemn. This is the heritage of the servants of the LORD, and their righteousness is of me, saith the LORD.

Rev 13:10: He that leadeth into captivity shall go into captivity: he that killeth with the sword must be killed with the sword. Here is the patience and the faith of the saints.

Isa 50:7-9: For the Lord GOD will help me; therefore shall I not be confounded: therefore have I set my face like a flint, and

I know that I shall not be ashamed. He is near that justifieth me; who will contend with me? Let us stand together: who is mine adversary? Let him come near to me. Behold, the Lord GOD will help me; who is he that shall condemn me? Lo, they all shall wax old as a garment; the moth shall eat them up.

Isa 54:15: Behold, they shall surely gather together, but not by me: whosoever shall gather together against thee shall fall for thy sake.

Praise and Worship

Prayer Points

1. Thou power of healing and deliverance, fall upon me now, in the name of Jesus.

2. Blood of Jesus, purge my foundation.

3. Every generational curse of disease and infirmity in my life, break by the power in the blood of Jesus, in the name of Jesus.

4. Every generational covenant of sickness in my life, break by the power in the blood of Jesus, in the name of Jesus.

5. Every generational bondage of sickness in my life, break by the power in the blood of Jesus, in the name of Jesus.

6. Every evil power from my father's house, transferring sickness into my life, die, in the name of Jesus.

7. Every evil power from my mother's house, transferring sickness into my life, die, in the name of Jesus.

8. Let God arise and let stubborn generational problems in my life die, in the name of Jesus.

9. Every cycle of generational hardship, break, in the name of Jesus.

10. Every destiny vulture of my father's house, die, in the name of Jesus.

11. Every evil power that pursued my parents, release me, in the name of Jesus.

12. I fire back every witchcraft arrow fired into my life as a baby, in the name of Jesus.

13. Fire of God, thunder of God, purse every generational pursuer, in the name of Jesus.

14. Holy Ghost fire, purge my blood from evil inheritance, in the name of Jesus.

15. Every evil power of my father's house that will not let me go, die, in the name of Jesus.

16. Every evil generational power designed to spoil my life, scatter, in the name of Jesus.

17. I kill every inherited sickness in my life with the blood of Jesus, in the name of Jesus.

18. Every power of the idols of my father's house, die, in the name of Jesus.

19. Every evil power using sickness to pursue me from my father's house, die, in the name of Jesus.

20. Every evil power using sickness to pursue me from my mother's house, die, in the name of Jesus.

21. Every witchcraft tree binding my placenta, die, in the name of Jesus.

22. Every idol of my father's house, lose your hold over my life, in the name of Jesus.

23. Every strongman of my father's house, die, in the name of Jesus.

24. I silence the evil cry of the evil powers of my father's house fashioned against me, in the name of Jesus.

25. All consequences of the worship of evil powers of my father's house upon my life, I wipe you off by the blood of Jesus.

26. Holy Ghost fire, burn down all spiritual shrines of my father's house, in the name of Jesus.

27. Sickness agenda of the evil powers of my father's house, die, in the name of Jesus.

28. Every blood speaking against my generational line, be silenced by the blood of Jesus.

29. Every evil power of my father's house, speaking against my health, scatter, in the name of Jesus.

30. I break all ancestral covenants with the evil powers of my father's house, in the name of Jesus.

31. Satanic investments in the foundation of my life, die, in the name of Jesus.

32. Hidden childhood poisons polluting my life, catch fire, in the name of Jesus.

33. Every tree that God the Father has not planted into my life, die, in the name of Jesus.

34. Let the consequences of satanic hands that carried me as a baby expire, in the name of Jesus.

35. Placental bondage, break by fire, in the name of Jesus.

36. My Father, walk to my childhood days and purge my life, in the name of Jesus.

37. Satanic seeds in my foundation, die, in the name of Jesus.

38. Serpents and scorpions planted by childhood polygamous witchcraft, die, in the name of Jesus.

39. Glory killers entrenched into my foundation, die, in the name of Jesus.

40. Blood of Jesus, arise in Your cleansing power and wash my roots, in the name of Jesus.

41. Every power of Herod tracing my star, I bury you now, in the name of Jesus.

42. Yokes buried inside the foundation of my life, break, in the name of Jesus.

43. Any problem buried in my childhood to pollute my future, die, in the name of Jesus.

44. Foundational failure magnet, catch fire, in the name of Jesus.

45. Plantations of darkness troubling my star, roast by fire, in the name of Jesus.

46. Anti-focus power troubling my destiny, die, in the name of Jesus.

Watch Two

Confessions: Psalm 68:1: Let God arise, let his enemies be scattered: let them also that hate him flee before him.

Isaiah 49:24-25: Shall the prey be taken from the mighty, or the lawful captive delivered? But thus saith the LORD, Even the captives of the mighty shall be taken away, and the prey of the terrible shall be delivered: for I will contend with him that contendeth with thee, and I will save thy children.

Job 5:12: He disappointeth the devices of the crafty, so that their hands cannot perform their enterprise.

Isa 54:17: No weapon that is formed against thee shall prosper; and every tongue that shall rise against thee in judgment thou shalt condemn. This is the heritage of the servants of the LORD, and their righteousness is of me, saith the LORD.

Rev 13:10: He that leadeth into captivity shall go into captivity:

he that killeth with the sword must be killed with the sword. Here is the patience and the faith of the saints.

Isa 50:7-9: For the Lord GOD will help me; therefore shall I not be confounded: therefore have I set my face like a flint, and I know that I shall not be ashamed. He is near that justifieth me; who will contend with me? let us stand together: who is mine adversary? let him come near to me. Behold, the Lord GOD will help me; who is he that shall condemn me? lo, they all shall wax old as a garment; the moth shall eat them up.

Isa 54:15: Behold, they shall surely gather together, but not by me: whosoever shall gather together against thee shall fall for thy sake.

Praise and Worship
Prayer Points

47.   Power to interpret the language of my star, come upon me now, in the name of Jesus.

48.   Power to read the handwriting of my star in the heavenlies, fall upon me, in the name of Jesus.

49.   Angels of the living God, possess my heavens, in the name of Jesus.

50. Angels of light, arise and fill my dark night, in the name of Jesus.

51. Angels of the living God, arise, fight and recover my high places, in the name of Jesus.

52. Lord Jesus, walk back into my childhood and correct my foundations, in the name of Jesus.

53. Every satanic plantation in my childhood, be dissolved by the fire of the Holy Ghost, in the name of Jesus.

54. Every effect of any bad thing I have swallowed or eaten as a child, be nullified, in the name of Jesus.

55. Powers assigned to capture my star, loose your hold, in the name of Jesus.

56. Any seed of wickedness planted in my childhood, Holy Ghost fire, dissolve it, in the name of Jesus.

57. Powers planted in my childhood to trouble my future, hear the word of the Lord. The Lord will cause dryness to come upon you today, in the name of Jesus.

58. Powers planted in my childhood to trouble my future, I dry up your river, even as Jordan was dried up, in the name of Jesus.

59. Powers planted in my childhood to trouble my future, I dry up your roots, even as the Lord caused the fig tree to dry up, in the name of Jesus.

60. Powers planted in my childhood to trouble my future, I knock down your gates, in the name of Jesus.

61. Every bitter water of sickness flowing in my family from the evil powers of my father's house, dry up, in the name of Jesus.

62. Any rope tying my family line to any evil power of my father's house, break, in the name of Jesus.

63. Every landlord spirit troubling my health, be paralysed, in the name of Jesus.

64. I recover my health stolen by the evil powers of my father's house, in the name of Jesus.

65. Where is the God of Elijah? Arise, disgrace every evil inheritance of the power of my father's house, in the name of Jesus.

66. Every satanic priest ministering in my family line, be retrenched, in the name of Jesus.

67. Arrows of sickness originating from idolatry, loose your hold, in the name of Jesus.

68. Every influence of the evil powers of my father's house, in my life, die, in the name of Jesus.

69. Every network of the evil powers of my father's house, in my place of birth, bringing sickness into my life, scatter, in the name of Jesus.

70. Every satanic dedication that speaks against me, be dismantled by the power in the blood of Jesus.

71. Every unconscious evil internal altar, be roasted, in the name of Jesus.

72. The voice of evil generational foundational powers of my father's house will never speak again, in the name of Jesus.

73. Every strongman assigned by the evil powers of my father's house against my life, die, in the name of Jesus.

74. Every satanic promissory note issued on my behalf by my ancestors, be reversed, in the name of Jesus.

75. Garments of opposition designed by evil powers of my father's house, roast, in the name of Jesus.

76. Every satanic cloud of sickness upon my life, scatter, in the name of Jesus.

77. Thou power of strange gods legislating against my health, scatter, in the name of Jesus.

78. Every seed of generational sickness in my life, die, in the name of Jesus.

79. Power of God, uproot generational sickness from my life, in the name of Jesus.

80. Every harsh weather confronting the fruit on my family tree, be arrested, in the name of Jesus.

81. Every flood of darkness assigned to my family tree, be disgraced, in the name of Jesus.

82.   Every warehouse of darkness caging the blessings of my family line, hear the word of the Lord: Release our blessings, in the name of Jesus.

83.   Every evil cycle in my blood line troubling our Israel, die, in the name of Jesus.

84.   The mistake of my parents will not become my tragedy, in the name of Jesus.

85.   The iniquity of my father's house shall not steal from me, in the name of Jesus.

86.   Whatsoever the enemy has set in motion against my family line, be reversed, in the name of Jesus.

87.   Every ancestral covenant strengthening suffering and sorrow in my family line, be broken, in the name of Jesus.

88.   Any curse under which my family labour, be broken by the power in the blood of Jesus.

89.   Lord Jesus, walk back into my foundations and carry out every reconstruction that will move my life forward.

90.   Lord, walk back 10 generations in my family line and erase every satanic instruction the enemy is using to torment me, in the name of Jesus.

91.   Every handwriting of the wicked programmed into my foundation through idol worship, be wiped off by the blood of Jesus, in the name of Jesus.

92.   My Father, purge my blood line, in the name of Jesus.

Watch Three

Confessions: Psalm 68:1: Let God arise, let his enemies be scattered: let them also that hate him flee before him.

Isaiah 49:24-25: Shall the prey be taken from the mighty, or the lawful captive delivered? But thus saith the LORD, Even the captives of the mighty shall be taken away, and the prey of the terrible shall be delivered: for I will contend with him that contendeth with thee, and I will save thy children.

Job 5:12:   He disappointeth the devices of the crafty, so that their hands cannot perform their enterprise.

Isa 54:17: No weapon that is formed against thee shall prosper; and every tongue that shall rise against thee in judgment thou shalt condemn. This is the heritage of the servants of the LORD, and their righteousness is of me, saith the LORD.

Rev 13:10: He that leadeth into captivity shall go into captivity: he that killeth with the sword must be killed with the sword. Here is the patience and the faith of the saints.

Isa 50:7-9:   For the Lord GOD will help me; therefore shall I not be confounded: therefore have I set my face like a flint, and I know that I shall not be ashamed. He is near that justifieth me; who will contend with me? let us stand together: who' is mine adversary? let him come near to me. Behold, the Lord GOD will help me; who is he that shall condemn me? lo, they all shall wax old as a garment; the moth shall eat them up.

Isa 54:15: Behold, they shall surely gather together, but not by me: whosoever shall gather together against thee shall fall for thy sake.

Praise and Worship
Prayer Points

93. Pattern of darkness in my family line, break, in the name of Jesus.

94. What my father did not enjoy, I will enjoy it, in the name of Jesus.

95. O God, backdate the blessings of my ancestors and give them to me, in the name of Jesus.

96. I make a contrary declaration to that of the enemy, in the name of Jesus.

97. Let my destiny be re-arranged to favour my life, in the name of Jesus.

98. I refuse to struggle for what my parents struggled for, in the name of Jesus.

99. Breakthrough miscarriage, die, in the name of Jesus.

100. Evil cycles in my bloodline, die, in the name of Jesus.

101. Whatever the enemy has set in motion, I reverse them, in the name of Jesus.

102. Materials coming down to me which the enemy has set in motion, be filtered through the Cross, in the name of Jesus.

103. I thank God for all the good I have inherited from my forefathers. I claim them and reject the evil ones, in the name of Jesus.

104. Blood of Jesus, flow through my family history and wash away every ground of satanic attack against my destiny, in the name of Jesus.

105. My Father, I ask in repentance for forgiveness of all my family sins, in the name of Jesus.

106. Every descending pattern that satan uses to perpetuate his destruction on my family line, be wiped off by the blood of Jesus.

107. Every power causing problem to escalate in my family line, die, in the name of Jesus.

108. Thou power of destructive patterns and habits, be destroyed by the power in the blood of Jesus.

109. My Father, send Your angels to bring each member of my family out of darkness into light, in the name of Jesus.

110. Thou dark power of my father's house repeating sickness and oppression in my life, die, in the name of Jesus.

111. Fire of God, burn off every inherited sickness and affliction from the evil powers of my father's house, in the name of Jesus.

112. Environmental oppression of the evil powers of my father's house, scatter by fire, in the name of Jesus.

113. Every tongue of the evil powers of my father's house, speaking sickness into my life, be silenced, in the name of Jesus.

114. Every attack against my health, from the womb, by the evil powers of my father's house, scatter, in the name of Jesus.

115. Every cycle of sickness and affliction of the evil powers of my father's house, be broken, in the name of Jesus.

116. Owners of evil loads of generational sickness, carry your load, in the name of Jesus.

117. Every generational arrester, be arrested, in the name of Jesus.

118. Every sickness planted in my foundation, scatter, in the name of Jesus.

119. Every serpent of sickness in my foundation, die, in the name of Jesus.

120. Every scorpion of sickness in my foundation, die, in the name of Jesus.

121. Holy Ghost fire, burn down all spiritual shrines of my father's house, in the name of Jesus.

122. Every generational transmission of sickness, break and die, in the name of Jesus.

123. Every generational transmission of disease, break and die, in the name of Jesus.

124. Every generational transmission of pains, break and die, in the name of Jesus.

125. Thou power of my family idol die, in the name of Jesus.

126. Every evil power of my family idol, what are you waiting for? Die, in the name of Jesus.

127. Every wicked foundation prepared for me by family idols die, in the name of Jesus.

128. I release myself from the cage of family idols, in the name of Jesus.

129. Blood of Jesus, break every blood connection between me and every family idol.

130. Powers planted in my childhood to trouble my future, I break in pieces your gates of brass, in the name of Jesus.

131. Powers planted in my childhood to trouble my future, I cut asunder your brass of iron, in the name of Jesus.

132. Powers planted in my childhood to trouble my future, I break down your walls, even as the walls of Jericho was broken down, in the name of Jesus.

133. Powers planted in my childhood to trouble my future, I cut off your cords and I cast them away, in the name of Jesus.

134. Powers planted in my childhood to trouble my future, I command you to bend your knee to Jesus.

135. Powers planted in my childhood to trouble my future, I put a cord around your tongue, in the name of Jesus.

136. Powers planted in my childhood, to trouble my future, I put a thorn in your jaw, in the name of Jesus.

137. Powers planted in my childhood to trouble my future, I take away your throne, in the name of Jesus.

138. Powers planted in my childhood to trouble my future, I command you to sit in the dust, in the name of Jesus.

Watch Four

Confessions: Psalm 68:1: Let God arise, let his enemies be scattered: let them also that hate him flee before him.

Isaiah 49:24-25: Shall the prey be taken from the mighty, or the lawful captive delivered? But thus saith the LORD, Even the captives of the mighty shall be taken away, and the prey of the terrible shall be delivered: for I will contend with him that contendeth with thee, and I will save thy children.

Job 5:12: He disappointeth the devices of the crafty, so that their hands cannot perform their enterprise.

Isa 54:17: No weapon that is formed against thee shall prosper; and every tongue that shall rise against thee in judgment thou shalt condemn. This is the heritage of the servants of the LORD, and their righteousness is of me, saith the LORD.

Rev 13:10: He that leadeth into captivity shall go into captivity: he that killeth with the sword must be killed with the sword. Here is the patience and the faith of the saints.

Isa 50:7-9: For the Lord GOD will help me; therefore shall I not be confounded: therefore have I set my face like a flint, and I know that I shall not be ashamed. He is near that justifieth me;

who will contend with me? let us stand together: who is mine adversary? let him come near to me. Behold, the Lord GOD will help me; who is he that shall condemn me? lo, they all shall wax old as a garment; the moth shall eat them up.

Isa 54:15: Behold, they shall surely gather together, but not by me: whosoever shall gather together against thee shall fall for thy sake.

Praise and Worship
Prayer Points

139. I break all curses or iniquities coming down my family line, in the name of Jesus.

140. I destroy the spiritual embargo on my mother's side and on my father's side, 10 generations backward, in the name of Jesus.

141. Any dark covenant with my place of birth, break, in the name of Jesus.

142. Every power of Ichabod upon my destiny, die, in the name of Jesus.

143. Every problem tormenting my glory, die, in the name of Jesus.

144. My legs, reject backwardness, in the name of Jesus.

145. The glory of my life stolen in the womb, I recover you by fire, in the name of Jesus.

146. Glory manipulators and glory robbers, let me go, in the name of Jesus.

147. Yoke magnetisers, hear the word of the Lord: Die, in the name of Jesus.

148. My days shall not be restless but shall be called the days of the Lord, in the name of Jesus.

149. Any good thing that died in my life when I was ignorant, come alive now, in the name of Jesus.

150. My eyes, open to see what God is doing, in the name of Jesus.

151. "I am that I am", arise and manifest Your power in my life and move me to my next level, in the name of Jesus.

152. O Lord, I plug my destiny to the socket of the Holy Ghost to receive divine elevation, in the name of Jesus.

153. O Lord, I plug my life to the socket of the Holy Ghost to receive divine acceleration, in the name of Jesus.

154. I mount on the horse of war and ride into the land of my breakthroughs, in the name of Jesus.

155. Hammer of God, break every evil leg walking against my elevation, in the name of Jesus.

156. Heavenly carpenter, nail to death every spiritual robber assigned against my elevation, in the name of Jesus.

157. All evil spirits in the air working against my elevation, scatter unto desolation, in the name of Jesus.

158. All evil spirits in the wind hindering the move of my progress, scatter unto desolation, in the name of Jesus.

159. All evil spirits in the water blocking steps to my elevation, scatter, in the name of Jesus.

160. I declare myself free from every evil dedication that speaks against me, in the name of Jesus.

161. Every yoke and burden of generational idolatry break, in the name of Jesus.

162. I rise above every power of foundational idolatry, in the name of Jesus.

163. I speak destruction unto every evil altar working against me, in the name of Jesus.

164. Every angry altar of my father's house crying against my breakthrough, die, in the name of Jesus.

165. Every idol seeking demotion of my destiny, die in the name of Jesus.

166. Every family cage sponsored by idols, break, in the name of Jesus.

167. Every evil chain linking me to family idol, break, in the name of Jesus.

168. My name, hear the word of the Lord. Depart from every evil altar.

169. Every evil power of my family idol, die, in the name of Jesus.

170. I withdraw my name from every evil altar, in the name of Jesus.

171. My life, receive deliverance from every cage of idolatry, in the name of Jesus.

172. Every evil priest ministering against me by any evil altar, receive the fire of God, in the name of Jesus.

173. Holy Ghost fire, burn every foundation altar working against me, in the name of Jesus.

174. Thou power of God, shatter every agenda of foundational idolatry designed against my life, in the name of Jesus.

175. I retire by fire, every occult priest divining against me, in the name of Jesus.

176. I shall not be a victim of destiny vandalisation, in the name of Jesus.

177. O altar of darkness, hear the word of the Lord. Be dismantled by fire, in the name of Jesus.

178. Every strange fire prepared by family idols, die, in the name of Jesus.

179. Let every shrine containing my name be wasted, in the name of Jesus.

180. Every evil connection with any dead relative, break, in the name of Jesus.

181. All satanic forces assigned against my elevation, scatter, in the name of Jesus.

182. O God, arise and send Your warrior angels to do battle for my family, in the name of Jesus.

183. I bind with a chain every evil king reigning in my family, in the name of Jesus.

184. Sacrifices done on my behalf, caging me from my root, die, in the name of Jesus.

Watch Five

Confessions: Psalm 68:1: Let God arise, let his enemies be scattered: let them also that hate him flee before him.

Isaiah 49:24-25: Shall the prey be taken from the mighty, or the lawful captive delivered? But thus saith the LORD, Even the captives of the mighty shall be taken away, and the prey of the terrible shall be delivered: for I will contend with him that contendeth with thee, and I will save thy children.

Job 5:12: He disappointeth the devices of the crafty, so that their hands cannot perform their enterprise.

Isa 54:17: No weapon that is formed against thee shall prosper; and every tongue that shall rise against thee in judgment thou shalt condemn. This is the heritage of the servants of the LORD, and their righteousness is of me, saith the LORD.

Rev 13:10: He that leadeth into captivity shall go into captivity: he that killeth with the sword must be killed with the sword. Here is the patience and the faith of the saints.

Isa 50:7-9: For the Lord GOD will help me; therefore shall I not be confounded: therefore have I set my face like a flint, and I know that I shall not be ashamed. He is near that justifieth me; who will contend with me? let us stand together: who is mine adversary? let him come near to me. Behold, the Lord GOD will help me; who is he that shall condemn me? lo, they all shall wax old as a garment; the moth shall eat them up.

Isa 54:15: Behold, they shall surely gather together, but not by me: whosoever shall gather together against thee shall fall for thy sake.

Praise and Worship
Prayer Points

185. Family spirits power and supervising powers in charge of my father's house, die, in the name of Jesus.

186. Foundational button pressed against my advancements, die, in the name of Jesus.

187. Strange animals in my roots, die, in the name of Jesus.

188. By the power in the blood of Jesus I renounce the gods that my ancestors or I have served, that have brought me into collective captivity, in the name of Jesus.

189. Thou power of collective demonisation in my family line, I destroy you, in the name of Jesus.

190. Every satanic odour coming out of the closet of my family, be neutralised, in the name of Jesus.

191. Every curse under which my family labour, be broken by the power in the blood of Jesus.

192. Every covenant under which my family labours, be broken by the power in the blood of Jesus.

193. Dedications that speak against my family line, be broken, in the name of Jesus.

194. Every power altering the destiny of my family, be scattered, in the name of Jesus.

195. Every affliction in my family line, die, in the name of Jesus.

196. Every satanic investment in the heavenlies expected to manifest seasonal evil in my family, be crushed, in the name of Jesus.

197. My Father, lay a new foundation for my family line, in the name of Jesus.

198. Every power of the wicked avenger upon my family line, be destroyed, in the name of Jesus.

199. Blood of Jesus neutralise any evil thing inherited from the blood of my parents, in the name of Jesus.

200. By the blood of Jesus I deliver my family tree from serpent and scorpion, in the name of Jesus.

201. Every satanic termite operating inside my family tree, dry up and die, in the name of Jesus.

202. Blood of Jesus and Holy Ghost fire, purge the foundation of every member of my family, in the name of Jesus.

203. Architects and builders of affliction in my family line, scatter, in the name of Jesus.

204. Every negative powers like father like son, like mother like daughter, clear away by the power in the blood of Jesus.

205. In the name of Jesus, I ruin the power of every strongman assigned to trouble my blood line, in the name of Jesus.

206. Every agent of wickedness in my bloodline, I bind and cast you out with all your roots, in the name of Jesus.

207. Every curse, evil covenant and enchantment militating against the star of my family, die, in the name of Jesus.

208. Strongmen behind stubborn problems in my family line, die, in the name of Jesus.

209. Anything buried or planted in my family compound that is reactivating ancient demons, catch fire, in the name of Jesus.

210. Any evil tree planted anywhere that speaks against my destiny, dry to the roots, in the name of Jesus.

211. Satanic panel set up against my family line, scatter, in the name of Jesus.

212. Every satanic law programmed against my elevation, die, in the name of Jesus.

213. Every ancestral law programmed into the heavenlies against my elevation, die, in the name of Jesus.

214. O God, arise and use every weapon at Your disposal to disgrace the enemies of my elevation, in the name of Jesus.

215. All evil wishes and desires programmed against my life, die, in the name of Jesus.

216. All hereditary seals upon my destiny, I break and dissolve you, in the name of Jesus.

217. All satanic vows against my destiny, die, in the name of Jesus.

218. All satanic sacrifices assigned against my destiny, die, in the name of Jesus.

219. All unconscious links with false prophets and visionaries, break, in the name of Jesus.

220. My dwelling place, be surrounded by the hedge of thorns, in the name of Jesus.

221. My dwelling place, be surrounded by a wall of fire, in the name of Jesus.

222. My dwelling place, be surrounded by a wall of faith, in the name of Jesus.

223. All spirits of bondage, I bind you with chains and fetters of iron, in the name of Jesus.

224. You enemies of my father's house, I forbid you to work against my destiny, in the name of Jesus.

225. All commandments issued against me by the powers of darkness, I cancel and render you null and void, in the name of Jesus.

226. I break the will of the enemy over every area of my life, in the name of Jesus.

227. I bring the mighty power of the resurrection of our Lord Jesus Christ against all powers of darkness, in the name of Jesus.

228. Holy Spirit, fight against those that are fighting against my destiny, in the name of Jesus.

229. Let the powers of wickedness be confounded and put to shame, in the name of Jesus.

230. O Lord, command Your light to shine in my darkness, in the name of Jesus.

Watch Six

Confessions: Psalm 68:1: Let God arise, let his enemies be scattered: let them also that hate him flee before him.

Isaiah 49:24-25: Shall the prey be taken from the mighty, or the lawful captive delivered? But thus saith the LORD, Even the captives of the mighty shall be taken away, and the prey of the terrible shall be delivered: for I will contend with him that contendeth with thee, and I will save thy children.

Job 5:12: He disappointeth the devices of the crafty, so that their hands cannot perform their enterprise.

Isa 54:17: No weapon that is formed against thee shall prosper;

and every tongue that shall rise against thee in judgment thou shalt condemn. This is the heritage of the servants of the LORD, and their righteousness is of me, saith the LORD.

Rev 13:10: He that leadeth into captivity shall go into captivity: he that killeth with the sword must be killed with the sword. Here is the patience and the faith of the saints.

Isa 50:7-9: For the Lord GOD will help me; therefore shall I not be confounded: therefore have I set my face like a flint, and I know that I shall not be ashamed. He is near that justifieth me; who will contend with me? let us stand together: who is mine adversary? let him come near to me. Behold, the Lord GOD will help me; who is he that shall condemn me? lo, they all shall wax old as a garment; the moth shall eat them up.

Isa 54:15: Behold, they shall surely gather together, but not by me: whosoever shall gather together against thee shall fall for thy sake.

Praise and Worship
Prayer Points

231. Any power gathering against my destiny, catch fire, in the name of Jesus.

232. Let the fuel of my problems dry up, in the name of Jesus.

233. Let the foundation stones of my life be washed in the blood of Jesus, in the name of Jesus.

234. Every power waging war against my testimony, fall down and die, in the name of Jesus.

235. Destiny thieves, release me, in the name of Jesus.

236. My body, my soul, my spirit, push out satanic plantations, in the name of Jesus.

237. Angels of the living God, pursue my pursuers, in the name of Jesus.

238. Every king Uzziah assigned to reposition my destiny, die by fire, in the name of Jesus.

239. Every yoke assigned to reposition my destiny to the back, clear away, in the name of Jesus.

240. Let the oil that will cause me to be celebrated come upon my destiny, in the name of Jesus.

241. Every power of the idols of my father's house, die, in the name of Jesus.

242. Every family idol crying against my destiny, die, in the name of Jesus.

243. Every seed of idolatry in my foundation, die, in the name of Jesus.

244. The voice of my family idol will not prevail over my destiny, in the name of Jesus.

245. Every grip of the evil consequences of the ancestral worship of my forefathers' god over my life and ministry, break by fire, in the name of Jesus.

246. Every unconscious evil soul-tie and covenant with the spirits of my dead grandfather, grandmother, occult uncles, aunties, custodians of family gods/oracles/shrines, be broken by the blood of Jesus.

247. Every decision, vow or promise made by my forefathers contrary to my divine destiny, loose your hold by fire, in the name of Jesus.

248. Every legal ground that ancestral/guardian spirits have in my life, be destroyed, by the blood of Jesus.

249. Every generational curse of God resulting from the sin of idolatry of my forefathers, loose your hold, in the name of Jesus.

250. Every ancestral evil altar conspiring against me, be dashed against the Rock of Ages, in the name of Jesus.

251. Every evil ancestral placental manipulation of my life, be reversed, in the name of Jesus.

252. Every ancestral life patterns, designed for me through vows, promises and covenants, be reversed, in the name of Jesus.

253. Every hold of any sacrifice ever offered in my family or on

my behalf, I break your power over my life, in the name of Jesus.

254. Any ancestral bloodshed of animals, or human beings affecting me, loose your hold by the blood of Jesus.

255. Any curse placed on my ancestral line by anybody who was cheated, maltreated, or at the point of death, break now, in the name of Jesus.

256. Every garment of ancestral infirmity, disease, sickness, untimely death, poverty, disfavour, dishonour, shame and failure at the edge of miracles passed down to my generation, be roasted by fire, in the name of Jesus.

257. Every evil ancestral river flowing down to my generation, I cut you off, in the name of Jesus.

258. Every evil ancestral habit and weakness of moral failures manifesting in my life, loose your grip and release me now, in the name of Jesus.

259. Any power from my family background seeking to make a shipwreck of my life and ministry, be destroyed by the fire of God, in the name of Jesus.

260. Every rage and rampage of ancestral and family spirits resulting from my being born again, be quenched by the liquid fire of God, in the name of Jesus.

261. I shall arise by the power of the Holy Ghost and disgrace my disgrace, in the name of Jesus.

262. Every area of satanic storm troubling my destiny, I scatter you today, in the name of Jesus.

263. Wherever demons are gathered against my elevation, I scatter their association by the power in the blood of Jesus.

264. I receive power to activate the covenant of Abraham's blessing and greatness to function in my life.

265. I speak to the womb of heaven and earth to work for my growth and increase my greatness, in the name of Jesus.

266. I paralyse every evil hand scattering my success and increase, in the name of Jesus.

267. Every satanic wind blowing away my virtues, expire, in the name of Jesus.

268. Every power fighting against my elevation and celebration, be paralysed, in the name of Jesus.

269. I dismantle every curse from my father's or mother's house working against my total freedom, in the name of Jesus.

270. Cycle of the dark in my family line, break, in Jesus' name.

271. The mistake of my parents will not become my tragedy, in the name of Jesus.

272. Iniquity of my father's house shall not steal from me, in the name of Jesus.

273. I place the cross of Jesus Christ between me and my ancestors, in the name of Jesus.

274. Blood of Jesus, flow through my family bloodline and wash away every ground of satanic attack against my destiny, in the name of Jesus.

275. Every evil pattern I have inherited from my family line, be destroyed by the blood of Jesus.

276. Every whirlwind of destruction flowing down from my family tree, I bury you now, in the name of Jesus.

Watch Seven

Confessions: Psalm 68:1: Let God arise, let his enemies be scattered: let them also that hate him flee before him.

Isaiah 49:24-25: Shall the prey be taken from the mighty, or the lawful captive delivered? But thus saith the LORD, Even the captives of the mighty shall be taken away, and the prey of the terrible shall be delivered: for I will contend with him that contendeth with thee, and I will save thy children.

Job 5:12: He disappointeth the devices of the crafty, so that their hands cannot perform their enterprise.

Isa 54:17: No weapon that is formed against thee shall prosper;

and every tongue that shall rise against thee in judgment thou shalt condemn. This is the heritage of the servants of the LORD, and their righteousness is of me, saith the LORD.

Rev 13:10: He that leadeth into captivity shall go into captivity: he that killeth with the sword must be killed with the sword. Here is the patience and the faith of the saints.

Isa 50:7-9: For the Lord GOD will help me; therefore shall I not be confounded: therefore have I set my face like a flint, and I know that I shall not be ashamed. He is near that justifieth me; who will contend with me? let us stand together: who is mine adversary? let him come near to me. Behold, the Lord GOD will help me; who is he that shall condemn me? lo, they all shall wax old as a garment; the moth shall eat them up.

Isa 54:15: Behold, they shall surely gather together, but not by me: whosoever shall gather together against thee shall fall for thy sake.

Praise and Worship
Prayer Points

277. Every family pattern by which satan pumps evil water into my family, die, in the name of Jesus.

278. Name each evil pattern and call the Lord to destroy it.

279. O heavens, arise and attack the powers of darkness inhabiting the garden of my family line, in the name of Jesus.

280. My Father, send Your angels to encamp about every member of my family and protect them, in the name of Jesus.

281. Every generational sin and iniquity in my family line, be terminated by the blood of Jesus.

282. I bind with a chain every evil king reigning in my family, in the name of Jesus.

283. Every power in my root magnetising my progress backward, die, in the name of Jesus.

284. Foundational inheritance from my parents, come out, in the name of Jesus.

285. Ancestral wall built around my glory, be pulled down, in the name of Jesus.

286. Let the blood of Jesus go into the foundation of my family line to wash me and redeem me, in the name of Jesus.

287. Every covenant, promise, oath, vow, dedication that my family line has made with demonic beings at various altars, I renounce you, in the name of Jesus.

288. I command future generations of my family line to be

released from every evil transaction that my ancestors have made, in the name of Jesus.

289. Oh earth, open and swallow every spiritual hired killer assigned against my family line, in the name of Jesus.

290. Every arrow that penetrated my life through my family line, be removed, in the name of Jesus.

291. Any ancestral power frustrating any area of my life in order to discourage me from following Christ, receive multiple destruction, in the name of Jesus.

292. Every ancestral chain of slavery binding my people from prospering in life, you are broken in my life by the hammer of God, in the name of Jesus.

293. The height nobody has attained in my generation, I will reach it, in the name of Jesus.

294. I recover every good thing stolen by ancestral spirits from my forefathers, my immediate family and myself, in the name of Jesus.

295. Every ancestral embargo, be lifted, and let good things begin to break forth in my life and in my family, in the name of Jesus.

296. Every negative pattern, character, behaviour and habit

flowing down from my family tree, I arrest you by the blood of Jesus.

297. Yokes, chains, fetters and bondage of my father's house, break, in the name of Jesus.

298. Thou cryptic demons and ancient dedications troubling my family line, vanish, in the name of Jesus.

299. Every satanic animal living on my family tree, catch fire and die, in the name of Jesus.

300. Fiery darts of the wicked targeting my family line, backfire, in the name of Jesus.

301. Oh heavens over the prosperity of my family line, open by fire, in the name of Jesus.

302. I refuse to be an extension of any failure of my father's house, in the name of Jesus.

303. The iniquity that swallowed my parents will not swallow me, in the name of Jesus.

304. All territorial spirits delegated against my family line, be arrested, in the name of Jesus.

305. Let thunder and fire destroy every satanic monitoring device working in my family line, in the name of Jesus.

306. All satanic embargo placed on my family line, be destroyed by fire, in the name of Jesus.

307. Every power aborting the plans of God for my family line, fall down and die, in the name of Jesus.

308. Anything spoken into the sun and the moon against my family line, be destroyed by the power in the blood of Jesus.

309. Every power drawing power from the heavenlies against my family line, fall down and die, in the name of Jesus.

310. I cut off the head of the Goliath of my family line, in the name of Jesus.

311. I terminate every terminator of my family line, in the name of Jesus.

312. All the friends of darkness in my family line, be exposed and disgraced, in the name of Jesus.

313. Every anti-prosperity curse flowing down from my family tree, break by the power in the blood of Jesus.

314. Every spirit of limitation flowing down from my family tree, die, in the name of Jesus.

315. Every financial handicap flowing down from my family tree, die, in the name of Jesus.

316. Every curse of untimely death flowing down from my family tree, break by the power in the blood of Jesus.

317. Blood of Jesus, scrub dirtiness off my blood line, in the name of Jesus.

318. Thou strongman supervising the woes in my family tree, fall to the ground and be buried, in the name of Jesus.

319. Every rage of witchcraft termites on my family tree, expire by fire, in the name of Jesus.

320. Angels of war, take hold of my family tree and shake off every defiling animal living on it, in the name of Jesus.

321. Let the purging fire of the Holy Ghost burn to ashes all satanic influences on my family tree, in the name of Jesus.

322. Every blood demon troubling my life, be cleared out by the blood of Jesus, in the name of Jesus.

323. Every generational liability troubling my life, get out of my life, in the name of Jesus.

324. Every storm of darkness raging against my family line, expire, in the name of Jesus.

325. Every drought attacking the leaves of my family tree, clear away, in the name of Jesus.

Bless God for His answers to your prayer.

Section Three

COMPLETE DELIVERANCE

CONFESSIONS

Philippians 2:9-11: Wherefore God also hath highly exalted him, and given him a name which is above every name: [10]That at the name of Jesus every knee should bow, of *things* in heaven, and *things* in earth, and *things* under the earth; [11]And *that* every tongue should confess that Jesus Christ *is* Lord, to the glory of God the Father.

Psalm 56:9: When I cry *unto thee*, then shall mine enemies turn back: this I know; for God *is* for me. **Psalms 18:37**: I have pursued min enemies, and overtaken them: neither did I turn again till they were consumed.

Obadiah 1:3-4: The pride of thine heart hath deceived thee, thou that dwellest in the clefts of the rock, whose habitation is high; that saith in his heart, Who shall bring me down to the ground? Though thou exalt thyself as the eagle, and though thou set thy nest among the stars, thence will I bring thee down, saith the LORD.

Isaiah 54:17: No weapon that is formed against thee shall prosper; and every tongue that shall rise against thee in judgment thou shalt condemn. This is the heritage of the servant of the LORD, and their righteousness if of me, saith the LORD.

Luke 10:19: Behold, I give unto you power to tread on serpents and scorpions, and over all the power of the enemy, and nothing shall by any means hurt you.

Jeremiah 1:19: And they shall fight against thee; but they shall not prevail against thee; for I am with thee, saith the LORD, to deliver thee.

Day One
Praise and worship

1. Thank the Lord for His power that is available to open your spiritual eyes.

2. Thank the Lord for the power in the blood of Jesus to save, to heal and to deliver.

3. Every doorway and ladder to satanic invasion in my life should be abolished forever by the Blood of Jesus.

4. I loose myself from curses, hexes, spells, bewitchments and evil domination directed against me through dreams in the name of Jesus.

2. I command you ungodly powers, release me in the name of Jesus.

3. Let all past satanic defeats in the dream be converted to victory, in the name of Jesus.

4. Let all test in the dream be converted to testimonies, in the name of Jesus.

5. Let all trials in the dream be converted to triumphs, in the name of Jesus.

6. Let all failures in the dream be converted to success, in the name of Jesus.

7. Let all scars in the dream be converted to stars, in the name of Jesus.

8. Let all bondage in the dream be converted to freedom in the name of Jesus.

9. Let all losses in the dream be converted to gains in the name of Jesus.

10. Let all opposition in the dream be converted to victory in the name of Jesus.

11. Let all weaknesses in the dream be converted to strength in the name of Jesus.

12. Let all negative in the dream be converted to positive, in the name of Jesus.

13. I release myself from every infirmity introduced into my life through dreams, in the name of Jesus.

14. Let all attempts by the enemy to deceive me through dreams fail woefully, in the name of Jesus.

15. I reject evil spiritual husband, wife, children, marriage, engagement, trading, pursuit, ornament, money, friend, relative, etc., in the name of Jesus.

16. Lord Jesus, wash my spiritual eyes, ears and mouth with Your blood.

17. The God who answereth by fire, answer by fire whenever any spiritual attacker comes against me, in the name of Jesus.

18. Lord Jesus, replace all satanic dreams with heavenly visions and divinely-inspired dreams.

19. Wonderful Lord, I reverse any defeat that I have ever suffered in the dream in the name of Jesus.

20. Any dream that I have dreamt that is good and for God, I receive it, and those that are satanic, I reject them, in the name of Jesus.

21. Every night and dream attacks and its consequences should be nullified, in the name of Jesus.

22. I claim freedom from satanic and restless dreams, in the name of Jesus.

23. I claim freedom from importing anxiety and shameful thoughts into my dream, in the name of Jesus.

24. I stand against dream defeats and its effects, in the name of Jesus.

25. Let all satanic designs of oppression against me in dreams and visions be frustrated, in the name of Jesus.

26. Let every demonic influence targeted at destroying my vision, dream and ministry receive total disappointment, in the name of Jesus.

27. Every witchcraft hand planting evil seeds in my life

through dream attacks, wither and burn to ashes, in the name of Jesus.

28. By the blood of Jesus, I rebuke all attacking and fearful dreams, in the name of Jesus.

29. Let the evil vision and dream on my life evaporate and condense in the camp of the enemy, in the name of Jesus.

30. Every cause of demotion in the dream in my life, be nullified by the blood of Jesus.

31. Every cause of confused and unprogressive dreams in my life, be nullified by the blood of Jesus.

32. Every cause of being harassed in the dreams by familiar faces in my life, be nullified by the blood of Jesus.

33. I send the arrows of any gun shot in the dream back to the senders, in the name of Jesus.

34. I paralyse all the night caterers and I forbid their foods in my dream, in the name of Jesus.

35. All pursuers in my dreams, begin to pursue yourself, in the name of Jesus.

36. Let all the contamination in my life through dreams be cleansed by the blood of Jesus.

37. I cancel every dream of backwardness, in the name of Jesus.

38. Every dream of demotions to junior school be dismantled. I shall go from glory to glory, in the name of Jesus.

39. By the power in the blood of Jesus, I cancel the maturity dates of any evil dreams with my life, in the name of Jesus.

40. You God of promotion, promote me beyond my wildest dreams, in the name of Jesus.

Day Two
Praise and worship

41. Every sickness planted in the dream into my life, get out now and go back to your sender, in the name of Jesus.

42. Let life be squeezed out of my dream attackers, in the name of Jesus.

43. By the power in the blood of Jesus, I command all my buried good dreams and visions to be exhumed, in the name of Jesus.

44. By the power in the blood of Jesus, I command all my polluted good dreams and visions to receive divine solution, in the name of Jesus.

45. By the power in the blood of Jesus, I command all dream and vision killers that are working against the manifestation of my good dreams and visions to be paralysed, in the name of Jesus.

46. By the power in the blood of Jesus, I command every good dream and vision that has been stolen away to be restored with fresh fire, in the name of Jesus.

47. By the power in the blood of Jesus, I command every good dream and vision that has been transferred to be restored with fresh fire, in the name of Jesus.

48. By the power in the blood of Jesus, I command every good dream and vision that has been poisoned to be neutralised, in the name of Jesus.

49. By the power in the blood of Jesus, I command every good dream and vision that has been amputated to receive divine strength, in the name of Jesus.

50. Let all the contamination in my life through dreams be cleansed by the blood of Jesus.

51. Any anti-progress material fired into my life through dreams, be nullified, in the name of Jesus.

52. I resist the threat of death in my dream by fire, in the name of Jesus.

53. Every evil dream that other people have had about me, I cancel them in the astral world, in the name of Jesus.

54. Every image of satan in my dream, I curse you to wither now, in the name of Jesus.

55. I command every dream of demotion to stop, in the name of Jesus.

56. Every arrow of death in the dream, come out and go back to your sender, in the name of Jesus.

57. Every sponsored dream of poverty by household wickedness against my life, vanish, in the name of Jesus.

58. I dash every poverty dreams to the ground, in the name of Jesus.

59. I cancel the manipulation of every satanic dream, in the name of Jesus.

60. You powers of the night, polluting my night dreams be paralysed, in the name of Jesus.

61. Every anti-prosperity dream, die, in the mighty name of Jesus.

62. Let all satanic designs of oppression against me in dreams and visions be frustrated, in the name of Jesus.

63. I paralyse the spirits that bring bad dreams to me, in the name of Jesus.

64. I cancel and wipe off all evil dreams, in the name of Jesus.

65. Let the blood of Jesus erase all evil dreams in my life, in the name of Jesus.

66. My dreams, my joys, my breakthroughs that have been buried in the dark world, be reversed now, in the name of Jesus.

67. Every dreaming serpent, go back to your sender, in the name of Jesus.

68. Every power planting affliction into my life in the dream, be buried alive, in the name of Jesus.

69. Any evil programme, programmed into my life from my dream, be dismantled now, in the name of Jesus.

70. I fire back every arrow of my family idols, in the name of Jesus.

71. Every evil power from my father's house, die, in the name of Jesus.

72. Every evil power from my mother's house, die, in the name of Jesus.

73. Let God arise and let stubborn problems die, in the name of Jesus.

74. Every cycle of hardship, break, in the name of Jesus.

75. Where is the Lord God of Elijah? Arise and manifest Your power, in the name of Jesus.

76. The voice of my enemy will not prevail over my destiny, in the name of Jesus.

77. Every terror of the night, scatter, in the name of Jesus.

78. Every witchcraft challenge of my destiny, die, in the name of Jesus.

79. Every seed of the enemy in my destiny, die, in the name of Jesus.

80. Every dream of demotion, die, in the name of Jesus.

Day Three
Prayer and Worship

81. Power of God, uproot wicked plantations from my life, in the name of Jesus.

82. Every destiny vulture, vomit my breakthroughs, in the name of Jesus.

83. Every evil power that pursued my parents, release me, in the name of Jesus.

84. I fire back every witchcraft arrow fired into my life as a baby, in the name of Jesus.

85. Fire of God, thunder of God, purse my pursuers, in the name of Jesus.

86. Holy Ghost fire, purge my blood from satanic injection, in the name of Jesus.

87. Every evil power of my father's house that will not let me go, die, in the name of Jesus.

88. Every power designed to spoil my life, scatter, in the name of Jesus.

89. Every herbal power working against my destiny, die, in the name of Jesus.

90. I kill every sickness in my life, in the name of Jesus.

91. Every power of the idols of my father's house, die, in the name of Jesus.

92. Every evil power pursuing me from my father's house, die, in the name of Jesus.

93. Every evil power pursuing me from my mother's house, die, in the name of Jesus.

94. Every witchcraft tree binding my placenta, die, in the name of Jesus.

95. Where is the Lord God of Elijah? Arise and fight for me, in the name of Jesus.

96. Every destiny-demoting dream, scatter, in the name of Jesus.

97. Every foundational bondage, break, in the name of Jesus.

98. Every dream sponsored by witchcraft, die, in the name of Jesus.

99. Every witchcraft vulture, vomit my destiny, in the name of Jesus.

100. I take authority over and order the binding of every strongman in every department of my life I bind and paralyse every strongman attached to any specific problem that I have, in the name of Jesus.

101. I withdraw all my properties in the possession of the strong man back, in the name of Jesus

102. I bind and paralyse every strong man of death and hell, in the name of Jesus.

103. I receive the mandate to release my children from the prison of any strong man, in the name of Jesus.

104. I release myself from the hold of any sexual strong man, in the name of Jesus.

105. You the strong man of my ancestors, release my blessings in your hands, in the name of Jesus

106. I take authority over and bind the strong man attached to the marriage department of my life, in the name of Jesus.

107. I bind every strong man from my father's and mother's sides attached to my marital life, in the name of Jesus.

108. I bind and paralyse every strong man of fear in my life, in the mighty name of Jesus

109. I take authority over and order the binding of the strong man of financial failure, in the name of Jesus.

110. I bind every strong man holding my privileges and rights captive, in the name of Jesus.

111. I bind, plunder and render to naught every strong man assigned to my . . . and marital life, in the name of Jesus.

112. Let all multiple strong men operating against me, be paralysed, in the name of Jesus. I bind the strong man attached to the life of . . . (mention the name of the person), from keeping him from receiving Jesus Christ as his Lord and Saviour, in the name of Jesus

113. I release myself from the hold of any evil strong man, in the name of Jesus.

114. I disgrace the strong man delegated by satan over my life, in the name of Jesus

115. You strong man of evil imagination paralysing the good things in my life, be paralysed, in the name of Jesus.

116. All the good thoughts that the strong man has paralysed in my life, receive life and be restored back into my life, in the name of Jesus

117. I bind, plunder and render to naught every strong man assigned to my womb, reproductive system and marital life, in the name of Jesus.

118. I bind the strong man behind my spiritual blindness and deafness and paralyse his operations in my life, in the name of Jesus.

119. Let the stubborn strong man delegated against me fall down to the ground and become impotent, in the name of Jesus.

120. Let the stubborn strong man delegated against me fall

down to the ground and become impotent, in the name of Jesus.

Day Four
Prayer and Worship

121. I bind the strongman over my life, in the name of Jesus.

122. I bind the strongman over my family, in the name of Jesus.

123. I bind the strongman over my blessings, in the name of Jesus.

124. I bind the strongman over my business, in the name of Jesus.

125. I bind and render useless every strongman assigned to my womb, reproductive system and marital life, in the name of Jesus.

126. I bind every strongman delegated to hinder my progress, in the name of Jesus

127. I bind and paralyse the strongman employed or delegated to disgrace me, in the name of Jesus.

128. Let the backbone of the strongman in charge of each problem be broken, in the name of Jesus.

129. Let the stubborn strongman delegated against me and my career fall down to the ground and become impotent, in the name of Jesus.

130. Let the stubborn strongman delegated against me fall down to the ground and become impotent, in the name of Jesus.

131. Any satanic strong man keeping my blessing as his goods, fall down and die. I recover my goods back now, in the name of Jesus.

132. You, the strong man of body destruction, lose your hold over my body, fall down and die, in the name of Jesus.

133. Every demon, strong man and associated spirits of financial collapse, receive the hailstones fire and be roasted beyond remedy, in the name of Jesus.

134. Let the finger of God unseat my household strong man, in the name of Jesus.

135. I bind the strong man in my life, and I clear my goods from your possession, in the name of Jesus.

136. You strong man of body destruction, be bound, in the name of Jesus.

137. You strong man of mind destruction, be bound, in the name of Jesus.

138. You strong man of financial destruction, be bound, in the name of Jesus.

139. Every strong man of bad luck attached to my life, fall down and die, in the name of Jesus.

140. I bind every strong man having my goods in his possessions, in the name of Jesus.

141. I bind and paralyse every strongman of death and hell, in the name of Jesus.

142. You evil strongman attached to my destiny, be bound, in the name of Jesus.

143. I paralyse every territorial strong man operating evil programme in _ _ _ hospital or clinic, in the name of Jesus.

144. I bind and plunder the goods of every strong man attached to my marriage, in the name of Jesus.

145. Let the stubborn strong man delegated against me and my career fall down to the ground and become impotent, in the name of Jesus.

146. Let the stubborn strongman delegated against me fall down to the ground and become impotent, in the name of Jesus.

147. I release my money from the house of the strong man, in the name of Jesus.

148. I bind every strong man delegated to hinder my progress, in the name of Jesus.

149. Every strong man of my father's house, die, in the name of Jesus.

150. Every strong man assigned by the evil powers of my father's house against my life, die, in the name of Jesus.

151. I consume the shrine of strong man in my family with the fire of God, in the name of Jesus.

152. The strong man from my father's side, the strong man from my mother's side, begin to destroy yourselves in the name of Jesus.

153. You strong man of body destruction lose your hold over my body, fall down and die, in the name of Jesus.

154. Every demon, strong man and associated spirits of financial collapse, receive the hailstones fire and be roasted beyond remedy, in the name of Jesus.

155. Let the finger of God unseat my household strong man, in the name of Jesus.

156. I bind the strong man in my life, and I clear my goods from your possession, in the name of Jesus.

157. You strong man of mind destruction, be bound, in the name of Jesus.

158. You strong man of financial destruction, be bound, in the name of Jesus.

159. Every strong man of bad luck attached to my life, fall down and die, in the name of Jesus.

Day Five

Praise and Worship

160. I bind every strong man militating against my home, in the name of Jesus.

161. I bind and paralyse every strong man of death and hell, in the name of Jesus.

162. You evil strong man attached to my destiny, be bound, in the name of Jesus.

163. Every strong man of my father's house, die, in the name of Jesus.

164. Every strong man assigned by the evil powers of my father's house against my life, die, in the name of Jesus.

165. Every strong man assigned to weaken my faith, catch fire, in the name of Jesus.

166. I bind and I render to nothing all the strong men that are currently troubling my life, in the name of Jesus.

167. Let the backbone of the stubborn pursuer and strong man break, in the name of Jesus.

168. I bind every strongman having my goods in his possessions, in the name of Jesus.

169. I clear my goods from the warehouse of the strong man, in the name of Jesus.

170. I withdraw the staff of the office of the strong man delegated against me, in the name of Jesus.

171. I bind every strong man delegated to hinder my progress, in the name of Jesus.

172. I bind the strong man behind my spiritual blindness and deafness and paralyse his operations in my life, in the name of Jesus.

173. Let the stubborn strong man delegated against me fall down to the ground and become impotent, in the name of Jesus.

174. I command the armour of the strong man to be roasted completely, in the name of Jesus.

175. I release myself from the hold of any religious spirit strong man, in the name of Jesus.

176. Every power siting on my divine promotion, clear away, in the name of Jesus.

177. My glory, my head, arise and shine, in the name of Jesus.

178. Every strong man behind poison of darkness in my body, come out now, in the name of Jesus.

179. Let the altars of affliction of the strong man assigned against my life, catch fire, in the name of Jesus.

180. Every strong man behind stubborn problems in my life, die, in the name of Jesus.

181. Every power behind the strong man of persistent problems in my life, die, in the name of Jesus.

182. Every strong man behind yokes acquired in the dreams, die, in the name of Jesus.

183. Every strong man behind plantation of infirmity in my family, die, in the name of Jesus.

184. Every strong man behind mocking yokes in my life, die, in the name of Jesus.

185. Let the habitation of cruelty assigned against me by the strong man of my father's house die, in the name of Jesus.

186. Every strange garment put on my spiritual body by the strong man, catch fire, in the name of Jesus.

187. Angels of God, gather your arrows and attack every strong man attached to my destiny, in the name of Jesus.

188. Every witchcraft judgement against me, scatter, in the name of Jesus.

189. Demonic pillars supporting every strong man assigned to my life, crumble, in the name of Jesus.

190. I will not die before my glory appears, in the name of Jesus.

191. Let the power in the name of Jesus, the name that is higher than all names, wipe out evil names of the strong man, in the name of Jesus.

192. Every witchcraft operation during my naming ceremony, die, in the name of Jesus.

193. I soak my name in the blood of Jesus.

194. I receive power to divide my Red Sea, in the name of Jesus.

195. After the order of Daniel, O Lord, deliver me from satanic lions, in the name of Jesus.

196. Thou altar of affliction, die, in the name of Jesus.

197. Power to be singled out for favour, fall upon me now, in the name of Jesus.

198. Every wicked conspiracy against my God-given dream, scatter, in the name of Jesus.

199. Every decision to slay me because of my dreams and vision, backfire, in the name of Jesus.

Day Six

Praise and Worship

200. In the presence of those saying, "We shall see what will become of his dreams," the God of Joseph shall land me on the throne, in the name of Jesus.

201. You wicked conspirators, wait and see what shall become of my dreams; my God shall arise on my behalf, in the name of Jesus.

202. By the power that made the boasts of Joseph's brothers expire, O Lord, complete your work in my life, in the name of Jesus.

203. You enemies of progress breathing fire against the pregnancy of God for my life, expire, in the name of Jesus.

204. The dream of God for my life shall not be slaughtered. O God, arise and manifest my dreams in full, in the name of Jesus.

205. My cry, provoke angelic violence against strongmen assigned to my life, in the name of Jesus.

206. Every plantation of failure in my foundation, die, in the name of Jesus.

207. Foundational witchcraft yoke, break, in the name of Jesus.

208. Every negative power flowing from my foundation to kill my destiny, die, in the name of Jesus.

209. Every dog of witchcraft barking against me, die, in the name of Jesus.

210. Every altar of witchcraft, I tear you down, in the name of Jesus.
211. Every assembly of witchcraft working against me, scatter, in the name of Jesus.
212. Every seed of witchcraft in my life, die, in the name of Jesus.
213. Every dream sponsored by witchcraft, die, in the name of Jesus.
214. Every power troubling my star, die, in the name of Jesus.
215. I declare war on every enchantment, in the name of Jesus.
216. Confidence of the wicked, be broken, in the name of Jesus.
217. Every serpent and scorpion of affliction, die, in the name of Jesus.
218. Every wicked plantation in the garden of my life, die, in the name of Jesus.
219. Every evil association working against me, O Lord, thunder upon them, in the name of Jesus.
220. I go from strength to strength by the power in the blood of Jesus.
221. Every evil power summoning my spirit, die, in the name of Jesus.
222. Every root of witchcraft in my family line, die, in the name of Jesus.
223. Every communal bondage limiting my breakthroughs, die, in the name of Jesus.

224. Every spell and enchantment, clear off, in the name of Jesus.

225. Every evil malpractice over my family, be crushed, in the name of Jesus.

226. Every witchcraft-marine power, be crushed to pieces, in the name of Jesus.

227. Every witchcraft agenda in my life, be destroyed, in the name of Jesus.

228. Every power using my life as a dumping bin, scatter, in the name of Jesus.

229. Every resurrection of affliction, die, in the name of Jesus.

230. Every evil game plan over my success, die, in the name of Jesus.

231. Every manufacturer of yokes, die, in the name of Jesus.

232. Every pregnancy of sorrow and setbacks, die, in the name of Jesus.

233. Every demonic setup against me, scatter, in the name of Jesus.

234. Every satanic imprisonment over my life, break away, in the name of Jesus.

235. Every satanic remote control against me, catch fire, in the name of Jesus.

236. Every power sponsoring repeated problems in my life, die, in the name of Jesus.

237. Let the voice of destruction be heard in the camp of every oppressor, in the name of Jesus.

238. Every wicked spirit working against my family, loose your hold and die, in the name of Jesus.

239. Let every satanic manipulating altars and their attending priests scatter, in the name of Jesus.

Day Seven

Praise and Worship

240. Every satanic yoke in my life, break, in the name of Jesus.

241. Every evil load heaped on my progress, clear away, in the name of Jesus.

242. Every satanic prayer against my destiny, scatter, in the name of Jesus.

243. Every evil-hindering-force militating against me, scatter by fire, in the name of Jesus.

244. Every witchcraft padlock hanging against my life, be smashed to pieces, in the name of Jesus.

245. Every witchcraft engagement over my success, break, in the name of Jesus.

246. Every demonic claim on my life, break, in the name of Jesus.

247. Every power of stagnation and limitation over my life, be destroyed, in the name of Jesus.

248. Every tree of failure in my lineage, be cut off, in the name of Jesus.

249. Every pin-up of witchcraft in my family, be destroyed, in the name of Jesus.

250. Every evil covenant working against me, break, in the name of Jesus.

251. Every witchcraft agenda for my life, be frustrated, in the name of Jesus.

252. Every witchcraft register bearing my name, catch fire, in the name of Jesus.

253. Every evil document against my life, be consumed by fire, in the name of Jesus.

254. Every evil informant assigned against my life, fall down and die, in the name of Jesus.

255. Every evil image carved in my name, catch fire, in the name of Jesus.

256. Every witchcraft authority over my life, break, in the name of Jesus.

257. Every evil tree planted against my freedom, be uprooted, in the name of Jesus.

258. Every curse of limitation in my life, be destroyed by fire, in the name of Jesus.

259. Every satanic road block, clear off by fire, in the name of Jesus.

260. Every millipede concoction working against my life, die, in the name of Jesus.

261. Every Beelzebub web cast over my life, clear off, in the name of Jesus.

262. Every satanic prophecy against my destiny, be nullified, in the name of Jesus.

263. Every witchcraft concourse against my life, crush to pieces, in the name of Jesus.

264. Every backbone of disfavour, break, in the name of Jesus.

265. I crush every witchcraft lion roaring against my favour, in the name of Jesus.

266. Every gate of evil delay, be broken, in the name of Jesus.

267. Every chain and shackle of limitation upon my life, break, in the name of Jesus.

268. Disappeared helpers, reappear to move my destiny forward, in the name of Jesus.

269. I stop my stoppers by fire, in the name of Jesus.

270. God arise and set my feet in a large room, in the name of Jesus.

271. Thou power of vain-labour, die, in the name of Jesus.

272. Every power wasting my efforts, die, in the name of Jesus.

273. Power of hard-labour assigned against my life, die, in the name of Jesus.

274. Anointing for turn-around breakthroughs, come upon my life, in the name of Jesus.

275. Thou mantle of divine accelerator, fall upon my life, in the name of Jesus.

276. God arise and confound the wicked, in the name of Jesus.

277. God, arise and ordain terrifying noises against my oppressors, in the name of Jesus.

278. Power-base of witchcraft in my place of birth, die, in the name of Jesus.

279. Every witchcraft meeting summoned for my sake, scatter, in the name of Jesus.

Day Eight

Praise and Worship

280. Every agent of darkness peeping into the spiritual world against me, receive blindness, in the name of Jesus.

281. God, arise and cut off every agent of darkness calling my life into any cauldron, in the name of Jesus.

282. Thou power of God, locate and destroy every spiritual pot assigned against my life, in the name of Jesus.

283. Every astral projection against my life, I cut you off, in the name of Jesus.

284. Creation, arise in battle against every agent of darkness attached to my life, in the name of Jesus.

285. Foundational yokes, foundational bondage, break, in the name of Jesus.

286. Foundation of marital distress, break, in the name of Jesus.

287. Every embargo on my glory from the womb, die, in the name of Jesus.

288. By the power that sank Pharaoh, let my stubborn problems, die, in the name of Jesus.

289. By the power that disgraced Goliath, let my stubborn problems, die, in the name of Jesus.

290. Holy Ghost fire, arise, attack my mountain, in the name of Jesus.

291. Every witchcraft incantation against my destiny, die, in the name of Jesus.

292. Every trouble of the night, bow to the name of Jesus.

293. Angels of God, scatter all those plotting against my destiny, in the name of Jesus.

294. Every demonic dragon working against my life, die, in the name of Jesus.

295. Thou terror of the night, scatter before me, in the name of Jesus.

296. I have dominion over every satanic challenge, in the name of Jesus.

297. I confront every witchcraft challenge by the power of God, in the name of Jesus.

298. Thou oppressor and thy weapons, drown in your own Red Sea, in the name of Jesus.

299. I cancel every weapon of discouragement, in the name of Jesus.

300. Holy Ghost, arise and link me with those who will bless me, in the name of Jesus.

301. Fire of God, shatter blindness and darkness in my life, in the name of Jesus.

302. My body, refuse to cooperate with every arrow of darkness, in the name of Jesus.

303. Every witchcraft broom sweeping away my blessings, die, in the name of Jesus.

304. Every yoke manufacturer, die with your yoke, in the name of Jesus.

305. Every satanic investment in my life, be wasted, in the name of Jesus.

306. Let my life experience divine acceleration, in the name of Jesus.

307. Satanic agenda for my life, vanish, in the name of Jesus.

308. Every satanic pregnancy for my life, die, in the name of Jesus.

309. Let my environment become too hot for any private enemy, in the name of Jesus.

310. Let all friendly witchcraft powers be exposed and disgraced, in the name of Jesus.

311. Every cooperation from the spirit of darkness around me, scatter, in the name of Jesus.

312. Lord, let Your light expose every hidden evil structure planted around me.

313. I shall arise and go forth, in the name of Jesus.

314. Any evil tree planted around me, be uprooted, in the name of Jesus.

315. I dismantle the powers stealing from the garden of my life, in the name of Jesus.

316. Every veil of darkness, be roasted by the fire of God, in the name of Jesus.

317. Let the power source of unfriendly friends be dissolved by the fire of God, in the name of Jesus.

318. I shake off any evil thing deposited into my body by friendly enemies, in the name of Jesus.

319. O God, arise in Your power and confuse my close oppressors, in the name of Jesus.

Day Nine

Praise and Worship

320. Lord, plant Your warring angels around me to dismantle and destroy evil stronghold of internal witchcraft.

321. Let my enemies make mistakes that would advance my course, in the name of Jesus.

322. Anything that the Father has not planted in my immediate environment, be uprooted, in the name of Jesus.

323. Listen to me satan, I plead the blood of Jesus over this environment.

324. Lord, take absolute control over my body, soul and spirit.

325. Lord Jesus, I surrendered every part of my life to You.

326. I receive the anointing of the warrior to drink the blood f the enemy, in the name of Jesus.

327. I charge my spiritual battle by the fire of the Holy Ghost, in the name of Jesus.

328. I challenge and destroy every satanic operation against my prayer life, in the name of Jesus.

329. I reject every involvement of the flesh and satan in my prayer, in the name of Jesus.

330. God, arise and let every evil presence around me scatter, in the name of Jesus.

331. Every power blocking me from the will of God, fall down and die, in the name of Jesus.

332. I pull down every stubborn stronghold protecting my enemy, in the name of Jesus.

333. I arrest every spirit of confusion by fire, in the name of Jesus.

334. I bring the blood of Jesus between me and the powers of darkness, in the name of Jesus.

335. Every problem (name it) harassing my life, I break your backbone by fire, in the name of Jesus.

336. I release myself from every evil spirit behind the problem, in the name of Jesus.

337. Let the backbone of the strongman in charge of each problem be broken, in the name of Jesus.

338. Every evil inflame fueling my problem, be disgraced by the blood of Jesus.

339. I command every evil monitoring spirit to leave me now, in the name of Jesus.

340. I renounce satan and his host and declare them to be my enemies, in the name of Jesus.

341. I exercise my authority over stubborn witchcraft and I pull down their structures, in the name of Jesus.

342. Listen to me satan, because of the blood of Jesus, you have no more power over me, no more place in me, in the name of Jesus.

343. I place the blood of Jesus upon myself and my family, in the name of Jesus.

344. I draw the bloodline of the Lord Jesus Christ around all my possessions, in the name of Jesus.

345. I draw the bloodline of Jesus around all my possessions and property, in the name of Jesus.

346. Rock of Ages, smash to pieces every foundation of witchcraft in my family, in the name of Jesus.

347. Let witchcraft powers eat their own flesh and drink their own blood, in the name of Jesus.

348. Every seat of witchcraft, receive the thunder fire of God, in the name of Jesus.

349. Let the habitation of witchcraft powers be desolate, in the name of Jesus.

350. Every throne of witchcraft, be dismantled by fire, in the name of Jesus.

351. Let the stronghold of witchcraft powers be pulled down by fire, in the name of Jesus.

352. Let the refuge of witchcraft powers be pulled down by fire, in the name of Jesus.

353. Let the network of witchcraft disintegrate, in the name of Jesus.

354. Let the communication systems of witchcraft powers, be destroyed by fire, in the name of Jesus.
355. Every transportation system of witchcraft powers, be destroyed by fire, in the name of Jesus.
356. Let the weapons of witchcraft powers turn against them, in the name of Jesus.
357. I withdraw my blessings from every bank or strongroom of the enemy, in the name of Jesus.
358. Altar of witchcraft, break, in the name of Jesus.
359. Every witchcraft padlock fashioned against me, break by fire, in the name of Jesus.

Day Ten

Praise and Worship

360. Every trap of witchcraft, catch your owners, in Jesus' name.
361. Every witchcraft utterance and projection made against me, be overthrown, in the name of Jesus.
362. I reverse every witchcraft burial fashioned against me, in the name of Jesus.
363. I deliver my soul from every witchcraft bewitchment, in the name of Jesus.
364. I reverse the effect of every witchcraft summoning of my spirit, in the name of Jesus.
365. Every witchcraft identification mark, be wiped off by the blood of Jesus.

366. I frustrate every witchcraft exchange of my virtues, in the name of Jesus.

367. Let the blood of Jesus block the flying route of witchcraft powers targeted against me.

368. Let every witchcraft curse break and be destroyed, in the name of Jesus.

369. Every covenant of witchcraft, melt by the blood of Jesus.

370. I withdraw every organ of my body from any witchcraft altar, in the name of Jesus.

371. Anything planted in my life by witchcraft, come out and die, in the name of Jesus.

372. Let the blood of Jesus cancel every witchcraft initiation fashioned against my destiny, in the name of Jesus.

373. Every witchcraft poison, be destroyed, in the name of Jesus.

374. I reverse every witchcraft pattern fashioned against my destiny, in the name of Jesus.

375. Every witchcraft cage fashioned against my life, be destroyed, in the name of Jesus.

376. Let every problem in my life that originated from witchcraft, receive divine and instant solution, in the name of Jesus.

377. I command all the damages done to my life by witchcraft to be repaired, in the name of Jesus.

378. Let every blessing confiscated by witchcraft spirits be released in the name of Jesus.

379. Every witchcraft power assigned against my life and marriage, receive .... (pick from the under listed), in the name of Jesus.

    - The thunder and lightning of God
    - Unbearable heat - raging fire
    - Hail and fire mingled with the blood of the Lamb
    - Concentrated acid
    - Continuous plagues
    - Destroying flood
    - Destruction
    - Failure
    - Confusion

380. I loose myself from any power of witchcraft, in the name of Jesus.

381. Every camp of witchcraft gathered against my prosperity, fall down and die, in the name of Jesus.

382. Every witchcraft pot working against me, I bring the judgment of God against you, in the name of Jesus.

383. I command every witchcraft pot using remote control against my health to be broken into pieces, in the name of Jesus.

384. Witchcraft opposition, receive the rain of affliction, in the name of Jesus.

385. Let the spirit of witchcraft attack the familiar spirits fashioned against me, in the name of Jesus.

386. I retrieve my integrity out of the hands of household witchcraft, in the name of Jesus.

387. I break the power of the occult, witchcraft and familiar spirits over my life, in the name of Jesus.

388. In the name of Jesus, I break and loose myself from all evil curses, chains, spells, jinxes, bewitchments, witchcraft or sorcery which may have been put upon me.

389. Let the thunder of God locate and dismantle the throne of witchcraft in my household, in the name of Jesus.

390. Let every seat of witchcraft in my household be roasted by the fire of God, in the name of Jesus.

391. Let the altar of witchcraft in my household be roasted, in the name of Jesus.

392. Let the thunder of God scatter beyond redemption, the foundation of witchcraft in my household, in the name of Jesus.

393. Every stronghold of refuge of my household witches, be destroyed, in the name of Jesus.

394. Every hiding place and secret place of witchcraft in my family, be exposed by fire, in the name of Jesus.

395. Let every local and international witchcraft network of my household witches, be shattered to pieces, in the name of Jesus.

396. Let the communication system of my household witches be frustrated, in the name of Jesus.

397. Let the terrible fire of God consume the transportation of my household witchcraft, in the name of Jesus.

398. Every agent ministering at the altar of witchcraft in my household, fall down and die, in the name of Jesus.

399. Let the thunder and the fire of God, locate the storehouses and strong rooms of the household witchcraft harbouring my blessings, and pull them down, in the name of Jesus.

Day Eleven

Praise and Worship

400. Let any witchcraft curse working against me be revoked by the blood of Jesus.

401. Every decision, vow and covenant of household witchcraft affecting me, be nullified by the blood of Jesus.

402. I destroy with the fire of God, every weapon of witchcraft used against me, in the name of Jesus.

403. Any material taken from my body and now placed on a witchcraft altar, be roasted by the fire of God, in the name of Jesus.

404. I reverse every witchcraft burial fashioned against me, in the name of Jesus.

405. Every trap set for me by witches, begin to catch your owners, in the name of Jesus.

406. Every witchcraft padlock fashioned against any area of my life, be roasted, in the name of Jesus.

407. Let the wisdom of household witches be converted to foolishness, in the name of Jesus.

408. Let the wickedness of household enemies overtake them, in the name of Jesus.

409. I deliver my soul from every witchcraft bewitchment, in the name of Jesus.

410. Any witchcraft bird flying for my sake, fall down, die and be roasted to ashes, in the name of Jesus.

411. Any of my blessings traded with by household witches, be returned to me, in the name of Jesus.

412. Any of my blessings and testimonies swallowed by witches, be converted to hot coals of fire of God and be vomited, in the name of Jesus.

413. I break myself loose from every bondage of witchcraft covenants, in the name of Jesus.

414. Any witchcraft coven where any of my blessings are hidden, be roasted by the fire of God, in the name of Jesus.

415. (Lay your right hand on your head) Every witchcraft spirit plantation, pollution, deposit and material in my body, melt by the fire of God and be flushed out by the blood of Jesus.

416. Every witchcraft hand planting evil seeds in my life through dream attacks, wither and burn to ashes, in the name of Jesus.

417. Every witchcraft hand planting evil seeds in my life through dream attacks, wither and burn to ashes, in the name of Jesus.

418. Every witchcraft obstacle put on the road to my desired miracle and success, be removed by the east wind of God, in the name of Jesus.

419. Every witchcraft chant, spell and projection made against me, I bind you and turn you against your owner, in the name of Jesus.

420. I frustrate every plot, device, scheme and project of witchcraft designed to affect any area of my life, in the name of Jesus.

421. Any witch projecting himself into the body of any animal in order to do me harm, be trapped in the body of such an animal forever, in the name of Jesus.

422. Any drop of my blood sucked by any witch, be vomited now, in the name of Jesus.

423. Any part of me shared out amongst household/ village witches, I recover you, in the name of Jesus.

424. Any organ of my body that has been exchanged for another through witchcraft operation, be replaced now, in the name of Jesus.

425. I recover any of my virtues/ blessings shared out amongst village/ household witches, in the name of Jesus.

426. I reverse the evil effect of any witchcraft invocation or summoning of my spirit, in the name of Jesus.

427. I loose my hands and feet from any witchcraft bewitchment or bondage, in the name of Jesus.

428. Let the blood of Jesus wash away every witchcraft identification mark on me or on any of my properties, in the name of Jesus.

429. I forbid any re-union or re-gathering of household and village witches against my life, in the name of Jesus.

430. Let the entire body system of my household witches begin to run amok until they confess all their wickedness, in the name of Jesus.

431. Let the mercies of God be withdrawn from them, in the name of Jesus.

432. Let them begin to grope in the daytime as in the thickness of a dark night, in the name of Jesus.

433. Let everything that has ever worked for them begin to work against them, in the name of Jesus.

434. Let them not have a cloth to cover their shame, in the name of Jesus.

435. Let as many of them that are stubbornly unrepentant, be smitten by the sun in the day and by the moon, in the night, in the name of Jesus.

436. Let each step they take lead them to greater destruction, in the name of Jesus.

437. But as for me, let me dwell in the hollow of God's hand, in the name of Jesus.

438. Let the goodness and mercies of God overwhelm me now, in the name of Jesus.

439. Any witchcraft operation under any water against my life, receive immediate judgment of fire, in the name of Jesus.

Day Twelve

Praise and Worship

440. Every witchcraft power, that has introduced spirit husband/ wife or child into my dreams, be roasted by fire, in the name of Jesus.

441. Every agent of witchcraft power, posing as my husband/ wife or child in my dreams, be roasted by fire, in the name of Jesus.

442. Every agent of witchcraft power, physically attached to my marriage to frustrate it, fall down now and perish, in the name of Jesus.

443. Every agent of witchcraft power, assigned to attack my finances through dream, fall down and perish, in the name of Jesus.

444. Let the thunderbolts of God, locate and destroy every witchcraft power coven, where deliberations and decisions were fashioned against me, in the name of Jesus.

445. Any water spirit from my village or place of birth, practicing witchcraft against me and my family, be amputated by the word of God, in the name of Jesus.

446. Any power of witchcraft, holding any of my blessings in bondage, receive the fire of God and release them, in the name of Jesus.

447. I loose my mind and soul, from the bondage of marine witches, in the name of Jesus.

448. Any witchcraft power chain, binding my hands and feet from prospering, be shattered to pieces, in the name of Jesus.

449. Every arrow, shot into my life from under any water through witchcraft, come out of me and go back to your sender, in the name of Jesus.

450. Any evil material, transferred into my body through contact with any witchcraft agent, roast by fire, in the name of Jesus.

451. Any evil done against me through witchcraft oppression or manipulation, be reversed by the blood of Jesus.

452. I bind every witchcraft control and mind-blinding spirit, in the name of Jesus.

453. I cast out every witchcraft arrow affecting my senses (sight, smell, taste, hearing), in the name of Jesus.

454. I command every witchcraft arrow to depart from my- spinal cord - spleen - navel - heart   -   throat - eyes - head

455. Let the blood of Jesus purge me of every witchcraft contaminating material, in the name of Jesus.

456. I destroy the hand of any witch-doctor working against me, in the name of Jesus.

457. Every witchcraft spirit attempting to build a wall against my destiny, fall down and die, in the name of Jesus.

458. I send the rain of affliction upon every witchcraft power working against me, in the name of Jesus.

459. Sun, moon, stars, earth, water and the elements, vomit every enchantment that is against me, in the name of Jesus.

460. Every power using the heavenlies against me, fall down and be disgraced, in the name of Jesus.

461. Let the stars of heaven begin to fight for me, in the name of Jesus.

462. God, arise and scatter every conspiracy in the heavenlies that is against me, in the name of Jesus.

463. I break with the blood of Jesus all evil soul-ties affecting my life, in the name of Jesus.

464. Spirit of the living God, come upon my life and place a shield of protection around me, in the name of Jesus.

465. Every chain of inherited witchcraft in my family, break, in the name of Jesus.

466. Every ladder used by witchcraft against me, be roasted, in the name of Jesus.

467. Any door that I have opened to witchcraft in any area of my life, be closed for ever by the blood of Jesus.

468. I revoke every witchcraft verdict on my marital life, in the name of Jesus.

469. I send confusion into the camp of household witchcraft, in the name of Jesus.

470. Stubborn witchcraft, release me, in the name of Jesus.

471. Every witchcraft power working against my destiny, fall down and die, in the name of Jesus.

472. Every incantation, ritual and witchcraft power against my destiny, fall down and die, in the name of Jesus.

473. I break the power of the occult, witchcraft and familiar spirits over my life, in the name of Jesus.

474. Witchcraft opposition, receive the rain of affliction, in the name of Jesus.

475. I cancel every witchcraft verdict against my life, in the name of Jesus.

476. I command every arrow of witchcraft in my life: Come out with all your roots, in the name of Jesus. (Lay your hands on your stomach and pray aggressively).

477. I command every witchcraft pot, using remote control against my health to be broken into pieces, in the name of Jesus.

478. I rebuke the spell of any witchcraft pot from my neck, in the name of Jesus.

479. I break every witchcraft pot over my life, in the name of Jesus.

Day Thirteen

Praise and Worship

480. Every council of witchcraft working against me will not prosper, in the name of Jesus.

481. I disentangle myself and my family from every witchcraft cage and pot, in the name of Jesus.

482. I retrieve my integrity from the hands of household witchcraft, in the name of Jesus.

483. Every witchcraft hand, planting evil seeds in my life through dream attacks, wither and burn to ashes, in the name of Jesus.

484. Let all friendly witchcraft powers be exposed and disgraced, in the name of Jesus.

485. Lord, plant your warring angels around me to dismantle and destroy evil stronghold of internal witchcraft, in the name of Jesus.

486. I exercise my authority, over stubborn witchcraft and I pull down its structure, in the name of Jesus.

487. Every placental witchcraft targeted against my destiny, what are you waiting for? Die, in the name of Jesus.

488. Placental witchcraft, manipulating my destiny, die, in the name of Jesus.

489. Every blessing that I have lost through placental witchcraft, I repossess you, in the name of Jesus.

490. Every witchcraft coven and marine banks, release my placenta, in the name of Jesus.

491. Every cage of family witchcraft, release my divine partner, in the name of Jesus.

492. Oh Lord, let my dreams and visions, reject every witchcraft projection, in the name of Jesus.

493. Satanic investments in the foundation of my life, die, in the name of Jesus.

494. Hidden childhood poisons polluting my life, catch fire, in the name of Jesus.

495. Every tree that God the Father has not planted into my life, die, in the name of Jesus.

496. Let the consequences of satanic hands that carried me as a baby expire, in the name of Jesus.

497. Placental bondage, break by fire, in the name of Jesus.

498. My Father, walk to my childhood days and purge my life, in the name of Jesus.

499. Satanic seeds in my foundation, die, in the name of Jesus.

500. Serpents and scorpions planted by childhood polygamous witchcraft, die, in the name of Jesus.

501. Glory killers entrenched into my foundation, die, in the name of Jesus.

502. Blood of Jesus, arise in Your cleansing power and wash my roots, in the name of Jesus.

503. Every power of Herod tracing my star, I bury you now, in the name of Jesus.

504. Yokes buried inside the foundation of my life, break, in the name of Jesus.

505. Any problem buried in my childhood to pollute my future, die, in the name of Jesus.

506. Foundational failure magnet, catch fire, in the name of Jesus.

507. Plantations of darkness troubling my star, roast by fire, in the name of Jesus.

508. Anti-focus power troubling my destiny, die, in the name of Jesus.

509. Power to interpret the language of my star, come upon me now, in the name of Jesus.

510. Power to read the handwriting of my star in the heavenlies, fall upon me, in the name of Jesus.

511. Angels of the living God, possess my heavens, in the name of Jesus.

512. Angels of light, arise and fill my dark night, in the name of Jesus.

513. Angels of the living God, arise, fight and recover my high places, in the name of Jesus.

514. Lord Jesus, walk back into my childhood and correct my foundations, in the name of Jesus.

515. Every satanic plantation in my childhood, be dissolved by the fire of the Holy Ghost, in the name of Jesus.

516. Every effect of any bad thing I have swallowed or eaten as a child, be nullified, in the name of Jesus.

517. Powers assigned to capture my star, loose your hold, in the name of Jesus.

518. Any seed of wickedness planted in my childhood, Holy Ghost fire, dissolve it, in the name of Jesus.

519. Powers planted in my childhood to trouble my future, hear the word of the Lord. The Lord will cause dryness to come upon you today, in the name of Jesus.

520. Powers planted in my childhood to trouble my future, I dry up your river, even as Jordan was dried up, in the name of Jesus.

Day Fourteen

Praise and Worship

521. Powers planted in my childhood to trouble my future, I dry up your roots, even as the Lord caused the fig tree to dry up, in the name of Jesus.

522. Powers planted in my childhood to trouble my future, I knock down your gates, in the name of Jesus.

523. Powers planted in my childhood to trouble my future, I break in pieces your gates of brass, in the name of Jesus.

524. Powers planted in my childhood to trouble my future, I cut asunder your brass of iron, in the name of Jesus.

525. Powers planted in my childhood to trouble my future, I break down your walls, even as the walls of Jericho was broken down, in the name of Jesus.

526. Powers planted in my childhood to trouble my future, I cut off your cords and I cast them away, in the name of Jesus.
527. Powers planted in my childhood to trouble my future, I command you to bend your knee to Jesus.
528. Powers planted in my childhood to trouble my future, I put a cord around your tongue, in the name of Jesus.
529. Powers planted in my childhood, to trouble my future, I put a thorn in your jaw, in the name of Jesus.
530. Powers planted in my childhood to trouble my future, I take away your throne, in the name of Jesus.
531. Powers planted in my childhood to trouble my future, I command you to sit in the dust, in the name of Jesus.
532. I break all curses or iniquities coming down my family line, in the name of Jesus.
533. I destroy the spiritual embargo on my mother's side and on my father's side, 10 generations backward, in the name of Jesus.
534. Any dark covenant with my place of birth, break, in the name of Jesus.
535. Every power of Ichabod upon my destiny, die, in the name of Jesus.
536. Every problem tormenting my glory, die, in the name of Jesus.
537. My legs, reject backwardness, in the name of Jesus.
538. The glory of my life stolen in the womb, I recover you by fire, in the name of Jesus.

539. Glory manipulators and glory robbers, let me go, in the name of Jesus.

540. Yoke magnetisers, hear the word of the Lord: Die, in the name of Jesus.

541. My days shall not be restless but shall be called the days of the Lord, in the name of Jesus.

542. Any good thing that died in my life when I was ignorant, come alive now, in the name of Jesus.

543. My eyes, open to see what God is doing, in the name of Jesus.

544. "I am that I am", arise and manifest Your power in my life and move me to my next level, in the name of Jesus.

545. Lord, I plug my destiny to the socket of the Holy Ghost to receive divine elevation, in the name of Jesus.

546. Lord, I plug my life to the socket of the Holy Ghost to receive divine acceleration, in the name of Jesus.

547. I mount on the horse of war and ride into the land of my breakthroughs, in the name of Jesus.

548. Hammer of God, break every evil leg walking against my elevation, in the name of Jesus.

549. Heavenly carpenter, nail to death every spiritual robber assigned against my elevation, in the name of Jesus.

550. All evil spirits in the air working against my elevation, scatter unto desolation, in the name of Jesus.

551. All evil spirits in the wind hindering the move of my progress, scatter unto desolation, in the name of Jesus.

552. All evil spirits in the water blocking steps to my elevation, scatter, in the name of Jesus.

553. All satanic forces assigned against my elevation, scatter, in the name of Jesus.

554. Every satanic law programmed against my elevation, die, in the name of Jesus.

555. Every ancestral law programmed into the heavenlies against my elevation, die, in the name of Jesus.

556. O god, arise and use every weapon at Your disposal to disgrace the enemies of my elevation, in the name of Jesus.

557. All evil wishes and desires programmed against my life, die, in the name of Jesus.

558. All hereditary seals upon my destiny, I break and dissolve you, in the name of Jesus.

559. All satanic vows against my destiny, die, in the name of Jesus.

Day Fifteen

Praise and Worship

560. All satanic sacrifices assigned against my destiny, die, in the name of Jesus.

561. All unconscious links with false prophets and visionaries, break, in the name of Jesus.

562. My dwelling place, be surrounded by the hedge of thorns, in the name of Jesus.

563. My dwelling place, be surrounded by a wall of fire, in the name of Jesus.

564. My dwelling place, be surrounded by a wall of faith, in the name of Jesus.

565. All spirits of bondage, I bind you with chains and fetters of iron, in the name of Jesus.

566. You enemies of my father's house, I forbid you to work against my destiny, in the name of Jesus.

567. All commandments issued against me by the powers of darkness, I cancel and render you null and void, in the name of Jesus.

568. I break the will of the enemy over every area of my life, in the name of Jesus.

569. I bring the mighty power of the resurrection of our Lord Jesus Christ against all powers of darkness, in the name of Jesus.

570. Holy Spirit, fight against those that are fighting against my destiny, in the name of Jesus.

571. Let the powers of wickedness be confounded and put to shame, in the name of Jesus.

572. Lord, command Your light to shine in my darkness, in the name of Jesus.

573. Any power gathering against my destiny, catch fire, in the name of Jesus.

574. Let the fuel of my problems dry up, in the name of Jesus.

575. Let the foundation stones of my life be washed in the blood of Jesus, in the name of Jesus.

576. Every power waging war against my testimony, fall down and die, in the name of Jesus.

577. Destiny thieves, release me, in the name of Jesus.

578. My body, my soul, my spirit, push out satanic plantations, in the name of Jesus.

579. Angels of the living God, pursue my pursuers, in the name of Jesus.

580. Every king Uzziah assigned to reposition my destiny, die by fire, in the name of Jesus.

581. Every yoke assigned to reposition my destiny to the back, clear away, in the name of Jesus.

582. Let the oil that will cause me to be celebrated come upon my destiny, in the name of Jesus.

583. I shall arise by the power of the Holy Ghost and disgrace my disgrace, in the name of Jesus.

584. Every area of satanic storm troubling my destiny, I scatter you today, in the name of Jesus.

585. Wherever demons are gathered against my elevation, I scatter their association by the power in the blood of Jesus.

586. I receive power to activate the covenant of Abraham's blessing and greatness to function in my life.

587. I speak to the womb of heaven and earth to work for my growth and increase my greatness, in the name of Jesus.

588. I paralyse every evil hand scattering my success and increase, in the name of Jesus.

589. Every satanic wind blowing away my virtues, expire, in the name of Jesus.

590. Every power fighting against my elevation and celebration, be paralysed, in the name of Jesus.

591. I dismantle every curse from my father's or mother's house working against my total freedom, in the name of Jesus.

592. Cycle of the dark in my family line, break, in the name of Jesus.

593. The mistake of my parents will not become my tragedy, in the name of Jesus.

594. Iniquity of my father's house shall not steal from me, in the name of Jesus.

595. I place the cross of Jesus Christ between me and my ancestors, in the name of Jesus.

596. Blood of Jesus, flow through my family bloodline and wash away every ground of satanic attack against my destiny, in the name of Jesus.

597. Every evil pattern I have inherited from my family line, be destroyed by the blood of Jesus.

598. Every whirlwind of destruction flowing down from my family tree, I bury you now, in the name of Jesus.

599. Every family pattern by which satan pumps evil water into my family, die, in the name of Jesus.

Day Sixteen
Praise and Worship

600. O heavens, arise and attack the powers of darkness inhabiting the garden of my family line, in the name of Jesus.

601. My Father, send Your angels to encamp about every member of my family and protect them, in the name of Jesus.

602. Every generational sin and iniquity in my family line, be terminated by the blood of Jesus.

603. I bind with a chain every evil king reigning in my family, in the name of Jesus.

604. Every power in my root magnetising my progress backward, die, in the name of Jesus.

605. Foundational inheritance from my parents, come out, in the name of Jesus.

606. Ancestral wall built around my glory, be pulled down, in the name of Jesus.

607. Let the blood of Jesus go into the foundation of my family line to wash me and redeem me, in the name of Jesus.

608. Every covenant, promise, oath, vow, dedication that my family line has made with demonic beings at various altars, I renounce you, in the name of Jesus.

609. I command future generations of my family line to be released from every evil transaction that my ancestors have made, in the name of Jesus.

610. Oh earth, open and swallow every spiritual hired killer assigned against my family line, in the name of Jesus.

611. Every arrow that penetrated my life through my family line, be removed, in the name of Jesus.

612. Every negative pattern, character, behaviour and habit flowing down from my family tree, I arrest you by the blood of Jesus.

613. Yokes, chains, fetters and bondage of my father's house, break, in the name of Jesus.

614. Thou cryptic demons and ancient dedications troubling my family line, vanish, in the name of Jesus.

615. Every satanic animal living on my family tree, catch fire and die, in the name of Jesus.

616. Fiery darts of the wicked targeting my family line, backfire, in the name of Jesus.

617. Oh heavens over the prosperity of my family line, open by fire, in the name of Jesus.

618. I refuse to be an extension of any failure of my father's house, in the name of Jesus.

619. The iniquity that swallowed my parents will not swallow me, in the name of Jesus.

620. All territorial spirits delegated against my family line, be arrested, in the name of Jesus.

621. Let thunder and fire destroy every satanic monitoring device working in my family line, in the name of Jesus.

622. All satanic embargo placed on my family line, be destroyed by fire, in the name of Jesus.

623. Every power aborting the plans of God for my family line, fall down and die, in the name of Jesus.

624. Anything spoken into the sun and the moon against my family line, be destroyed by the power in the blood of Jesus.

625. Every power drawing power from the heavenlies against my family line, fall down and die, in the name of Jesus.

626. I cut off the head of the Goliath of my family line, in the name of Jesus.

627. I terminate every terminator of my family line, in the name of Jesus.

628. All the friends of darkness in my family line, be exposed and disgraced, in the name of Jesus.

629. Every anti-prosperity curse flowing down from my family tree, break by the power in the blood of Jesus.

630. Every spirit of limitation flowing down from my family tree, die, in the name of Jesus.

631. Every financial handicap flowing down from my family tree, die, in the name of Jesus.

632. Every curse of untimely death flowing down from my family tree, break by the power in the blood of Jesus.

633. Blood of Jesus, scrub dirtiness off my blood line, in the name of Jesus.

634. Thou strongman supervising the woes in my family tree, fall to the ground and be buried, in the name of Jesus.

635. Every rage of witchcraft termites on my family tree, expire by fire, in the name of Jesus.
636. Angels of war, take hold of my family tree and shake off every defiling animal living on it, in the name of Jesus.
637. Let the purging fire of the Holy Ghost burn to ashes all satanic influences on my family tree, in the name of Jesus.
638. Every blood demon troubling my life, be cleared out by the blood of Jesus, in the name of Jesus.
639. Every generational liability troubling my life, get out of my life, in the name of Jesus.

Day Seventeen
Praise and Worship

640. Every storm of darkness raging against my family line, expire, in the name of Jesus.
641. Every drought attacking the leaves of my family tree, clear away, in the name of Jesus.
642. Every harsh weather confronting the fruit on my family tree, be arrested, in the name of Jesus.
643. Every flood of darkness assigned to my family tree, be disgraced, in the name of Jesus.
644. Every warehouse of darkness caging the blessings of my family line, hear the word of the Lord: Release our blessings, in the name of Jesus.

645. Every evil cycle in my blood line troubling our Israel, die, in the name of Jesus.

646. The mistake of my parents will not become my tragedy, in the name of Jesus.

647. The iniquity of my father's house shall not steal from me, in the name of Jesus.

648. Whatsoever the enemy has set in motion against my family line, be reversed, in the name of Jesus.

649. Every ancestral covenant strengthening suffering and sorrow in my family line, be broken, in the name of Jesus.

650. Any curse under which my family labour, be broken by the power in the blood of Jesus.

651. Lord Jesus, walk back into my foundations and carry out every reconstruction that will move my life forward.

652. Lord, walk back 10 generations in my family line and erase every satanic instruction the enemy is using to torment me, in the name of Jesus.

653. Every handwriting of the wicked programmed into my foundation through idol worship, be wiped off by the blood of Jesus, in the name of Jesus.

654. My Father, purge my blood line, in the name of Jesus.

655. Pattern of darkness in my family line, break, in the name of Jesus.

656. What my father did not enjoy, I will enjoy it, in the name of Jesus.

657. God, backdate the blessings of my ancestors and give them to me, in the name of Jesus.

658. I make a contrary declaration to that of the enemy, in the name of Jesus.

659. Let my destiny be re-arranged to favour my life, in the name of Jesus.

660. I refuse to struggle for what my parents struggled for, in the name of Jesus.

661. Breakthrough miscarriage, die, in the name of Jesus.

662. Evil cycles in my bloodline, die, in the name of Jesus.

663. Whatever the enemy has set in motion, I reverse them, in the name of Jesus.

664. Materials coming down to me which the enemy has set in motion, be filtered through the Cross, in the name of Jesus.

665. I thank God for all the good I have inherited from my forefathers. I claim them and reject the evil ones, in the name of Jesus.

666. Blood of Jesus, flow through my family history and wash away every ground of satanic attack against my destiny, in the name of Jesus.

667. My Father, I ask in repentance for forgiveness of all my family sins, in the name of Jesus.

668. Every descending pattern that satan uses to perpetuate his destruction on my family line, be wiped off by the blood of Jesus.

669. Every power causing problem to escalate in my family line, die, in the name of Jesus.

670. Thou power of destructive patterns and habits, be destroyed by the power in the blood of Jesus.
671. My Father, send Your angels to bring each member of my family out of darkness into light, in the name of Jesus.
672. God, arise and send Your warrior angels to do battle for my family, in the name of Jesus.
673. I bind with a chain every evil king reigning in my family, in the name of Jesus.
674. Sacrifices done on my behalf, caging me from my root, die, in the name of Jesus.
675. Family spirits power and supervising powers in charge of my father's house, die, in the name of Jesus.
676. Foundational button pressed against my advancements, die, in the name of Jesus.
677. Strange animals in my roots, die, in the name of Jesus.
678. By the power in the blood of Jesus I renounce the gods that my ancestors or I have served, that have brought me into collective captivity, in the name of Jesus.
679. Thou power of collective demonisation in my family line, I destroy you, in the name of Jesus.

Day Eighteen

Praise and Worship

680. Every satanic odour coming out of the closet of my family, be neutralised, in the name of Jesus.

681. Every curse under which my family labour, be broken by the power in the blood of Jesus.

682. Every covenant under which my family labours, be broken by the power in the blood of Jesus.

683. Dedications that speak against my family line, be broken, in the name of Jesus.

684. Every power altering the destiny of my family, be scattered, in the name of Jesus.

685. Every affliction in my family line, die, in the name of Jesus.

686. Every satanic investment in the heavenlies expected to manifest seasonal evil in my family, be crushed, in the name of Jesus.

687. My Father, lay a new foundation for my family line, in the name of Jesus.

688. Every power of the wicked avenger upon my family line, be destroyed, in the name of Jesus.

689. Blood of Jesus neutralise any evil thing inherited from the blood of my parents, in the name of Jesus.

690. By the blood of Jesus I deliver my family tree from serpent and scorpion, in the name of Jesus.

691. Every satanic termite operating inside my family tree, dry up and die, in the name of Jesus.

692. Blood of Jesus and Holy Ghost fire, purge the foundation of every member of my family, in the name of Jesus.

693. Architects and builders of affliction in my family line, scatter, in the name of Jesus.

694. Every negative powers like father like son, like mother like daughter, clear away by the power in the blood of Jesus.

695. In the name of Jesus, I ruin the power of every strongman assigned to trouble my blood line, in the name of Jesus.

696. Every agent of wickedness in my bloodline, I bind and cast you out with all your roots, in the name of Jesus.

697. Every curse, evil covenant and enchantment militating against the star of my family, die, in the name of Jesus.

698. Strong men behind stubborn problems in my family line, die, in the name of Jesus.

699. Anything buried or planted in my family compound that is reactivating ancient demons, catch fire, in the name of Jesus.

700. Any evil tree planted anywhere that speaks against my destiny, dry to the roots, in the name of Jesus.

701. Satanic panel set up against my family line, scatter, in the name of Jesus.

702. Thou power of deliverance, fall upon me now, in the name of Jesus.

703. Blood of Jesus, purge my foundation.

704. Every foundational curse in my life, break, in the name of Jesus.

705. Every foundational covenant in my life, break, in the name of Jesus.

706. Every foundational bondage in my life, break, in the name of Jesus.

707. Every foundational arrester, be arrested, in the name of Jesus.

708. Every darkness planted in my foundation, scatter, in the name of Jesus.

709. Every serpent in my foundation, die, in the name of Jesus.

710. Every scorpion in my foundation, die, in the name of Jesus.

711. Let God arise and let all foundational witchcraft scatter, in the name of Jesus.

712. Every seed of witchcraft in my foundation, die, in the name of Jesus.

713. Every foundation of confusion in my life, die, in the name of Jesus.

714. Holy Spirit, shake down every foundational stronghold, in the name of Jesus.

715. Every foundational familiar spirit, I bind you and cast you out, in the name of Jesus.

716. Every foundational marine power, bow, in the name of Jesus.

717. Every seed of poverty in my foundation, die, in the name of Jesus.

718. Every foundational padlock, break, in the name of Jesus.

719. I repent from all ancestral idol worship, in the name of Jesus.

Day Nineteen

Praise and Worship

720. Every idol of my father's house, lose your hold over my life, in the name of Jesus.

721. Every strongman of the idol of my father's house, die, in the name of Jesus.

722. I silence the evil cry of any idol fashioned against me, in the name of Jesus.

723. All consequences of ancestral idol worship upon my life, I wipe you off by the blood of Jesus.

724. Holy Ghost fire, burn down all spiritual shrines of my father's house, in the name of Jesus.

725. Oppression agenda of my family idol, die, in the name of Jesus.

726. Every blood speaking against my generational line, be silenced by the blood of Jesus.

727. Every idol power speaking against my destiny, scatter, in the name of Jesus.

728. I break all ancestral covenants with any idol power, in the name of Jesus.

729. Every bitter water flowing in my family from any idol, dry up, in the name of Jesus.

730. Any rope tying my family line to any family idol break, in the name of Jesus.

731. Every landlord spirit troubling my destiny, be paralysed, in the name of Jesus.

732. Every outflow of satanic family name, die, in the name of Jesus.

733. I recover every benefit stolen by idol powers, in the name of Jesus.

734. Where is the God of Elijah? Arise, disgrace every family idol, in the name of Jesus.

735. Every satanic priest ministering in my family line, be retrenched, in the name of Jesus.

736. Arrows of affliction originating from idolatry, loose your hold, in the name of Jesus.

737. Every influence of idol worship in my life, die, in the name of Jesus.

738. Every network of idol power in my place of birth, scatter, in the name of Jesus.

739. Every satanic dedication that speaks against me, be dismantled by the power in the blood of Jesus.

740. I vomit every food with idolatrous influence that I have eaten, in the name of Jesus.

741. Let the stone of hindrance constructed by family idol be rolled away, in the name of Jesus.

742. The voice of foundational idols will never speak again, in the name of Jesus.

743. Every strongman assigned by the idols of my father's house against my life, die, in the name of Jesus.

744. Every satanic promissory note issued on my behalf by my ancestors, be reversed, in the name of Jesus.

745. Garments of opposition designed by ancestral idols, roast, in the name of Jesus.

746. My glory, buried by family idols, come alive by fire, in the name of Jesus.

747. Thou power of strange gods legislating against my destiny, scatter, in the name of Jesus.

748. Idols of my place of birth, I break your chain, in the name of Jesus.

749. Every problem attached to my family name, be neutralized, in the name of Jesus.

750. Every power searching the oracle to know my progress, die, in the name of Jesus.

751. Family idols, receive the consuming fire of God, in the name of Jesus.

752. I release myself from any bondage present in my family line, in the name of Jesus.

753. Any evil pattern laid by my ancestors, break, in the name of Jesus.

754. No enchantment shall hold me captive, in the name of Jesus.

755. I break the pattern of darkness that locked me up, in the name of Jesus.

756. I release my life from the yoke of my village, in the name of Jesus.

757. Every curse that came to me through the sins of my ancestors, break by the blood of Jesus.

758. Every ancestral transmission of affliction, break and die, in the name of Jesus.

759. Every ancestral transmission of failure, break and die, in the name of Jesus.

Day Twenty

Praise and Worship

760. Every ancestral transmission of backsliding, break and die, in the name of Jesus.

761. Every ancestral transmission of poverty, break and die, in the name of Jesus.

762. Every ancestral transmission of untimely death, break and die, in the name of Jesus.

763. Every ancestral transmission of disease and infirmity, break and die, in the name of Jesus.

764. Every ancestral transmission of bad luck, break and die, in the name of Jesus.

765. I render every aggressive altar impotent, in the name of Jesus.

766. Every evil altar erected against me, be disgraced, in the name of Jesus.

767. Anything done against my life under demonic anointing, be nullified, in the name of Jesus.

768. I curse every local altar fashioned against me, in the name of Jesus.

769. Let the hammer of the Almighty God smash every evil altar erected against me, in the name of Jesus.

770. Lord, send Your fire to destroy every evil altar fashioned against me, in the name of Jesus.

771. Every evil priest ministering against me at the evil altar, receive the sword of God, in the name of Jesus.

772. Let the thunder of God smite every evil priest working against me on the evil altar and burn them to ashes, in the name of Jesus.

773. Let every satanic priest ministering against me at evil altars fall down and die, in the name of Jesus.

774. Any hand that wants to retaliate or arrest me because of all these prayers I am praying, dry up and wither, in the name of Jesus.

775. Every stubborn evil altar priest, drink your own blood, in the name of Jesus.

776. I possess my possession stolen by the evil altar, in the name of Jesus.

777. I withdraw my name from every evil altar, in the name of Jesus.

778. I withdraw my blessings from every evil altar, in the name of Jesus.

779. I withdraw my breakthroughs from every evil altar, in the name of Jesus.
780. I withdraw my glory from every evil altar, in the name of Jesus.
781. I withdraw my prosperity from every evil altar, in the name of Jesus.
782. I withdraw anything representing me from every evil altar, in the name of Jesus.
783. Mention the organ that you know is not behaving the way it should. When you have done this, begin to say, "I withdraw you from every evil altar, in the name of Jesus." Say this seven hot times.
784. Let the wind of the Holy Spirit bring every scattered bone together now, in the name of Jesus.
785. I use the blood of Jesus to reverse every poor record of the past about my life, in the name of Jesus.
786. I refuse to accept satanic substitute for my destiny, in the name of Jesus.
787. I refuse to be caged by the enemy of good things, in the name of Jesus.
788. Let every internal coffin in my life receive the fire of God and be roasted now, in the name of Jesus.
789. Every destiny-paralysing power fashioned against my destiny, fall down and die, in the name of Jesus.
790. Every inherited evil limitation in any area of my life, depart now, in the name of Jesus.

791. Every architect of spiritual coffins, I command you to fall down and die, in the name of Jesus.
792. Every cloud of uncertainty, clear away now, in the name of Jesus.
793. I refuse to be converted to a living dead, in the name of Jesus.
794. Let every evil laying on of hands and shaking of evil hands be nullified, in the name of Jesus.
795. Every satanic consultation concerning my life, be nullified, in the name of Jesus.
796. Every decision taken against my life by witchcraft spirits, be nullified, in the name of Jesus.
797. I reject aborted victories in every area of my life, in the name of Jesus.
798. Every caged star, be released now, in the name of Jesus.
799. My imagination and dreams will not be used against me, in the name of Jesus.

Day Twenty-One
Praise and Worship

800. God, arise and visit all shrines assigned against me with thunder and earthquake, in the name of Jesus.
801. All satanic altars, erected against my destiny, be overthrown by fire, in the name of Jesus.
802. God, arise and set unquenchable fire upon every coven of darkness assigned against me, in the name of Jesus.

803. All images, carved against my life, break into pieces after the order of dagon, in the name of Jesus.

804. God, arise and cause confusion in the camp of my enemies, in the name of Jesus.

805. I decree that my oppressors shall consult their powers in their confusion, but there will be no response, in the name of Jesus.

806. Holy Ghost fire, arise and stir up civil war in the camp of my enemies, in the name of Jesus.

807. I command every satanic intermediary working against me to loose heart, in the name of Jesus.

808. God, arise and bring the plans of my oppressors to nothing, in the name of Jesus.

809. My Father, set up a fierce king against my oppressors and let the king treat them with great torture, in the name of Jesus.

810. Let the power of God intimidate and frustrate all diviners assigned against me, in the name of Jesus.

811. God, arise and wipe out the understanding of my stubborn pursuers, in the name of Jesus.

812. God, pour out the spirit of dizziness upon all evil spiritual consultants speaking against me, in the name of Jesus.

813. Let these evil spiritual consultants stagger in all they do as a drunkard staggers in his vomit, in the name of Jesus.

814. By the power in the blood of Jesus, let all soothsayers, witch doctors, enchanters arrange against me be cut off, in the name of Jesus.

815. Heavens, O earth, hear the word of the Lord: you must not execute the counsel of my enemies, in the name of Jesus.
816. God, pass through the camp of my enemies with affliction and drain the anointing of wickedness, in the name of Jesus.
817. Every power assigned to wreck my destiny, your end has come, die, in the name of Jesus.
818. I de-programme and cancel all negative prophecies pronounced against me, in the name of Jesus.
819. Lord, guide me into the mysteries of my life.
820. Lord, give me the keys to unlock the hidden riches of secret places.
821. All ancient doors that have hindered the plan of God for my life, be unlocked by fire, in the name of Jesus.
822. I destroy every agreement made at covens and satanic centres against me, in the name of Jesus.
823. Every secret code, evil registers and archives of the enemy in my place of birth, be roasted, in the name of Jesus.
824. God, arise and cast abominable filth upon witches and wizards and set them as gazing stock, in the name of Jesus.
825. Let the tables of witches and wizards become snares unto them, in the name of Jesus.
826. Let the eyes of witches monitoring my life be darkened, in the name of Jesus.
827. Let the covens of witchcraft become desolate, let there be no one to dwell in them, in the name of Jesus.
828. I command crash-landing of witches and wizards assigned against my breakthrough, in the name of Jesus.

829. I command the sun to smite my oppressors in the day and the moon and stars to smite them at night, in the name of Jesus.

830. I command the stars in their courses to fight against my stubborn pursuers, in the name of Jesus.

831. God, arise, roar and prevail over my enemies, in the name of Jesus.

832. Let the gathering of the wicked against me be harvested for judgement, in the name of Jesus.

833. God, arise and hang every Hamaan assigned against my life, in the name of Jesus.

834. Every stumbling block to God's prophetic agenda on my life, be rooted out, in the name of Jesus.

835. All negative words that have been spoken against me by evil men, die, in the name of Jesus.

836. All evil records, evil marriage certificates and registers that are kept in satanic archives against me, be wiped off by the blood of Jesus.

837. I programme divine health, divine favour, long life, spiritual advancement into my life by the power in the blood of Jesus.

838. I close down every spiritual ship carting away my benefits, in the name of Jesus.

839. O God, arise and lay waste all the operations of dark forces working against me, in the name of Jesus.

Section Four

PRAYERS TO UNVEIL MYSTERIES AND SCERETS

The prayers in this section are vomited by the Holy Spirit to enable you to access secrets and mysteries that will birth your deliverance from the bondage of the enemy as well as gain victory over his kingdom and cohorts.

Pray them with unwavering faith, violence and persistence. The God that answers by fire will reveal great and mighty things to you.

(A)　　　**KNOW THE SECRETS**
　　　　(Prayer to find out secrets things from the Lord)

Praise worship

Scripture Reading: Daniel 2

Confession: Daniel 2:2, Eph. 1:17

1.　　Thank God for the Holy Spirit
2.　　Lord, give unto me the spirit of revelation and wisdom in the knowledge of Yourself
3.　　Lord, remove spiritual cataracts from my eyes

4. Lord, Forgive me for every false motive or thought that has been formed in my heart since the day I was born.

5. Lord, forgive me for any lie that I have ever told against any person, system or organisation

6. Lord, deliver me from the bondage and sin of spiritual laziness.

7. Lord, open up my understanding.

8. Lord, teach me deep and secret things.

9. Lord, reveal to me every secret behind any problem that I have.

10. Lord, bring to light everything planned against me in darkness

11. Lord, ignite and revive my beneficial potential

12. Ask the Lord for divine wisdom to operate your life.

13. Lord, let every veil preventing me from having plain spiritual vision be removed.

14. Father in the name of Jesus, I ask to know your mind about.... (slot in the appropriate situation).

15. Let the spirit of prophecy and revelation fall upon the totality of my being, in the name of Jesus.

16. Holy Spirit, reveal deep and the secret things to me about......

17. I bind every demon that pollutes spiritual vision and dreams, in the name of Jesus

18. Let every dirtiness blocking my communication pipe with the living God be washed clean with the blood of Jesus.

19. I receive power to operate with sharp spiritual eyes that cannot be deceived, in the name of Jesus.

20. Let the glory and the power of the Almighty God fall upon my life in a mighty way, in the name of Jesus.

21. I remove my name from the book of those who grope and stumble in darkness, in the name of Jesus.

22. Lord, make me a vessel capable of knowing your secret thing

23. Divine revelations, spiritual visions, dreams and information will not become a scarce commodity in my life, in the name of Jesus.

24. I drink to the full in the well of salvation and anointing, in the name of Jesus.

25. Pray in the Spirit for at least 15 minutes before going to bed.

(B)   REVELATION KNOWLEDGE PRAYERS

Praise Worship
Scripture Reading – Deut. 29:29; *Daniel* 2:22
Confession – Psalm 20:7-8

Deuteronomy 29:29: The secret things belong unto the LORD our God: but those things which are revealed belong unto us and to our children forever, that we may do all the words of this law.
Psalm 5:8: Lead me, O LORD, in thy righteousness because of

mine enemies; make thy way straight before my face. Psalm 25:14: The secret of the LORD is with them that fear him; and he will shew them his covenant. Daniel 2:22: He revealeth the deep and secret things: he knoweth what is in the darkness, and the light dwelleth with him. Ephesians 1:17: That the God of our Lord Jesus Christ, the Father of glory, may give unto you the spirit of wisdom and revelation in the knowledge of him.

1. Every secret, covenant and vow affecting my destiny, be broken, in the name of Jesus.

2. Every ancestral secret retarding my progress, be revealed, in the name of Jesus.

3. Evil secret activities currently affecting my life, be exposed and disgraced, in the name of Jesus.

4. Every secret I need to know to excel spiritually and financially, be revealed, in the name of Jesus.

5. Every secret hidden in the marine kingdom, affecting my elevation, be exposed and disgraced, in the name of Jesus.

6. Every secret hidden in the satanic archive, crippling my elevation, be exposed and disgraced, in the name of Jesus.

7. Every secret I need to know about my environment, be revealed, in the name of Jesus.

8.   Secrets of wicked elders behind my challenges, be exposed and disgraced, in the name of Jesus.

9.   Every secret I need to know about my father's lineage, be revealed, in the name of Jesus.

10.   Every secret I need to know about my mother's lineage, be revealed, in the name of Jesus.

11.   Every secret I need to know about my hometown, be revealed, in the name of Jesus.

12.   Every secret I need to know about the work I am doing, be revealed, in the name of Jesus.

13.   Every power that wants my efforts to turn against me, I pull you down, in the name of Jesus

14.   O Lord, lift evil stones away from my body, in the name of Jesus.

15.   O God, arise and stir the winds to bring me restoration, in the name of Jesus.

16.   O Lord, call forth new patterns in my life that will promote me in the name of Jesus.

17.   Evil winds blowing against me, be reversed, in the name of Jesus.

18.   Afflictions, hear the word of the Lord, become promotions, in the name of Jesus.

19.   Let my glory be perfected by fire, in the name of Jesus.

20.   Blood of Jesus, stand between me and every strange altar, in the name of Jesus.

21. Blood of Jesus, secure my portion, secure and my destiny, in the name of Jesus.
22. Blood of Jesus, walk through my family and scatter every witchcraft operation, in the name of Jesus.
23. Blood of Jesus, open up all gates shut against me, in the name of Jesus.
24. O God, restore the structure of my life in the perfection in which you ordained it, in the name of Jesus.
25. O God, rebuild the damaged walls of my life, in the name of Jesus.
26. Every strange altar of fear, scatter, in the name of Jesus.
27. I destroy every covenant of fear by the blood of the Lamb, in the name of Jesus.
28. You dead works in my life, get out now, in the name of Jesus.
29. Every secret agenda of_____ (pick from the following), assigned against my life, scatter, in the name of Jesus.
    - Star hijacker
    - desert spirit
    - evil mark
    - destiny killer
    - Iron-like curse
    - evil spirit marriage
    - territorial demotion
    - head manipulator
    - Gate of evil

- satanic poison
- progress arrester
- placental manipulator
- Arrow of fruitless efforts
- poverty activator
- unfriendly friend
- spirit of tragedy
- Coffin spirit
- evil observer
- strange money
- evil bullet
- Vagabond anointing
- rain of affliction
- wicked broadcaster
- dark agent
- Witchcraft handwriting
- children killer
- business bewitchment
- marriage killer
- Evil reinforcement
- arrow of infirmity
- spirit of death and hell
- pocket with holes

30. Lord give unto me the Spirit of revelation and wisdom in the knowledge of yourself, in the name of Jesus.

31. O Lord, make Your way plain before my face on this issue, in the name of Jesus.
32. O Lord, remove spiritual cataract from my eyes, in the name of Jesus.
33. O Lord, forgive me for every false motive or thought that has ever been formed in my heart since the day I was born, in the name of Jesus.
34. O Lord forgive me for any lie that I have ever told against any person, system or organisation, in the name of Jesus.
35. O Lord, deliver me from the bondage and sin of spiritual laziness, in the name of Jesus.
36. O Lord, open up my eyes to see all I should see on this issue, in the name of Jesus.
37. O Lord, teach me deep and secret things, in the name of Jesus.
38. O Lord, reveal to me every secret behind any problem that I have, in the name of Jesus.
39. O Lord, bring to the light everything planned against me in darkness, in the name of Jesus.
40. O Lord, ignite me and revive my beneficial potential, in the name of Jesus.
41. O Lord, give me divine wisdom to operate my life, in the name of Jesus.
42. O Lord, let every veil preventing me from having plain spiritual vision be removed, in the name of Jesus.

43.   O Lord, give unto me the spirit of revelation and wisdom in the knowledge of You, in the name of Jesus.

44.   O Lord, open up my spiritual understanding, in the name of Jesus.

45.   O Lord, let me know all I should know about this issue, in the name of Jesus.

46.   O Lord, reveal to me every secret behind the particular issue whether beneficial or not, in the name of Jesus.

47.   O Lord, remove from me any persistent buried grudges, half-acknowledge enmity against anyone and every other thing that can block my spirit vision, in the name of Jesus.

48.   O Lord, teach me to know that which is worth knowing and love that which is worth loving and to dislike whatsoever is not pleasing to Your eyes, in the name of Jesus.

49.   O Lord, make me a vessel capable of knowing Your secret things, in the name of Jesus.

50.   Father in the name of Jesus, I ask to know Your mind about____(slot in the appropriate situation) situation.

51.   Let the spirit of prophesy and revelation fall upon the totally of my being, in the name of Jesus.

52.   Holy Spirit, reveal deep and the secret things to me about____, in the name of Jesus.

53.   I bind every demon that pollutes spiritual vision and dreams, in the name of Jesus.

54. Let every dirtiness blocking my communication pipe with the living God be washed clean with the blood of Jesus, in the name of Jesus.

55. I receive power to operate with sharp spiritual eyes that cannot be deceived, in the name of Jesus.

56. Let the glory and power of the Almighty God, fall upon my life in a mighty way, in the name of Jesus.

57. I remove my name from the book of those who grope and stumble in darkness, in the name of Jesus.

58. Divine revelations, spiritual visions, dreams and information will not become scarce commodity in my life, in the name of Jesus.

59. I drink to the full in the well of salvation and anointing, in the name of Jesus.

60. O God, to whom no secret is hidden, make know unto me whether_____ (mention the name of the thing) is your choice for me, in the name of Jesus.

61. Let every idol present consciously or unconsciously in my heart concerning the issue be melted away by the fire of the Holy Spirit, in the name of Jesus.

62. I refuse to fall under the manipulation of the spirits of confusion, in the name of Jesus.

63. I refuse to make foundational mistakes in my decision making, in the name of Jesus.

64. Father Lord, guide and direct me in knowing your mind on this particular issue, in the name of Jesus.

65.   I stand against all satanic attachments hat may seek to confuse my decision, in the name of Jesus.

66.   If_____(mention the name of the thing) is not for me, O Lord redirect my steps.

67.   I bind the activities of_____(pick from the list below) in my life, in the name of Jesus.

  (i)   lust
  (ii)   Ungodly infatuation
  (iii)   ungodly family pressure
  (iv)   demonic manipulation in dreams and visions
  (v)   attachment from/to the wrong choice
  (vi)   confusing revelation
  (vii)   spiritual blindness and deafness
  (viii) unprofitable advice
  (ix)   ungodly impatience

(C)   MAKE YOUR WAY PLAIN BEFORE MY FACE

Confessions:

Deut. 29:29: The secret thing belongs unto the LORD our God: but those things which are revealed belong unto us and to our children forever, that we may do all the words of this law.

Psalm 25:14: The secret of the LORD is with them that fear him; and he will shew them his covenant.

Daniel 2:22: He revealeth the deep and secret things: he knoweth what is in the darkness, and the light dwelleth in him.

Ephesians 1:17: That the God of our Lord Jesus Christ, the Father of glory, may give unto you the spirit of wisdom and revelation in the knowledge of him.

Prayer Points

Praise Worship

1. Thank God for the revelation power of the Holy Spirit.
2. O Lord, give unto me the Spirit of revelation and wisdom in the knowledge of Yourself, in the name of Jesus.
3. O Lord, make your way plain before my face on this issue, in the name of Jesus.
4. O Lord, remove spiritual cataract from my eyes, in the name of Jesus
5. O Lord, forgive me for every false motive or thought that has ever been formed in my heart since the day I was born, in the name of Jesus.
6. O Lord, forgive me for any lie that I have ever told against any person, system or organisation, in the name of Jesus.

7.   O Lord, deliver me from the bondage and sin of spiritual laziness, in the name of Jesus.

8.   O Lord, open up my eyes to see all I should see on this issue, in the name of Jesus.

9.   O Lord, teach me deep and secret things, in the name of Jesus.

10.   O Lord, reveal to me every secret behind any problem that I have, in the name of Jesus.

11.   O Lord, bring to the light everything planned against me in darkness, in the name of Jesus.

12.   O Lord, ignite and revive my beneficial potential, in the name of Jesus.

13.   O Lord, give me divine wisdom to operate my life, in the name of Jesus.

14.   O Lord, let every veil preventing me from having plain spiritual vision be removed, in the name of Jesus.

15.   O Lord, give unto me the spirit of revelation and wisdom in the knowledge of you, in the name of Jesus.

16.   O Lord, open up my spiritual understanding, in the name of Jesus

17.   O Lord, let me know all I should know about this issue, in the name of Jesus

18.   O Lord, reveal to me every secret behind the particular issue whether beneficial or not, in the name of Jesus.

19. O Lord, remove from me any persistent buried grudges, half knowledge enmity against anyone and every other thing that can block my spiritual vision.

20. O Lord, teach me to know that which is worth knowing and love that which is worth loving and to dislike whatsoever is not pleasing to your eyes.

21. O Lord, make me a vessel capable of knowing your secret things.

22. Father in the name of Jesus I ask to know your mind about............ (Slot in the appropriate situation) Situation

23. Let the spirit of prophesy and revelation fall upon the totality of my being, in the name of Jesus.

24. Holy Spirit, reveal deep and the secret things to me about........, in the name of Jesus.

25. I bind every demon that pollutes spiritual vision and dreams, in the name of Jesus.

26. Let every dirtiness blocking my communication pipe with the living God be washed clean with the blood of Jesus, in the name of Jesus.

27. I receive power to operate with sharp spiritual eyes that cannot be deceived, in the name of Jesus.

28. Let the glory and the power of the Almighty God, fall upon my life in a mighty way, in the name of Jesus.

29. I remove my name from the Book of those who grope and stumble in darkness, in the name of Jesus.

30. Divine revelations, Spiritual visions, dreams and information will not become scarce commodity in my life, in the name of Jesus.

31. I drink to the full in the well of salvation and anointing, in the name of Jesus.

32. O God, to whom no secret is hidden, make know unto me whether...................... (mention the name of the thing) is your choice for me, in the name of Jesus.

33. Let every idol present consciously or unconsciously in my heart concerning this issue be melted away by the fire of the Holy Spirit, in the name of Jesus.

34. I refuse to fall under the manipulation of the Spirits of confusion, in the name of Jesus.

35. I refuse to make foundational mistakes in my decision making, in the name of Jesus.

36. Father Lord, guide and direct me in knowing your mind on this particular issue, in the name of Jesus.

37. I stand against all satanic attachements that may seek to confuse my decision, in the name of Jesus.

38. If .... (mention the name of the thing) is not for me, O Lord, redirect my steps.

39. I bind the activities of .... (Pick from the list below) In my life, in the name of Jesus.

(i)   Lust

(ii)   Ungodly infatuation

(iii) Ungodly family pressure

(iv) Demonic manipulation in dreams and visions

(v)   Attachment from/ to the wrong choice

(vi) Confusing revelations

(vii) Spiritual blindness and deafness

(viii) unprofitable advice

(ix) Ungodly impatience

40.   O God, you who reveals secret things, make known unto me your choice for me in this issue, in the name of Jesus.

41.   Holy Spirit, open my eyes and help me to make the right decision, in the name of Jesus.

42.   Thank you Jesus for your presence and the good testimonies that will follow.

43.   Pray in the Spirit for at least 15 minutes before going to bed.

(D)   PRAYERS TO DAMAGE YOUR IGNORANCE AND OPEN YOUR SPIRITUAL EYES

Confession: Hosea 4:6a: My people are destroyed for lack of knowledge:

II Kings 6:17: And Elisha prayed, and said, Lord, I pray thee, open his eyes that he may see. And the Lord opened the eyes of the young man; and he saw: behold, the mountain was full of horses and chariots of fire round about Elisha.

1. Holy Spirit, lay Your hands on me again, until I see clearly, in the name of Jesus.

2. Every hypocrisy in my life, making me to focus on the minor, be destroyed in the name of Jesus.

3. Every ideology of men that I have held unto religiously for years, be destroyed completely in the name of Jesus.

4. Every word that has been spoken to me, that make me believe that I have no future, die, in the name of Jesus.

5. Any power planning for my downfall, I will always be ahead of you, in the name of Jesus.

6. O Lord, surround me with people whose eyesight and insight are sharper than mine, in the name of Jesus.

7. O God Arise and damage my ignorance in the name of Jesus.

8. Every power incubating the eggs of ignorance in my life, die with your eggs, in the name of Jesus.

9. You the mountain of ignorance blocking the glory of my destiny, be wasted unto desolation, in the name of Jesus.

10. Arrows of chronic ignorance working overtime in my life, die, in the name of Jesus.

11. You the breeding ground of ignorance in my life: be vacated by the power in the blood of Jesus, in the name of Jesus.

12. Chains of ignorance, holding me captive your time is up, break, in the name of Jesus.

13. You the scaffold of lies supporting the high-rise of ignorance on my foundation, expire and crumble, in the name of Jesus.

14. Powers sponsoring ignorance and supervising destruction of good things in my life, expire and be disgraced, in the name of Jesus.

15. Every power rejecting the knowledge of God in my life, you are a liar. I reject you, die, in the name of Jesus.

16. Wherever I go, Holy Ghost fire, overshadow my life, in the name of Jesus.

17. O Lord, open my eyes that I will see what is going on in my environment spiritually, in the name of Jesus.

18. I shall not labour in vain.. Another person shall not eat the fruit of my labour, in the name of Jesus

19. As from today, Holy Ghost, control my thought and my mind, in the name of Jesus.

20. Lord Jesus, feed me with the food of the Champions, in the name of Jesus.

21. I receive the unsearchable wisdom in the Holy Ghost, to excel in life, in the name of Jesus.

Section Five

PRAYERS THAT PROVOKE DIVINE ENCOUNTER

SCRIPTURES: Gen.32:22-30; Exod. 3:3-4;
Confession: Ps102:13

1. My Father, my Father, my Father, arise and have mercy upon me now, in the name of Jesus.
2. O God, reveal Yourself to me and give me a turnaround experience, in the name of Jesus.
3. Father Lord, let me have a Peniel encounter after the order of Jacob, in the name of Jesus.
4. O Lord, give me a divine dream that will change my life like Joseph, in the name of Jesus.
5. Powers assigned against my divine manifestation, die by fire, in the name of Jesus.
6. O God, arise and let me experience my own personal Pentecost, in the name of Jesus.
7. Fresh divine encounter that will make eternal impact on my life, manifest now, in the name of Jesus.
8. Where is the Lord God of Elijah? Arise and manifest in my life by Your fire, in the name of Jesus.
9. Father, let me hear Your still small voice as You spoke to Samuel, in the name of Jesus.

10. Enemies of my divine manifestation, what are you waiting for me? Scatter and die, in the name of Jesus.

11. Divine favour that makes a man to become uncommon, locate me now, in the name of Jesus.

12. Father purge and purify my life with Your fire, in the name of Jesus.

13. O God my Father, move me from Jacob to Israel, in the name of Jesus.

14. I receive fresh baptism of fire, in the name of Jesus.

15. Power to do exploits for the kingdom of God, my life is available enter, in the name of Jesus.

16. Father, let me experience the glory of Your Presence in a new way, in the name of Jesus.

17. Powers assigned against the move of God's power in my life, you shall not prosper, die by fire, in the name of Jesus.

18. Whether the devil likes it or not, I shall become what the Lord has destined me to become, in the name of Jesus.

19. O God, arise and make me relevant in my generation, in the name of Jesus.

20. The voice of my glory, refuse to be silent, in the name of Jesus.

21. By Your power, O God, let me become a voice that cannot be silenced by evil powers, in the name of Jesus.

22. O God, my Father, let me know You more and more, in the name of Jesus.

23. O God of wonders, arise and make me a divine phenomenon, in the name of Jesus.

Section Six

JOURNEY BACK TO THE WOMB

Confession: Psalm 118: 10-16

All nations compassed me about: but in the name of the Lord will I destroy them. They compassed me about; yea, they compassed me about: but in the name of the Lord I will destroy them. They compassed me about like bees; they are quenched as the fire of thorns: for in the name of the Lord I will destroy them. Thou hast thrust sore at me that I might fall: but the Lord helped me. The Lord is my strength and song, and is become my salvation. The voice of rejoicing and salvation is in the tabernacles of the righteous: the right hand of the Lord doeth valiantly. The right hand of the Lord is exalted: the right hand of the Lord doeth valiantly.

1. Lord Jesus, wash me from the impurity and stigma of the past, in the name of Jesus.

2. Help me Lord, to discover my real self.

3. Lord, make known to me the secrets of my inner life.

4. Holy Ghost, occupy me now, in the name of Jesus.

5. Lord Jesus, walk back into every second of my life and deliver me where I need deliverance, heal me where I need healing, transform me where I need transformation.

6. Womb related problems in my life, manifest and come out in the name of Jesus.

7. Let my divine destiny appear, let my perverted destiny disappear, in the name of Jesus.

8. Any problem that came into my life by parental invitation, depart and die, in the name of Jesus.

9. Every problem of stillbirth and threatened abortion that has landed my life in trouble, die, in the name of Jesus.

10. Any pot in the house of native doctor used to suspend my pregnancy in my mother's womb for any reason, presently troubling my life, break, in the name of Jesus.

11. Covenant of safe delivery and child birth, between my parent and the devil, break, in the name of Jesus.

12. Any agent of darkness that has tampered with:

    - My Hair

    - My Placenta

    - My Blood

    - My Glory and

- Water used to birth me after delivery, die, in the name of Jesus.

13. Any evil altar where my parents has consciously and unconsciously submitted my name, catch fire, in the name of Jesus.

14. Bloodline problems, from ten generations in my lineage, be broken over my life, in the name of Jesus.

15. Deep rooted problems in my life, hear the word of the Lord, die, in the name of Jesus.

16. Death contractors hired against me from my mothers womb, kill yourselves in the name of Jesus.

17. Any tree that parental error has planted in my life, I cut you down, in the name of Jesus.

18. Fountain of discomfort in my life, dry up now, in the name of Jesus.

19. Foundational related problems in my life, leave me alone, die, in the name of Jesus.

20. Any power meeting to decide untimely death for my life, scatter unto desolation, in the name of Jesus.

21. Powers that defeated my parents, you will not overcome me, die, in the name of Jesus.

Section Seven

PRAYERS TO CORRECT PARENTAL MISTAKES

Scriptures: Ps 51:1-9; Lam. 5:7.

Confession: Gal.3:13-14.

1. Powers assigned to visit the errors of my parents upon my life, fall down and die, in the name of Jesus.
2. Any evil transactions made by my parents now troubling my life, be terminated by the Blood of Jesus, in the name of Jesus.
3. Every demonic libation poured on my behalf, be neutralised by the blood of Jesus, in the name of Jesus.
4. Evil blood crying against my destiny, be silenced by the power in the Blood of Jesus, in the name of Jesus
5. I refuse to pay for what I did not buy in the satanic market, in the name of Jesus.
6. O God, arise and correct the consequences of my parents' errors upon my life and destiny, in the name of Jesus.
7. The faulty shoes of my parents shall not size my feet, in the name of Jesus.

8.   Acquired yokes, inherited bondage of my father's house, of my mother's house, break and release my life, in the name of Jesus.

9.   Ancestral spiritual padlocks assigned to lock up my blessings, be blast open by the fire of God, in the name of Jesus.

10.   O God, arise and let Your mercy speak for me, in the name of Jesus.

11.   Covenant Blood of Jesus, cancel any evil blood covenant speaking against my life, in the name of Jesus.

12.   Powers that want to revenge the wickedness of my father's house upon my life, let the righteousness of Jesus defend my cause, in the name of Jesus.

13.   Limitating powers of my father's house, of my mother's house, I am not your candidate, break and die in the name of Jesus.

14.   Inherited curses, inherited evil covenants of my mother's house, break by fire, in the name of Jesus.

15.   Boasting powers of my father's house and mother's house, claiming this is how far you can go, you are all liars. I overcome you by the power of God in th the order according of David and Goliath, in the name of Jesus.

16.   O God, arise, expose and disgrace every masquerading power of my parents' families, in the name of Jesus.

17. Powers that stopped my parents shall not stop me by the power, in the Blood of Jesus.

18. Lord Jesus, visit my life and destroy every deposit of parental mistakes, in the name of Jesus.

19. Evil carry over of my father's house and my mother's house, my case is different, catch fire, burn to ashes for my sake, in the name of Jesus.

20. O God, settle my case and give me rest from effects of parental errors, in the name of Jesus.

21. By Your name called JAH, O God arise let the world know that You are my God, in the name of Jesus.

Section Eight

DESTINY RECOVERY AND
REPOSITIONING PRAYERS

Confession: Jeremiah 30:16
"Therefore, all they that devour me shall be devoured; and all mine adversaries, everyone of them, shall go into captivity; and they that spoil me shall be a spoil, and all that prey upon me will God give for a prey."

Psalm 126:1-2: When the LORD turn again the captivity of Zion, we were like them that dream; then was our mouth filled with laughter and our tongue with singing; then said they among the heathen: the Lord hath done great things for them.

1.   O Lord fine-tune my destiny for total recovery, in the name of Jesus.
2.   Powers that did not allow my parents to succeed, leave me alone, die, in the name of Jesus.
3.   Activities of household enemies over my life, expire, in the name of Jesus.
       Joel 2:25, the Bible says "And I will restore to you the years that the locust hath eaten, the cankerworm, and the caterpillar, and the palmerworm, my great army which I send among you".

4.	Power to recover all, fall upon my life, in the name of Jesus.

	Isaiah 22:25, the Bible says "In that day, saith the Lord of hosts, shall the nail that is fastened in the sure place be removed, and be cut down, and fall; and the burden that was upon it shall be cut off: for the Lord hath spoken it".

5.	Any wicked nail fastened to any ancient wall or evil tree in order to torment my life; be removed by fire in the name of Jesus.

6.	Glory Restorer, Jesus Christ, restore all that ignorance has stolen from my destiny, in the name of Jesus.

7.	Battles that have jumped into my life from my parents; jump out now and disappear, in the name of Jesus.

8.	The height my parents could not attain; the level they could not get to, I shall get there, bt the power in the Blood of Jesus, in the name of Jesus.

9.	The level at which parents stopped, shall be my starting point in the name of Jesus.

10.	Spirit of inadequacy, leave my life alone and die, in the name of Jesus.

11.	Any ancient tree troubling my life and that of my family, be uprooted in the name of Jesus.

12.	O God of Elijah, it is my time of manifestation; arise and manifest Yourself in my life, in the name of Jesus.

13.	All those who have gathered together against my rising up, scatter and die, in the name of Jesus.

14.   My destiny, escape from the cage of failure, in the name of Jesus.

15.   Satanic investment over my destiny when I was a baby, scatter, in the name of Jesus.

16.   I enter into my prophetic destiny, by the power in the Blood of Jesus.

17.   The leaf of my destiny shall not wither, in the name of Jesus.

18.   Thou Lion of Judah, pursue affliction out of my destiny, in the name of Jesus.

19.   I shall not serve my enemies; my enemies shall bow down to me, in the name of Jesus.

20.   I declare with my mouth that nothing shall be impossible with me, in the name of Jesus.

21.   Let my point of ridicule be converted to my source of miracle, in the name of Jesus.